ENCYCLOPEDIA
OF
MAN-MADE
CATASTROPHES

Also by Lee Davis

Encylopedia of Natural Disasters*
* *Available in paperback from Headline*

Encyclopedia
of
Man-made
Catastrophes

Lee Davis

HEADLINE

First published in Great Britain in 1994
by HEADLINE BOOK PUBLISHING

10 9 8 7 6 5 4 3 2 1

ISBN 0 7472 4353 0

Typeset by
Letterpart Limited, Reigate, Surrey

Printed and bound in Great Britain by
HarperCollins Manufacturing, Glasgow

HEADLINE BOOK PUBLISHING
A division of Hodder Headline PLC
Headline House
79 Great Titchfield Street
London W1P 7FN

To Lisa.
That's all.

Contents

Acknowledgments

It is the custom, as if it were an awards ceremony, to thank everybody but your dog and your least favorite relative for help in the birthing of a book. That is not going to be the practice on this page. If I were to name all of the people over the passage of three years who, while I was writing about and therefore living through some of the world's worst times, kept me from getting depressed to the point of paralysis, I would compile a cast of – well – hundreds.

So, I won't, but will, instead, express my gratitude to the major players in this drama of disasters:

Particularly to Mary Lou Barber, who forfeited half a summer to help me endlessly and immeasurably in the accumulation of a small mountain range of reference material;

To Diane Johnston, who cut through a continent of red tape at the New York Public Library and made the portion of my life spent there infinitely more productive than it otherwise would have been;

To Jean Kaleda, Edana McCaffery Cichanowicz, Joanne Brooks, Patricia S. Tormey and the rest of the research staff at the Riverhead Free Library; to Shirley Van Derof, Phyllis Acard, Karen Hewlett, Susan La Vista, Jane Vail, Elva Stanley, Robert Allard, Jan Camarda and Nancy Foley of the Westhampton Free Library; to Selma Kelson and the research staff of the Patchogue-Medford Library; to the research staff of the library at the Southampton Campus of Long Island University; to the research staff of the print division of the Library of Congress;

To Elizabeth Hooks, of the American Red Cross photo library; to Reynaldo Reyes, of the United Nations photo library; to Pedro Soto, of the CARE photo library; to Michael Benson, Larry Crabil and particularly Bill McGruder of the National Transportation Safety Board; to Tim Cronen of the library of the Smithsonian Institution Air and Space Museum;

To Tom Deja for his picture research; to Fred Robertson for his patient photography of disintegrating copies of old newspapers;

To my agents, Elizabeth and Ed Knappman, for causing this to happen in the first place;

To my editors at Facts On File, during the long course of the birth of this book: Kate Kelly and Neal Maillet.

And to all of those unnamed friends and spiritual advisors who kept me sane for three years – my deepest and heartfelt thanks.

Lee Davis
Westhampton, N.Y.

Introduction

Stupidity.
Neglect.
Avariciousness.
The three weird sisters, the archetypal three of man-made disasters, wend their way through practically every one of the several hundred entries in this volume, often in triplicate and duplicate.

Although 'human error' is the euphemism that is used in journalism to describe the reasons for most man-made disasters, it is not altogether accurate. True, the mistakes that a conductor or engineer makes in judging distances when rounding a blind curve are human errors, as are the misreadings of instruments in an industrial plant about to blow apart. Human error is present when an airline pilot, using his best judgment, miscalculates the fuel left in rapidly emptying tanks or the distance to a runway. And human error is present when a navigator of a ship, in a panic situation, steers out of the safety of deep water into the disaster of a reef.

But more often than not, other forces have made that human error easy to commit, and certain to cause a cataclysm. Human sloth and corporate greed often figure in the faulty instrument provided the engineer in the doomed plant, in the failure to provide a proper evacuation plan for a nuclear facility, in the decision of a captain who goes to bed and leaves the bridge to a midshipman in treacherous waters, in the failure of the management of a building or a discotheque to provide the proper fire exits for its patrons, in the neglect of the owners of a shipping line to provide the proper number of lifeboats or the correct filling in life jackets for its passengers.

And in man-made disasters, government often plays an ill-starring role. The cover-ups that are universally present after nuclear disasters have occurred, the misinformation before they happen and the failure to conduct proper inspections of such vital parts as the O-rings in space vehicles have all indicated government culpability.

If, then, there is any constant thread that weaves through the fabric of man-made disasters, it is the presence of those three weird sisters, Stupidity, Neglect and Avariciousness, their pervasiveness before, during and after the disasters and the uncomfortable truth that without them, some of the worst of these disasters never would have occurred.

To carry the Shakespearian analogy still further:

Another basic characteristic of man-made disaster is its inevitability, the inexorable passage of fate once a particular person or group of persons sets that fate in motion. The Shakespearian tragic hero (as distinguished from the Greek tragic hero) has a series of choices. If he makes the correct choice, he wins and faces only complications that result in comedy. If he makes the wrong choice, or a series of wrong choices, he faces his ineluctable doom. For once the first domino has been knocked over, that's it. The rest are bound to follow, with all the inevitability of a law in physics.

And that, too, is another characteristic of many man-made disasters. One error in design is committed; one fatal shortcut is tried by management; one chance too many is taken by a pilot or an engineer; one unwise challenge to fate or inevitability is made by anyone, and the rest is sadness.

At least in the realm of natural disasters, which seem to conform to the Greek theory of tragedy, one can blame it on fate itself, represented by the overwhelming presence of the overpowering forces of nature. People may admittedly be in the wrong place at the wrong time when a tidal wave or a hurricane or an earthquake strikes. But they did not *initiate* the coming of the tidal wave or hurricane or earthquake.

And in the broad spectrum of man-made disasters, it is true that natural forces *have* taken a hand. Ships have gone down in sudden storms and faceless fogs; airliners have been struck by lightning or have been the victims of sudden wind shears; small fires have been fanned into conflagrations by sudden wind gusts. Freezing temperatures certainly played a role in bringing about the *Challenger* space disaster. And it might even be argued that natural, explosive gases in coal mines were placed there, not by man, but by nature.

But except for very few instances, these presences are *secondary*, and it is what occurs *before* or *during* these emergencies that matters in man-made disasters. The judgment of the captain of a ship or an airplane, the decisions made by fire chiefs or rescue squads, the advice given by experts to engineers fighting to bring an industrial plant under control spell the difference between disasters and accidents. And once those Shakespearian dominoes have been set in motion by that act of bad judgment, ignorance, badly placed cowardice or misplaced bravado, the dividing line between trouble and cataclysm is crossed. And there is no going back.

Now, a word about degree:

In his introduction to his play *Death of a Salesman*, Arthur Miller separates the merely pathetic from the truly tragic by using the image of a man being hit by a falling piano.

The situation is this:

A piano is being moved into a fifth-floor apartment via a block and tackle. It hovers outside a window, five stories above a city sidewalk.

An unsuspecting man turns the corner, whistling. He strolls down the sidewalk, and then, just as he gets underneath the piano, a rope breaks. The piano falls, crushing the man.

The next day, an article, headed 'Man Hit by Falling Piano,' appears in the newspapers. It reports the facts and nothing else.

Is that, asks Miller, pathetic or tragic?

It's pathetic, according to Miller, because you don't know where the man came from or where he was going. If, on the other hand, you knew, for instance, that he had just paid the last installment on his mortgage and was on the way to the jewelry store to pick up the engagement ring to give to the love of his life, it would be tragic. Summing it up, Miller concludes, 'You are in the presence of tragedy when you are in the presence of a man who has missed his joy. But the awareness of the joy, and the awareness that it has been missed must be there.'

Well, there is both tragedy and patheticness in *Man-made Catastrophes*. Because of its encyclopedic nature, there is neither the space nor the information to include on these pages all of the joys that have been missed by the millions who have died. But it is there, by implication, and wherever it has been possible, it has been included.

There is no greater disaster than the one that occurred to you last year, yesterday or in the last instant. And the reason for this is that you knew the joy and you know the vacuum that is left when it has been missed. So, in the catastrophes that consume this volume, there are millions of people to whom that particular disaster was far more than pathetic. It was the supreme tragedy of their existence.

And all of this would be terribly depressing, if that were all. But there is a reason that we revere our tragedies more than our comedies, why we feel, when they are over, the uplift that the Greeks termed catharsis and that Aristotle, in his *Poetics*, decreed must be present in every true tragedy. It's composed of two qualities: bravery and knowledge. Tragic heroes go to their deaths bravely and learn from their errors before they die.

So, while there is terrible, horrible, disgusting cowardice on these pages – particularly, for some odd
reason, in the recital of maritime disasters (they seem
to have brought out the very worst in us) – there is also
noble bravery, too. Time after time, there are vignettes
of remarkable, indelible acts of courage that shine like
stars in an otherwise dark sky of disaster: The families
who went back to their cabins and donned their
evening clothes before stoically going down with the
Titanic, for instance; the heroic conductors and engineers of out-of-control trains who hurtled to their
deaths with their hands on brakes that burned out
beneath them; the rescuers that risked their lives to go
into burning buildings or soon-to-explode mine shafts;
the pilots of planes that brought their crippled birds in
with minimum loss of life; the flight attendants and
crews who faced down terrorists. The list is long and
bright, and proof that there is a goodness and a courage
in human beings that no disaster can entirely destroy.

It is hoped, then, that, utilizing this criterion, this
volume of man-made cataclysms does contain some
nobility, some surviving dignity and an ultimate sense
that, even given catastrophic circumstances, some of
us, as King Arthur says at the end of *Camelot*, 'do
shine.'

Air Crashes

The Worst Recorded Air Crashes

N.B.: For air crashes caused by
terrorist bombs or hijacking, see
CIVIL UNREST AND TERRORISM.
* Detailed in text

Africa
* Mediterranean coast
(Dec. 21, 1923) French
dirigible *Dixmude*

Antarctica
* (Nov. 28, 1979) New
Zealand DC-10

Atlantic Ocean
(Aug. 1, 1948) French
Latecoere 631 Flying
Boat
* (Aug. 14, 1958) KLM
Super Constellation
* (Feb. 8, 1965) Eastern
DC7-B
(June 23, 1985) Air India
Boeing 747SR

Austria
* Innsbruck (Feb. 29, 1964)
British Eagle
International Britannia

Belgium
Berg (Feb. 15, 1961)
Sabena Boeing 707
Bali (April 27, 1974) Pan
Am Boeing 707

Brazil
Azul (July 16, 1961)
Argentine Airlines
Boeing 707
Rio de Janeiro (Feb. 25,
1960) U.S. Navy
transport; REAL
DC-3

Cameroon
* Douala (Mar. 4, 1962)
Trans-African British
Caledonian DC-7C

Canada
Newfoundland
* Gander (Dec. 12, 1985)
Arrow Air DC-8
Ontario
* Toronto (July 5, 1970)
Air Canada DC-8
Quebec
* Issoudun (Aug. 11, 1957)
Maritime Central Airways
DC-4
* Montreal (Nov. 29, 1963)
Trans-Canada DC-8 F

Chile
* Andes Mountains (Feb.
6, 1965) Chilean Linea
Aera Nacionale
DC-6B

China
Shanghai (Dec. 25, 1946)
3 China Air transport
planes
Nanjing (July 31, 1992)
Yakovlev-4Z

Colombia
* Bogota (July 24, 1938)
Colombian military
stunt plane
Bogota (Feb. 15, 1947)
Avianca DC-4

Cyprus
Nicosia (April 20, 1967)
Swiss Globe Britannia

Czechoslovakia
* Bratislava (Nov. 24, 1966) TABSO Bulgarian Ilyushin-18

Dominican Republic
Santo Domingo (Feb. 15, 1970) Dominican DC-9

Egypt
Aswan (Mar. 20, 1969) United Arab IL-18
Cairo (Aug. 31, 1950) TWA Constellation
* Cairo (May 20, 1965) Pakistan International Boeing 707

France
* Beauvais (Oct. 5, 1930) British dirigible R-101
* Grenoble (Nov. 13, 1950) Canadian Curtis-Reid Air-Tours
Nice (Sept. 11, 1968) Air France Caravelle
Paris
* (June 3, 1962) Air France Boeing 707
(July 11, 1973) Brazilian Boeing 707
* (Mar. 3, 1974) Turkish Airlines Douglas DC-10
Pyrenees (June 3, 1967) British Air Ferry Ltd. DC-6

Germany
* East Berlin (Aug. 14, 1972) Interflug Ilyushin-62
Edelweiler (Aug. 11, 1955) 2 U.S. Air Force Flying Boxcars
* Johannisthal (Oct. 17, 1913) German naval dirigible LZ-18

* Munich (Dec. 17, 1960) U.S. Air Force C-131 Convair

Great Britain
England
* London (June 18, 1972) BEA Trident 1
Wales
* Cardiff (Mar. 12, 1950) British Avro Tudor V

Greece
Athens (Dec. 8, 1969) Olympia Airways DC-6B

Guam
(Sept. 19, 1960) World Airways DC6-B

India
Bombay
(July 7, 1962) Alitalia DC-8
* (Jan. 1, 1978) Air India Boeing 747
* New Delhi (June 14, 1972) Japan Airlines DC-8

Indonesia
Bali (April 27, 1974) Pan Am Boeing 707

Iran
Tehran (Feb. 9, 1993) Iran Air passenger jet; military jet

Ireland
Shannon (Sept. 19, 1961) President Airlines DC-6

Italy
Milan (June 26, 1959) TWA Super Constellation
* Palermo (May 5, 1972) Alitalia DC-8

Japan
Hokkaido (Feb. 1, 1954)
U.S. Air Force C-46
* Morioka (July 30, 1971)
All-Nippon Boeing 727;
Japanese Air Force
F-86
* Mount Fuji (Mar. 5,
1966) BOAC Boeing
707
* Mount Ogura (Aug. 12,
1985) Japan Airlines
Boeing 747SR
Tokyo
* (June 18, 1953) U.S. Air
Force C-124
* (Feb. 4, 1966) All-Nippon
Airways Boeing 727

Libya
Ghadames (May 10, 1961)
Air France Starliner

Mexico
Guadalajara (June 2,
1958) Lockheed
Constellation

Morocco
Casablanca
(May 18, 1958) Sabena
DC-6B
* (July 12, 1961)
Czechoslovak
Ilyushin-18
Imzizen (Aug. 3, 1975)
Alia Boeing 707
Mt. Mallaytine (Dec. 23,
1973) Sabena Caravelle
Rabat (Sept. 12, 1961)
Air France Caravelle

Nepal
Katmandu (July 30, 1992)
A310–300 Airbus

Netherlands
Amsterdam (Oct. 4, 1992)
El Al Boeing 747 Cargo
Jet

New Guinea
* Biak Island (July 16,
1957) KLM Super
Constellation

Nigeria
(Nov. 20, 1969) Nigerian
Airlines DC-10
(Jan. 22, 1973) Nigerian
Airlines Boeing 707
Lagos (Sept. 26, 1992)
Hercules C-130

Pacific Ocean
(Mar. 16, 1962) Flying
Tiger Super
Constellation

Pakistan
* Karachi (Mar. 3, 1953)
Canadian Pacific Comet
Jet

Peru
Cuzco (Aug. 9, 1970)
Peruvian Electra
Jungle (Dec. 24, 1971)
Peruvian Electra
* Lima (Nov. 27, 1962)
Varig Airlines Boeing
707

Puerto Rico
* San Juan (April 11, 1952)
Pan Am DC-4

Saudi Arabia
* Jidda (July 11, 1991)
Canadian Charter DC-8
* Riyadh (Aug. 19, 1980)
Saudi Airlines
Lockheed Tristar

South Vietnam
(Dec. 24, 1966) U.S.
military C-44
Saigon (April 4, 1975)
U.S. Air Force Galaxy
C-58

Spain
* Barcelona (July 3, 1970)
Dan-Air British Comet

* Lakehurst (May 6, 1937)
  German zeppelin
  Hindenburg
New York
* Brooklyn (Dec. 16, 1960)
  United DC-8; TWA
  Super Constellation
* Cove Neck, L.I. (Jan. 25,
  1990) Avianca Boeing
  707
New York City
* (July 28, 1945) Army Air
  Corps B-25
  (May 29, 1947) United
  DC-4
* (Feb. 3, 1959) American
  Lockheed Electra
  (Mar. 1, 1962) American
  Boeing 707
  (June 24, 1975) Eastern
  Boeing 727
North Carolina
* Hendersonville (July 19,
  1967) Piedmont Boeing
  727; Cessna 310
Ohio
* Ava (Sept. 3, 1925) U.S.
  Army dirigible
  Shenandoah
Pennsylvania
  Mt. Carmel (June 17,
  1948) United DC-6
Texas
* Dawson (May 3, 1968)
  Braniff Lockheed
  Electra
Utah
* Bryce Canyon (Oct. 24,
  1947) United DC-6
Virginia

* Richmond (Nov. 8, 1961)
  Imperial Airlines
  Lockheed Constellation
Washington
* Moses Lake (Dec. 20,
  1952) U.S. Air Force
  C-124
Washington, D.C.
  (Nov. 1, 1949) Eastern
  DC-4; Bolivian P-38
Wyoming
  Laramie (Oct. 6, 1955)
  United DC-4

USSR
  Irkutsk (Aug. 11, 1971)
  Soviet Aeroflot
  Tupolev-104
  Kanash (Oct. 17, 1958)
  Soviet Aeroflot
  Tupolev-104
  Kharkov (May 18, 1972)
  Soviet Aeroflot
  Tupolev-104
* Kranaya Polyana (Oct.
  14, 1972) Aeroflot
  Ilyushin-62
  Leningrad (Dec. 31, 1970)
  Soviet Aeroflot
  Ilyushin-18

Venezuela
* La Coruba (Mar. 16,
  1969) Venezuelan DC-8

West Indies
* Guadaloupe (June 22,
  1962) Air France
  Boeing 707

Yugoslavia
* Ljubljana (Sept. 1, 1966)
  Britannia Airways 102

Chronology

N.B.: For air crashes caused by terrorist bombs or hijacking, see CIVIL UNREST AND TERRORISM.
* Detailed in text

1913
Oct. 17
   * Johannisthal, Germany; German naval dirigible LZ-18
1923
Dec. 21
   * Mediterranean coast of Africa; French dirigible *Dixmude*
1925
Sept. 3
   * Ava, Ohio; US Army dirigible *Shenandoah*
1930
Oct. 5
   * Beauvais, France; British dirigible R-101
1933
April 14
   * Coast of New Jersey; U.S. dirigible *Akron*
1937
May 6
   * Lakehurst, New Jersey; German zeppelin *Hindenburg*
1938
July 24
   * Bogota, Colombia; Colombian military stunt plane
1945
July 28
   * New York, New York; Army Air Corps B-25

1946
Dec. 25
   Shanghai, China; 3 China Air transport planes
1947
Feb. 15
   Bogota, Colombia; Avianca DC-4
May 29
   New York, New York; United DC-4
May 30
   Fort Deposit, Maryland; Eastern DC-4
Oct. 24
   * Bryce Canyon, Utah; United DC-6
1948
June 17
   Mt. Carmel, Pennsylvania; United DC-6
Aug. 1
   Atlantic Ocean; French Latecoere 631 Flying Boat
1949
July 12
   Simi Mountains, California; Standard Airlines
Nov. 1
   Washington, D.C.; Eastern DC-4; Bolivian P-38
1950
Mar. 12
   * Cardiff, Wales; British Avro Tudor V
Aug. 31
   Cairo, Egypt; TWA Constellation

Nov. 13
  * Grenoble, France;
      Canadian Curtis Reid
      Air-Tours

1951
Dec. 16
    Elizabeth, New Jersey;
      Miami Airlines C-46

1952
April 11
  * San Juan, Puerto Rico;
      Pan Am DC-4
Dec. 20
  * Moses Lake, Washington;
      U.S. Air Force C-124

1953
Mar. 3
  * Karachi, Pakistan;
      Canadian Pacific Comet
      Jet
June 18
  * Tokyo, Japan; U.S. Air
      Force C-124

1954
Feb. 1
    Hokkaido, Japan; U.S.
      Air Force C-46

1955
Mar. 22
    Honolulu, Hawaii; U.S.
      Navy DC-6
Aug. 11
    Edelweiler, Germany; 2
      U.S. Air Force Flying
      Boxcars
Oct. 6
    Laramie, Wyoming;
      United DC-4

1956
June 20
    Asbury Park, New Jersey;
      Venezuelan
      Constellation

June 30
  * Grand Canyon, Arizona;
      TWA Super
      Constellation; United
      DC-7

1957
July 16
  * New Guinea; KLM Super
      Constellation
Aug. 11
  * Quebec, Canada;
      Maritime Central
      Airways DC-4

1958
May 18
    Casablanca, Morocco;
      Sabena DC-6B
June 2
    Guadalajara, Mexico;
      Lockheed
      Constellation
Aug. 14
  * Atlantic Ocean; KLM
      Super Constellation
Oct. 17
    Kanash, USSR; Soviet
      Aeroflot Tupolev-104

1959
Feb. 3
  * New York, New York;
      American Lockheed
      Electra
June 26
    Milan, Italy; TWA Super
      Constellation

1960
Feb. 25
    Rio de Janeiro, Brazil;
      U.S. Navy transport;
      REAL DC-3
Sept. 19
    Guam; World Airways
      DC6-B

Oct. 4
* Boston, Massachusetts;
  Eastern Electra

Dec. 16
* Brooklyn, New York;
  United DC-8; TWA
  Super Constellation

Dec. 17
* Munich, Germany; U.S.
  Air Force C-131
  Convair

1961

Feb. 15
  Berg, Belgium; Sabena
  Boeing 707

May 10
  Ghadames, Libya; Air
  France Starliner

July 12
* Casablanca, Morocco;
  Czechoslovak
  Ilyushin-18

July 16
  Azul, Brazil; Argentine
  Airlines Boeing 707

Sept. 1
  Hinsdale, Illinois; TWA
  Constellation

Sept. 10
  Shannon, Ireland;
  President Airlines DC-6

Sept. 12
  Rabat, Morocco; Air
  France Caravelle

Nov. 8
* Richmond, Virginia;
  Imperial Airlines
  Lockheed Constellation

1962

Mar. 1
  New York, New York;
  American Boeing 707

Mar. 4
* Douala, Cameroon;
  Trans-African British
  Caledonian DC-7C

Mar. 16
  Pacific Ocean; Flying
  Tiger Super
  Constellation

June 3
* Paris, France; Air France
  Boeing 707

June 22
* Guadaloupe, West Indies;
  Air France Boeing 707

July 7
  Bombay, India; Alitalia
  DC-8

Nov. 27
* Lima, Peru; Varig
  Airlines Boeing 707

1963

Feb. 4
  Ankara, Turkey; Turkish
  Air Force C-47

June 3
* Anchorage, Alaska;
  Northwest DC-7 charter

Sept. 2
  Zurich, Switzerland;
  Swissaire Caravelle

Nov. 29
* Montreal, Canada;
  Trans-Canada DC-8F

Dec. 8
* Elkton, Maryland; Pan
  Am Boeing 707

1964

Feb. 29
* Innsbruck, Austria;
  British Eagle
  International Britannia

Mar. 1
  Lake Tahoe, California;
  Paradise Airlines
  Constellation

Oct. 2
* Granada, Spain; Union
  transports Africain
  DC-6

1965

Feb. 6
* Andes Mountains, Chile;
  Chilean Linea Aera
  Nacionale DC-6B

Feb. 8
* Atlantic Ocean; Eastern
  DC7-B

May 20
* Cairo, Egypt; Pakistan
  International Boeing
  707

June 25
El Toro, California; U.S.
Air Force C-135

1966

Feb. 4
* Tokyo, Japan; All
  Nippon Airways
  Boeing 727

Mar. 5
* Mount Fuji, Japan;
  BOAC Boeing 707

Sept. 1
* Ljubljana, Yugoslavia;
  Britannia Airways 102

Nov. 24
* Bratislava,
  Czechoslovakia;
  TABSO Bulgarian
  Ilyushin-18

Dec. 24
South Vietnam; U.S.
military C-44

1967

April 20
Nicosia, Cyprus; Swiss
Globe Britannia

June 3
Pyrenees, France; British
Air Ferry Ltd. DC-6

July 19
* Hendersonville, North
  Carolina; Piedmont
  Boeing 727; Cessna
  310

1968

May 3
* Dawson, Texas; Braniff
  Lockheed Electra

Sept. 11
Nice, France; Air France
Caravelle

1969

Mar. 16
* La Coruba, Venezuela;
  Venezuelan DC-8

Mar. 20
Aswan, Egypt; United
Arab IL-18

Aug. 9
* Shelbyville, Indiana;
  Allegheny DC-9; Piper
  Cherokee

Nov. 20
Nigeria; Nigerian Airlines
DC-10

Dec. 8
Athens, Greece;
Olympia Airways
DC-6B

1970

Feb. 15
Santo Domingo,
Dominican Republic;
Dominican DC-9

July 3
* Barcelona, Spain;
  Dan-Air British Comet

July 5
Toronto, Canada; Air
Canada DC-8

Aug. 9
    Cuzco, Peru; Peruvian
    Electra
Dec. 31
    Leningrad, USSR; Soviet
    Aeroflot Ilyushin-18

1971
July 30
    * Morioka, Japan;
    All-Nippon Boeing 727;
    Japanese Air Force F-86
Aug. 11
    Irkutsk, USSR; Soviet
    Aeroflot Tupolev-104
Sept. 4
    * Juneau, Alaska; Alaska
    Airlines Boeing 727
Dec. 24
    Jungle, Peru; Peruvian
    Electra

1972
Jan. 7
    * Ibiza, Spain; Iberia
    Caravelle
Mar. 18
    Kharkov, USSR; Soviet
    Aeroflot Tupolev-104
May 5
    * Palermo, Italy; Alitalia
    DC-8
June 14
    * New Delhi, India; Japan
    Airlines DC-8
June 18
    * London, Great Britain;
    BEA Trident 1
Aug. 14
    East Berlin, Germany;
    Interflug Ilyushin-62
Oct. 14
    * Kranaya Polyana,
    USSR; Aeroflot
    Ilyushin-62

Dec. 3
    * Santa Cruz de Tenerife,
    Canary Islands;
    Spantax Airlines
    Convair 990-A

1973
Jan. 22
    Nigeria; Nigerian Airlines
    Boeing 707
April 10
    * Basel, Switzerland; BEA
    Vanguard
July 11
    Paris, France; Brazilian
    Boeing 707
July 31
    * Boston, Massachusetts;
    Delta DC-9
Dec. 23
    Mt. Mallaytine, Morocco;
    Sabena Caravelle

1974
Mar. 3
    * Paris, France; Turkish
    Airlines Douglas
    DC-10
April 27
    Bali, Indonesia; Pan Am
    Boeing 707
Dec. 4
    Colombo, Sri Lanka;
    Dutch DC-8

1975
April 4
    Saigon, South Vietnam;
    U.S. Air Force Galaxy
    C-58
June 24
    New York, New York;
    Eastern Boeing 727
Aug. 3
    Imzizen, Morocco; Alia
    Boeing 707

1977

Mar. 27
  * Santa Cruz de Tenerife,
    Canary Islands; KLM
    Boeing 747; Pan Am
    Boeing 747

1979

May 25
  * Chicago, Illinois;
    American DC-10

Nov. 8
  * Antarctica; New Zealand
    DC-10

1980

Aug. 19
  * Riyadh, Saudi Arabia;
    Saudi Airlines
    Lockheed Tristar

1985

June 23
    Atlantic Ocean; Air India
    Boeing 747SR

Aug. 12
  * Mount Ogura, Japan;
    Japan Airlines Boeing
    747SR

Dec. 12
  * Gander, Newfoundland,
    Canada; Arrow Air
    DC-8

1990

Jan. 25
  * Cove Neck, Long Island,
    New York; Avianca
    Boeing 707

1991

April 6
    Brunswick, Georgia;
    Southeast Airlines
    turbo-prop commuter
    plane

May 26
  * Suphan Buri, Thailand;
    Lauda Air Boeing
    767–300

July 11
  * Jidda, Saudi Arabia;
    Canadian Charter
    DC-8

Dec. 1
    Los Angeles, California;
    USAIR Boeing 737;
    commuter plane

1992

July 30
    Katmandu, Nepal;
    A310–300 Airbus

July 31
    Nanjing, China;
    Yakovlev-42

Sept. 26
    Lagos, Nigeria; Hercules
    C-130

Oct. 4
    Amsterdam, Netherlands;
    El Al Boeing 747 Cargo
    Jet

1993

Feb. 9
    Tehran, Iran; Iran Air
    passenger jet; military
    jet

Air Crashes

Commercial air travel has come a long way from the days of the old Ford Tri-Star. In 1928, a trip on TWA (Transcontinental and Western Airlines then) was a true adventure. Improvements were clearly necessary. By 1933, the commercial airliner as we know it today had been built, at least in an elementary outline. Its configuration – a pilot's cabin up front, engines encased in cowlings on the wings, a row of portholes through which passengers peered (apprehensively or otherwise) at the clouds, the sky and the arrival or departure of the ground – was established early in the DC-1 (D for Douglas, C for Commercial, 1 for first).

The craft was a model of noisy luxury. Each of its upholstered seats had a reading lamp and a footrest. The galley at the rear was equipped with electric hot plates and a lavatory. The cabin was heated and contained a ventilation system designed to let in more air than noise, and the 'stewardess' was, before her transformation into 'flight attendant,' more than a waitress and psychiatrist. She was also a registered nurse.

And so began a multibillion dollar industry that now makes practically every corner of the globe accessible to those who use it – and millions do, every year.

And yet, large segments of the public are still deathly afraid of flying. Some refuse to fly. Some fly with their hearts in their throats and their fingers digging into armrests or their companion's arms. Others board flights with grim resignation. And their resignation has a basis: Once aboard an airplane, the passenger is, admittedly, helpless. There's no stopping the plane in midflight to debark, no way of seeing ahead or behind, no escape hatch in the sky. Strapped into his or her seat, the airline passenger is at the total mercy of the crew in the cockpit and the fates surrounding the plane.

And, unfortunately, those crews have not always been skillful, nor has fate been kind. As in any man-made disaster, human failure has played a feature role. And there are a huge number of people who can fail in the chain of command behind the orderly flying of a commercial airliner. There are the engineers who design the craft, the mechanics who service it, the flight personnel who fly it and the controllers who guide it from airport to airport. There are the groups who make the rules regulating commercial flying, and the politicians behind the regulatory bodies.

As the skies become more and more crowded, as they inevitably will, air control, pilot training and the technology to prevent turning the more than 2,000 near misses that occur in the sky into fatal collisions will become more and more of an issue and a burning necessity, overseen by government agencies and government policy-makers.

Having said all of this, the one human failure that no amount of technology or skill can cure is that of bad judgment under pressure. As highly trained, as experienced and as cool under grueling circumstances as airline pilots are today, they are nevertheless human and can make mistakes. And, in the case of commercial aviation, as the following section will show, these mistakes can – and often do – result in terrible tragedy.

There are other factors besides human failures: Faulty design and the metal fatigue that comes from long use have caused crashes. Weather has been a constant hazard. And terrorism, whether individual or state sponsored, has picked the airlines as its prime target.

So, the fear of flying, which is really a fear of crashing, has its realistic roots. The statistics are grim, and although air crashes occur infrequently now, they receive enormous media coverage because of the sheer magnitude of the loss of life.

New technology – transponders, three-dimensional radar, wind-shear protection, etc. – is being developed in the interest of safer flying. Efforts to build better, safer airports will certainly diminish the number of crashes, for the statistics reveal that most troubles with aircraft and consequent crashes occur during landing or takeoff. And that has held true, whether the aircraft is a lighter-than-air blimp or a jetliner.

There is no doubt that air travel is safe. And there is also no doubt that it could be safer.

The criteria for inclusion of crashes in this section centered upon the number of fatalities and the severity of the crash. But statistics alone were not the constant arbiters, and for a logical reason: A 1990 casualty figure could not realistically be applied to the 1930s, when planes were smaller and fewer people were flying. Thus the casualty figures were matched with the time in which they occurred.

Other, lesser crashes were included if they were of a particularly unusual nature or the only crash of a particular type.

Airplane disasters involving terrorism can be found in the section CIVIL UNREST AND TERRORISM.

AFRICA – MEDITERRANEAN COAST
December 21, 1923

The state-of-the-art airship Dixmude, *one of France's proudest lighter-than-air ships, exploded when it was struck by lightning over the Mediterranean coast of Africa, on December 21, 1923. All 52 crew members aboard died.*

ANTARCTICA
November 28, 1979

An Air New Zealand DC-10 on a sightseeing flight, hampered by low visibility, unpredictable wind currents and a possibly malfunctioning navigation system,

*slammed into the side of the 12,400-foot-high volcano
Mount Erebus on November 28, 1979. Two hundred
fifty-seven died in the crash.*

Air New Zealand began a series of sightseeing flights
over Antarctica in 1978. Popular with tourists, they
were looked on askance by representatives of the
National Science Foundation, the coordinators of an
extensive scientific program in Antarctica. The planes
disrupted both wildlife and the atmosphere, as they
dipped and circled over the scientific encampments at
the end of the earth.

On November 28, 1979 the fourth flight of the season
took off from Auckland, New Zealand at 8:21 A.M. It
was a nonstop flight that was scheduled to circle over
the South Pole and then land at Christchurch at about 5
P.M. There was a low cloud cover near Mount Erebus, a
12,400-foot active volcano located on Ross Island, off
the Antarctica coast about 30 miles north of the U.S.
military and scientific station at McCurdo Sound. This
was a disappointment; a circle of the volcano was
always a high point of the tour.

The temperature in the area was approximately 15
degrees Fahrenheit, and, at that time of year, there was
daylight almost around the clock.

At 1 P.M., the pilot of the DC-10, Captain Tim
Collins, radioed Auckland that he was descending from
his 10,000-foot altitude to 2,000 feet, apparently in an
attempt to pierce the cloud cover and give the sightseers a closer, unimpeded view of the volcano.

It was the last anyone would hear from the Air New
Zealand flight. It slammed into the side of the mountain about 1,500 feet from its base, exploded and
caught fire. No one would survive.

Only 90 of the 257 bodies would ever be found. The
rest, rescuers reasoned, had slipped into crevices or
were buried too deeply under the snow to be found.

The 'black box' flight recorder was retrieved, and its
story was one of instantaneous disaster with almost no

warning. Seconds before impact, an alarm sound reverberated in the cockpit from the ground proximity warning system, telling the crew that the plane had descended too low.

ATLANTIC OCEAN
August 14, 1958

KLM Flight 607-E, a Super Constellation, bound from Brussels to New York exploded over the North Atlantic 130 miles off the Irish coast at 11:35 P.M. on August 14, 1958. There were no survivors.

ATLANTIC OCEAN
February 8, 1965

Sabotage was suspected in the crash, shortly after takeoff from Kennedy Airport, of Eastern Airlines Flight 663, a DC7-B, off the coast of Long Island. All 84 aboard died.

AUSTRIA – INNSBRUCK
February 29, 1964

A British Eagle International Airlines Bristol Britannia failed to make an instrument landing at Innsbruck Airport on the night of February 29, 1964 and smashed into Mount Glungezer. All 88 aboard were killed.

There are scary descents into certain airports in the world. Several Caribbean islands are noted for 'white knuckle' landing sites, including the St. Thomas airport in the U.S. Virgin Islands. But at least these airports are situated in areas in which the weather is usually clear and placid.

Not so the airport at Innsbruck, Austria, in the heart of the Austrian Alps and the midst of some of the best ski country on earth. Ringed by 8,000-foot-high mountains, it lies in a bowl that requires a steep and rapid descent from 10,000 feet. Few unseasoned travelers who have ever landed there forget the experience or wish to repeat it.

The night of February 29, 1964 was foggy and still. British Eagle International Airlines, Britain's largest independent airline in 1964, flew regularly from London to Innsbruck, and one of its Bristol Britannias, piloted by Captain E. Williams, attempted an instrument landing in the midst of the fog. The plane never made it to the runway.

Some 12 miles from the airport, flying 100 feet below the necessary altitude to clear the surrounding peaks, the plane smashed into Mount Glungezer, cracked apart and slid into a gorge. All 88 people aboard were killed.

CAMEROON – DOUALA
March 4, 1962

There has never been an explanation for the crash on takeoff of a Trans-African British Caledonian DC-7C at Douala Airport, in Cameroon, on March 4, 1962. All 111 aboard died in the crash.

The mystery of the sudden crash, on takeoff, of a Caledonian DC-7C from Douala Airport in Cameroon on March 4, 1962 has never been solved. A charter owned by the Trans-African Coach Company and loaded with 111 persons, it had originated in Mozambique and had made an eventless stop at Lisbon. Its destination was Luxembourg.

All seemed to be in order as the DC-7C left the runway on the last leg of its journey. But a mere two minutes after it became airborne, the plane plunged to the ground, bursting into flames and killing all 111 aboard. No incendiary device was discovered in the wreckage, no distress call was radioed to the airport and no mechanical failure was found in the smoldering wreckage of the plane.

CANADA – NEWFOUNDLAND, GANDER
December 12, 1985

A combination of human error and malfeasance on the part of Arrow Air Charter combined to send an Arrow Air DC-8 plunging to earth after takeoff from Newfoundland's Gander Airport on December 12, 1985. All 258 American servicemen aboard died.

CANADA – ONTARIO, TORONTO
July 5, 1970

Incorrectly deployed wing spoilers caused the crash of an Air Canada DC-8 on landing at Toronto Airport on July 5, 1970. All 108 aboard were killed.

CANADA – QUEBEC, ISSOUDUN
August 11, 1957

An overloaded maritime Central Charter DC-4, piloted by a man with a record of intentionally causing accidents, was flung to the ground in a fierce thunderstorm over Issoudun, near Quebec, on the morning of August 11, 1957. There was one survivor – a baby. Seventy-seven passengers and crew died.

Bizarre as it may seem, Norman Ramsay, the pilot of the ill-fated Maritime Central Charter DC-4 that plunged to earth near Quebec on the morning of August 11, 1957, had been discharged three years previously by Trans-Canada Airlines for intentionally plunging his aircraft into the ground. Since that time he had been under psychiatric care.

That incident had involved a Super Constellation flight from Tampa, Florida to Toronto on December 17, 1954. Coming in for a landing 400 feet below the minimum required altitude, he had simply flown the plane into the turf near the runway. Miraculously, none of the 44 passengers or crew was seriously injured.

Three years later, after his psychiatrist had pronounced him unfit to fly (all of this was revealed in the later board of inquiry findings), Captain Ramsay was piloting an overloaded charter, packed with veterans of the Canadian contingent of the British Expeditionary Force in France, who had gone back to view the battlefields where they had fought in World War I. The DC-4 had been designed to carry 49 passengers. On this trip, from London to Toronto, it would be carrying 73.

The plane took off from Heathrow Airport in London at 5:55 P.M. on the night of August 10. The overloaded plane had difficulty clearing the runway but finally managed it, and the weather report signaled clear weather all the way to Montreal. Refueling stops were planned in Reykjavik, Iceland and Montreal, unless headwinds forced an earlier stop in Quebec.

By the time the plane left Iceland, at 1:12 A.M., the crew had been on duty for 20 hours and had flown almost constantly for 15 or 16 hours. It would be daylight before they would reach Seven Island and Mont Joli, near Quebec city. When they did, they had a mere 122 gallons of fuel left. Most pilots would have elected to land and refuel. Ramsay elected to continue on. He radioed his position.

It would be the last communication received from the plane.

West of Quebec, an enormous thunderstorm loomed up directly in the flight's path. Had they had extra fuel, the flight crew could have climbed above it or skirted around it. Ramsay had only one choice: He entered the storm, and that proved to be a fatal decision. Somewhere over Issoudun, near Quebec, the forces of the thunderstorm flung the DC-4 into the ground with such force that some of its fuselage and all of its motors dug in to depths of up to 84 feet. There was only one survivor – an infant child, whom rescuers, arriving a disgraceful five and a half hours later, discovered sitting in the unoccupied pilot's seat, a considerable distance from the main body of the wreck.

Only 20 bodies could be identified. The others were damaged beyond recognition. Local authorities were given the responsibility of protecting the site until Department of Transport crash investigators could arrive the next day. But these local authorities apparently ignored their mandate. Hundreds of curious souvenir hunters from Quebec and elsewhere roamed the wreckage, carrying away personal possessions of the dead passengers and removing thousands of small parts of the aircraft that might have pieced together the last moments of the doomed flight.

CANADA – QUEBEC, MONTREAL
November 29, 1963

Trans-Canada Flight 831, a DC-8F, encountered severe turbulence after taking off from Montreal Airport on November 29, 1963 and plunged to the ground. All 118 aboard were killed.

CHILE – ANDES MOUNTAINS
February 6, 1965

An ill-maintained Aera Nacionale DC-6B with 87 tourists aboard lost radio contact with Santiago, Chile on February 6, 1965, entered a cloud bank and crashed into the side of San Jose Mountain. All aboard were killed.

It may be fortunate that the jets of the major airlines fly at altitudes too high to view the majestic but dangerous peaks of the Andes. Most adventurous tourists view them close at hand, at ground level. But others, particularly those who want to get an intimate glimpse of the famous statue of Christ of the Andes, erected in Uspallata Pass on the Argentine-Chilean border, must take smaller, propeller-driven planes, which are subjected to the unpredictable air currents and weather of the high Andes.

Such was the case when a soccer team, sightseers and tourists climbed aboard an Aera Nacionale DC-6B at the Santiago airport on February 6, 1965. It was the height of the summer tourist season, and the plane was packed with 87 passengers eager to catch a glimpse of the fabled statue and the peaks that surround it.

The plane was old and, some said afterward, ill maintained. No reason is known for its loss of radio contact 20 minutes after takeoff. A heavy cloud cover shrouded the Andes near Santiago and completely obscured San Jose Mountain and its ancient gorge, El Volcan Pass. The DC-6B disappeared into the cloud cover.

A waterworks engineer spotted it flying overhead, in the direction of the pass. A loud explosion followed, and the engineer immediately reported his sighting to the Santiago airport. Some time later, rescuers discovered the wreckage of the aircraft strewn along the slope of the mountain. There were no survivors.

COLOMBIA – BOGOTA
July 24, 1938

A military stunt plane flying too close to the packed stands at a military air show at the opening of the Campo de Marte in Bogota, Colombia on July 24, 1938 broke up and slashed through the crowd of 50,000. Fifty-three spectators were killed by falling debris.

The 155th anniversary of the birth of Simon Bolivar, the patriot-dictator who liberated South America from Spain, and the opening of the Campo de Marte, a military exercise field, were celebrated in Bogota, Colombia with a military air show. Fifty thousand spectators packed several metal-roofed stands that sunny afternoon to applaud the daredevil acrobatics of a hand-picked group of military fliers.

The low-flying antics of these pilots did not please Dr. Eduardo Santos, president of Colombia, and he complained more than once to War Minister Alberto Pumarejo about the reckless disregard of safety unfolding before them.

The president's evaluation of the situation turned out to be correct. Within minutes after his last complaint to the war minister, a plane piloted by a Lieutenant Abadia clipped the end of one stand with its wing tip, rolled sideways, sheered away a set of steps leading to the stand and burst into flame. The propeller, separated from its engine, preceded the flaming wreck as it plowed into the stands, incinerating and slashing hundreds of screaming, terrified and trapped spectators.

Some, their clothes on fire, bolted for the open fields; others were pinned to their seats by pieces of wreckage. Fifty-three persons perished in this needless disaster.

CZECHOSLOVAKIA – BRATISLAVA
November 24, 1966

An Ilyushin-18 owned by TABSO Airlines disappeared into a snowstorm on the night of November 24, 1966 and plunged into a peak of the Carpathian Mountains near Bratislava, Czechoslovakia. All 82 aboard died.

EGYPT – CAIRO
May 20, 1965

Hampered by dangerous landing conditions at Egypt's Cairo Airport, a Pakistan International Airways Boeing 707 crashed on landing on the night of May 20, 1965. All 124 aboard were killed.

Cairo Airport in the early 1960s was a nightmare. For years it had been the talk of the industry, and finally, by 1965, members of the International Pilots' Association refused to make night landings at Cairo.

There were numerous hazards. First, there was inadequate lighting, making it difficult to define the parameters of each runway. In addition, some of the runways were eccentrically configured. One in particular was heavily sloped and approachable only by an abrupt dropping of a plane for a distance of almost 1,000 feet. Finally there was a shortage of rescue equipment.

Heeding the boycott by the IPA, authorities had begun to make improvements. But their priorities and the way they deployed them were mysterious. Their first purchase was up-to-date rescue equipment, but this was kept locked away.

The price for this laxity was paid by 124 people who died in the wreckage of a Pakistan International Airways Boeing 707, which, approaching the airport at far too steep a decline, crash-landed on the night of May 20, 1965. The tragedy finally brought about the improvements that could have prevented it.

FRANCE – BEAUVAIS
October 5, 1930

A combination of bad weather, bad judgment and faulty design sent the R-101, Britain's mammoth dirigible, to the ground on October 5, 1930. Forty-nine died.

The R-101, Britain's entry in the speed and passenger sweepstakes of giant dirigibles in the 1920s and 1930s, was buffeted by an enormous storm on the night of October 5, 1930. Its passengers and crew were flung from one side of the gondola to the other. Yet Lieutenant H. C. Irwin, the commander of the dirigible, radioed to his home base in Cardington, England: 'After an excellent supper our distinguished passengers smoked a final cigar and, having sighted the French coast, have now gone to rest after the excitement of the leave-taking.'

A sister ship to the R-100, the R-101 was an imposing construction. Seven hundred seventy-seven feet in length, it had a hydrogen capacity of five million cubic feet. Powered by six Rolls-Royce Condor engines, it was capable of lifting 150 tons and had accommodations for 100 passengers.

But the R-101 had been in trouble from the first moment out of the factory. On its maiden voyage, on October 14, 1929, its engines had malfunctioned. The fabric of its skin had seemed faulty.

The British government had been aware of these problems, and yet, in an international dirigible competition with Germany and France, it had still pushed for a long trip.

Thus, on October 5, 1930, 52 crew members and four distinguished observers, including Lord Thomson, who had argued most strongly in Parliament for the trip, boarded the R-101 for a trip to the Orient.

There were two portents of disaster. Four tons of water used as ballast were accidentally thrown overboard while the dirigible was still tied to its mooring. Second, a storm was brewing on the Channel, and that was exactly where the R-101 was heading.

Nevertheless, at 6:40 P.M., the R-101 left its mooring mast and headed directly into the storm. Cruising altitude was supposed to be 1,000 feet, but it could not maintain that altitude, dropping abruptly to 700, then shooting up to 1,100. One of the engines stopped partway across the Channel. Still, Lieutenant Irwin pressed cheerily on.

The storm did not abate when they passed over the French coastline. Thirty-five-knot winds buffeted the R-101, driving it lower and lower. By 1:00 A.M., at a village called Poix, the ship's altitude was a mere 250 feet and descending.

An hour later, the R-101 had reached Beauvais. It was now skimming trees and rooftops, headed for what seemed like a gentle and safe landing in a large field outside town. The field, however, was not altogether without obstacles. At one end was a ridge of hills, and the R-101 headed straight for it, crashing into the ridge and igniting its load of hydrogen. The entire ship was consumed in roaring flames in an instant, and 48 crew members and Lord Thomson were burned to death.

FRANCE – GRENOBLE
November 13, 1950

Bad weather forced a Canadian Curtis-Reid Air-Tours charter flight to ram into Mont Obiou, near Grenoble, France, on November 13, 1950. There were no survivors.

FRANCE – PARIS
June 3, 1962

Pilot error in failing to abort the takeoff of an overloaded Air France Boeing 707 from Paris's Orly Airport on June 3, 1962 was blamed for its fiery crash. One hundred thirty passengers and crew members were killed; two flight attendants survived.

FRANCE – PARIS
March 3, 1974

In the worst crash in the history of aviation to that date, Turkish Airlines Flight 981, a Douglas DC-10, suddenly lost compression and control when a faulty cargo door blew off, forcing the craft to crash in a turnip field near Paris. All 346 people aboard perished.

GERMANY – EAST BERLIN
August 14, 1972

One hundred fifty-six persons died in the midair explosion of an Interflug Ilyushin-62 flying from East Berlin to Burgas, Bulgaria. No official explanation for the tragedy has been released by East German authorities.

GERMANY – JOHANNISTHAL
October 17, 1913

A ripped hull, overheated gas and faulty design were responsible for the crash of the German naval dirigible LZ-18 on October 17, 1913 over Johannisthal, Germany. Twenty-eight died in the fiery crash.

GERMANY – MUNICH
December 17, 1960

A U.S. Air Force C-131 Convair went out of control over Munich, Germany on December 17, 1960 and plunged into the crowded city. Fifty-three people died; 20 were on the plane, 33 on the ground.

GREAT BRITAIN – ENGLAND, LONDON
June 18, 1972

Overloading was the apparent cause of the crash of a BEA Trident 1 shortly after takeoff from Heathrow Airport in London on June 18, 1972. All 118 aboard died, and no official reason for the crash was ever given.

A worldwide pilots' strike had been threatened for the summer of 1972, in protest over the lackadaisical attitude individual Western governments had taken toward the steadily increasing incidents of air terrorism and skyjacking. As a result, flights in Europe in June 1972 were full and occasionally overfull.

This was apparently the case with a British European Airways Trident 1, bound for Brussels, at London's Heathrow Airport on June 18, 1972. The weather was clear; flying conditions were ideal. The plane had been inspected and appeared to be taking off normally, if sluggishly. It was overloaded with 118 passengers and crew.

The plane cleared the runway and retracted its landing gear, preparatory to climbing to cruising altitude. And then, like a wounded bird, it fell out of the sky into a field beyond the runway it had just cleared. The aircraft split upon impact, scattering bits and pieces of its fuselage, wings and engines all over the field.

Rescue crews rushed to the scene immediately, dousing the huge fires fed by the large amount of jet fuel aboard. Two passengers survived the impact but died later: A young girl was pulled from the wreckage by police, but she expired before an ambulance could arrive for her. An older man, found in the field, was taken to a London hospital, but he too died before the end of the day. The precise cause of the crash was never determined.

GREAT BRITAIN – WALES, CARDIFF
March 12, 1950

No reason has been given for the crash on landing of a charter Avro Tudor V at Cardiff, Wales on March 12, 1950. Eighty soccer fans and crew members died; three men survived.

The legion of unexplained crashes under ideal conditions seems to be endless. One such incident is the odd crash of a chartered Avro Tudor V prop plane that carried 78 Welsh soccer fans returning from a triumphant match in Dublin to their deaths.

It was a one-hour, commuter-length flight from Dublin. The weather was nonthreatening; Llandow Airport at Cardiff was clear and ready to accept the landing of the aircraft.

The Avro circled and approached – far too low. Just short of the runway, the plane's forward section hit the ground, and the plane flipped over.

There was no fire, just an eerie, other-worldly silence surrounding this bizarre but fatal accident. Evan Thomas, a farmer who was one of the first rescuers on the scene, reported to the newspapers, 'The smoke from the engines was curling from the wreckage. Through it walked two men. They were the only things that moved.'

Three men survived the crash. Eighty other soccer fans and crew members were crushed to death.

INDIA – BOMBAY
January 1, 1978

No official explanation was given for the midair explosion of an Air India Boeing 747 over Bombay on January 1, 1978. All 213 aboard were killed.

INDIA – NEW DELHI
June 14, 1972

Terrorism was suspected but never proved in the midair explosion of a Japan Airlines DC-8 over New Delhi on June 14, 1972. Eighty-seven died; six survived.

A suspicion of terrorist sabotage surrounded the mysterious crash of a Japan Airlines DC-8 jet at New Delhi's Palam International Airport on June 14, 1972. Only two weeks before, Japanese terrorists had massacred 25 innocent people in the International Airport in Tel Aviv, and threats of retaliation had been made. But investigators would never adequately prove this theory.

The plane had departed from Tokyo and was proceeding with a normal, clear-weather landing when it suddenly burst into flames, heeled over and crashed into the farmland that rimmed the airport, near the Jamuna River. Authorities reasoned that there was an explosion, either before or on impact, since pieces of the plane and its passengers were strewn over a two-mile radius. Eighty-seven died in the wreck and six survived, but their testimony cast no light upon the events that led to the crash.

ITALY – PALERMO
May 5, 1972

Pilot error caused the crash of an Alitalia DC-8 into Montagna Lunga, near Palermo, on May 5, 1972. All 115 aboard were killed.

JAPAN – MORIOKA
July 30, 1971

A Japanese Air Force F-86 Sabre jet without radar collided in midair with an All-Nippon Boeing 727 on July 30, 1971. Pilot error was blamed in this crash that killed all 162 passengers aboard the jet. The military jet pilot parachuted to safety.

The year 1971 was particularly bad for near collisions in the sky. There were 600 of these near misses reported in the United States that year, and 200 in Japan. There were just too many civilian and military aircraft flying in close proximity to one another in the two countries, and experts felt that a tragedy was bound to occur. It did, on July 30, over Morioka, in the so-called Japanese Alps.

Flight 58, an All-Nippon Boeing 727 was loaded largely with members of a Japanese society dedicated to the memory of war dead. They had just been to Hokkaido on a pilgrimage and were heading back to Tokyo. The takeoff from Chitose Airport was uneventful; it was a clear day, and visibility was good. They reached their cruising level of 28,000 feet easily and without incident.

In the same area, Sergeant Yoshimi Ichikawa, a student pilot with 21 hours in the air, was at the controls of a Japanese Air Force F-86 Sabre jet. Neither he nor his instructor, Captain Tamotsu Kuma, who was flying in another Sabre jet, had the benefit of radar.

The airliner did, and thus it is somewhat puzzling

that its commander did not see the military aircraft until it was too late. The planes collided in midair. The airliner exploded upon impact, and pieces of it and its passengers were scattered over mountaintops. All 162 jet passengers would die in this tragedy, but Ichikawa, the student pilot of the jet, would parachute to safety.

He was immediately arrested and charged with involuntary homicide, but he would be acquitted.

JAPAN – MOUNT FUJI
March 5, 1966

Pilot error and wind conditions claimed a BOAC Boeing 707 on March 5, 1966. The aircraft collided with Mount Fuji, killing 124 people.

JAPAN – MOUNT OGURA
August 12, 1985

Improper repairs of a Japan Airlines Boeing 747SR led to the loss of part of the airplane's tail section and loss of control of the aircraft, which crashed into the side of Mount Ogura, Japan. The worst air disaster in the world involving a single passenger plane, it claimed 475 lives. Forty-nine passengers survived.

The worst air disaster in the world involving a single passenger plane occurred on a mountainside in central Japan on the evening of Monday, August 12, 1985. A Japan Airlines jumbo jet veered eratically in an uncontrolled path and slammed into the side of Mount Ogura, one of Japan's highest peaks. There were 524 people aboard; only 49 of them survived.

Japan Airlines Flight 123 left Tokyo's Haneda Airport at 6:15 P.M. for its 250-mile flight to Osaka. Travel had been especially heavy in the last few days. Thousands of Japanese were returning to their hometowns for a traditional midsummer festival known as Obon, in which the souls of ancestors are honored.

The plane was a Boeing 747SR, especially configured for Japan, where flights with 500 passengers were not uncommon. This one was completely filled.

The aircraft had seen a lot of service and, seven years before, had made a hard landing at Osaka. The impact had damaged the lower rear fuselage, and Boeing maintenance people had supposedly repaired it.

Thirteen minutes after takeoff, Flight 123 was clearly in trouble. The pilot, Masami Takahama, radioed that the right rear passenger door had 'broken.' One of the survivors, Yumi Ochia, an off-duty assistant purser for Japan Airlines, said later that there was a loud noise that originated in the rear of the plane and over her head. Following it, there was an instant 'whiteout' as a thick fog filled the cabin – a sure indication that the cabin pressure had dropped and water vapor had condensed.

The plane had reached its cruising altitude of 24,000 feet by now, and the crew immediately radioed Tokyo for permission to drop to 20,000 feet.

But a far greater problem than reduced cabin pressure had been created by whatever caused the loud noise heard by the off-duty purser. The impact of it had been great enough to force the plane's nose up. And worse, it had apparently done something major to the craft's control system. Among the 43 sensors placed throughout the airliner, the one in the rear, near the horizontal stabilizer, had registered the greatest shock. It had broken off. Captain Takahama was unable to control the plane.

'Immediate trouble, request turn back to Haneda,' a crew member radioed to Tokyo at 6:25 P.M., seconds after the first transmission. Four times over the next 30 minutes, the captain radioed that he had no control of the plane. He was attempting to steer it by alternately increasing and throttling down engine power.

By 6:45, the plane had lost an appreciable amount of altitude. It was flying at only 9,300 feet, and the captain had all but lost complete control. 'We may be finished,' he said to his co-pilot. At the same time, the black box recorder picked up a voice in the background announcing emergency-landing instructions in the cabin.

Ten minutes later, Tokyo radioed Flight 123 that it could land either at Haneda or at a U.S. air base in Yokota, northwest of Tokyo.

But by then, Flight 123 had stopped answering. One minute after the clearance had been given for an emergency landing, it had slammed into the side of Mount Ogura, in Gumma prefecture, 70 miles northwest of Tokyo. It exploded on impact, setting fire to acres of forest on the side of the mountain.

An eyewitness later told the Japan Broadcasting Corporation that she had watched the plane crash in 'a big flame' after it flew over her house. The explosion was 'followed by a white smoke which turned into a black mushroom-like-cloud,' she said.

It would be 14 hours before the first rescue teams, composed of three dozen airborne troops, could be lowered onto the mountain by helicopters, joined by local police who hiked through a steady rain to the crash site.

At first, sabotage was thought to be the culprit. But a Japanese Navy destroyer on routine patrol reported finding a section of the plane's tail in Sagami Bay, just off the Miura Peninsula, southwest of Tokyo and 80 miles southeast of the crash site. The tail had apparently fallen off.

Now the history of the aircraft began to help solve the mystery of the crash and the 32 terrible minutes that preceded it. One of the first questions to be solved was what had caused the rudder and other hydraulic systems to stop functioning.

The answer was in the repairs made seven years previously to a ruptured bulkhead. They had been improperly made, even though they had been done by a team flown by Boeing to Japan. Shaped somewhat like an umbrella canopy, the bulkhead was at the very back of the passenger cabin and separated the highly pressurized cabin, from the unpressurized tail section, which was immediately behind it.

A single line of rivets was used for part of the repair, instead of the double line of rivets called for in the manual. With the expected metal fatigue brought on by seven years of constant use, the improper repair eventually gave way. And the results were monumentally tragic.

The blame apparently was not entirely Boeing's, at least in the minds of some officials and employees of Japan Airlines. Shortly after the findings of the investigative panel were released, there was a major shake-up in the executive structure of Japan Airlines. The president and two executives were replaced.

But this was not the end of the aftermath of this record catastrophe. On September 21, police in Yokohama were called to the home of Hiro Tominaga, a Japan Airlines maintenance official who had been negotiating compensation payments with families of the crash victims.

Tominaga was found on the floor of his home, dead of knife wounds inflicted to his neck and chest. A four-inch-long knife was found near his body. A note nearby read, 'I am atoning with my death.'

JAPAN – TOKYO
June 18, 1953

Unspecified engine trouble caused the crash of a U.S. Air Force C-124 Globemaster shortly after takeoff from Tachikawa Air Base, near Tokyo, on June 18, 1953. All 129 aboard perished.

JAPAN – TOKYO
February 4, 1966

No official reason was ever given for the crash of an All-Nippon Airways Boeing 727 landing at Tokyo

*International Airport on February 4, 1966. All 133
persons aboard died.*

MOROCCO – CASABLANCA
July 12, 1961

*A fear of exposing Soviet military secrets to the West
caused the pilot of a Czechoslovakian Airlines
Ilyushin-18 to ignore instructions to divert from fog-
bound Casablanca Airport to a nearby U.S. air base.
The plane crashed, killing all 72 aboard.*

International politics seem to have figured prominently
in the terrible tragedy that befell the passengers in a
Ceskoslovenske Aerolinie (Czechoslovakian Airlines)
Ilyushin-18 flight from Zurich to Prague, via Morocco.
   The flight was scheduled to stop at Casablanca on the
evening of July 12, 1961. But Casablanca was completely blanketed with a heavy fog, and the airport had
closed down. Josef Mikus, the veteran pilot captaining
the flight, was denied permission to land and told to
divert to the U.S. air base at Nouasseur, a mere 15
minutes away. It was still open and relatively fog free.
   The plane had plenty of fuel. It could easily have
made the distance to the U.S. air base. However,
Captain Mikus knew that there were several Soviet
flying instructors aboard, on their way to train revolutionaries in Ghana and Guinea. Furthermore, there
was a huge cargo load of films and pamphlets also
destined for these two insurrection-torn African republics. To Mikus, landing at an American military base
was tantamount to landing in the arms of the enemy.
   At least that was the explanation given by authorities
afterward, after Mikus ignored the instructions of the
control tower at Casablanca and nosed his turboprop in
for an instrument landing. But without help from the
controllers, Mikus and his plane had no chance of
success. Midway to its landing, the aircraft hit a power
line. The heavy cable ripped two engines from the

plane's wings, hurling them into midair, where they exploded. Two towers collapsed inward, toward the plane, which was flung heavily to earth.

It would take 25 minutes for rescuers to reach the scene of the crash, and even then, according to the *I.C.A.O.* (International Civil Aviation Organization) *Accident Digest*, Number 13, 'When the police arrived at the scene . . . calls for help were heard coming from the wreckage, and an attempt was made to rescue the passengers, but a fire started, and it was impossible to continue operations.'

All 72 persons aboard died.

NEW GUINEA – BIAK ISLAND
July 16, 1957

An unexplained engine explosion hurtled a KLM Super Constellation into the sea shortly after takeoff from Biak Island, New Guinea on July 16, 1957. Fifty-seven died.

PAKISTAN – KARACHI
March 3, 1953

Pilot error was blamed for the first fatal jetliner crash in history, on takeoff from Karachi Airport on March 3, 1953. On a test run, the Canadian Pacific Comet 1A turbojet burst into flames on impact, killing all 11 men aboard.

PERU – LIMA
November 27, 1962

No explanation was given for the crash, in clear weather in the Andes near Lima, of a Varig Airlines Boeing 707 on November 27, 1962. All 97 aboard perished.

PUERTO RICO – SAN JUAN
April 11, 1952

The failure of airline personnel to follow basic safety procedures during a ditch at sea near San Juan killed 52 people aboard a Pan American DC-4 on April 11, 1952. Seven survived.

A failure to follow basic procedure by the cabin and cockpit crew aboard a Pan American DC-4 on April 11, 1952 accounted for 52 needless fatalities.

The flight took off uneventfully from San Juan, Puerto Rico bound for New York. But nine minutes into the flight, the plane developed engine trouble. With one of its motors inoperable, it began to descend. The pilot had time to decide between ditching the plane in the sea, four miles from Puerto Rico, or taking his chances over land. He opted to go down at sea and informed the San Juan tower of his intent.

Once this course had been determined, it was up to the crew to prepare the passengers for the ditching effort by informing them of the location of life jackets and rubber rafts – both of which were aboard in sufficient quantity to save everyone. But this crucial and elementary drill was never carried out.

As a result, when the aircraft struck the water and floated, passengers panicked. To compound the terror, the crew opened the wrong doors to debark the passengers and let enormous amounts of water into the cabin, thus hastening the sinking of the craft. Terrified, confused and without life jackets, the passengers huddled on the plane's wing. Only one life raft was inflated, and this floated off with only seven survivors aboard.

Three minutes later, the aircraft sank beneath 15-foot waves, carrying 52 passengers to a watery death. A handful managed to stay afloat until ships could rescue them.

SAUDI ARABIA – JIDDA
July 11, 1991

All 250 passengers and 11 crew members died when a Canadian Charter DC-8 crashed shortly after takeoff from King Abdel-Aziz airport. It was the tenth worst crash in commercial airline history.

The *hajj*, an annual Muslim pilgrimage to the holy cities of Mecca and Medina, has frequently been marred by tragedy. In 1990, 1,426 pilgrims died in a stampede in a tunnel (see CIVIL UNREST, p. 95). Before that, terrorist attacks had disrupted the pilgrimage. But the 1991 *hajj* was a relatively peaceful one, free from unrest and calamity – until after it concluded.

On July 11, 250 Nigerian Muslims boarded their charter jet at King Abdel-Aziz Airport in Jidda, Saudi Arabia, for the return trip to Sokoto, Nigeria. The DC-8 was a Canadian Charter, owned by the Montreal-based carrier Nationair and leased by a Nigerian Company, Holdtrade. It was a prestigious arrangement; Holdtrade was set up to exclusively carry Muslim pilgrims by Ibrahim Dasuki, the son of the spiritual leader of Nigeria's Muslims, the Sultan of Sokoto.

The weather was clear and hot; the takeoff was uneventful. But shortly after the plane cleared the sands of the Saudi desert, the control tower at King Abdel-Aziz Airport began to receive rapidly delivered distress signals from the Canadian pilot of the jet. There was a fire in the plane's landing gear.

Officials at the airport advised the pilot to dump his fuel and return to the airport, but within instants of this command, the plane nosed over and dove for the tarmac. With a bone-rattling, thunderous explosion, the jet erupted on impact, flinging pieces of the airplane and the bodies of its passengers and crew far into the desert.

It was a grisly sight. Dismembered bodies and

white robes blackened to torn tatters littered the grounds of the airport and the nearby sands. All 250 passengers and 11 crew members died, making this the tenth worst crash in commercial airline history.

SAUDI ARABIA – RIYADH
August 19, 1980

A combination of the failure of airline personnel to follow evacuation procedures and the Saudi Airlines practice of cooking over open butane stoves aboard its aircraft resulted in death by fire aboard a Saudi Airlines Lockheed L-1011 TriStar on the ground at Riyadh, Saudi Arabia on August 19, 1980. All 310 aboard died.

Three hundred ten passengers and crew were aboard a Saudi Airlines Lockheed L-1011 TriStar on the afternoon of August 19, 1980. The flight had originated in Karachi, Pakistan and was on its way to Jidda, after a short stopover in Riyadh. Among the passengers were some devout Muslims, who were allowed to bring two butane cooking stoves aboard so that they could observe their dietary laws in flight. Western carriers would blanch at this practice, but it was routine in the Middle East.

The flight departed from Riyadh without incident. But shortly after takeoff, when the plane was approximately 80 miles from the airport, the pilot radioed that there was a fire aboard and he was returning. He was given clearance and landed safely. The plane taxied to the end of the runway and onto a side area.

Rescue teams rushed to it, expecting the passengers to pour from the escape hatches. But before fire fighters could reach the plane, it burst thunderously into flames. Heavy smoke billowed from every opening, and the heat was intense. No one could approach the aircraft, not even in a protective asbestos suit. Fire trucks sprayed the consumed airliner with foam. It was all that could be done for the moment.

When teams were finally able to cut their way into the wreckage, they found an appalling sight. Passengers were piled up in mounds of fused and charred flesh near the escape hatches. There had obviously been a stampede when the plane landed. But none of the hatches were open or even unlocked. The crew's escape hatch in the cockpit was also, strangely, firmly latched. Every single person on the aircraft had died in the fire.

There was a fire extinguisher alongside one of the butane cooking stoves, and this must have been where the fire began. But why hadn't the crew opened the escape hatches?

Investigators posited three possibilities:

1. From the position of the bodies, it was obvious that there had been mass panic aboard the craft. Those in the back had rushed to the front, and this mayhem might have blocked the efforts of the crew to open the exits.

2. It was entirely possible that by the time the plane had taxied to a stop at Riyadh airport, all aboard had been asphyxiated.

3. The escape system on the plane was designed so that the hatches could not be opened from the inside unless the cabin had been depressurized. For some reason, the cabin pressure had not been released by the crew, and thus the escape hatches could not be opened by anyone.

A series of lawsuits by relatives of some of the 310 who perished aboard the plane attempted to prove negligence in the use of flammable materials within the aircraft, and that certainly contributed to the intensity of the blaze. But the reason that the plane remained sealed will never be known.

SPAIN – BARCELONA
July 3, 1970

No official reason was given for the disappearance of a Dan-Air Airlines Comet over the Mediterranean near Barcelona on July 3, 1970. All 112 persons aboard died.

SPAIN – CANARY ISLANDS, SANTA CRUZ DE TENERIFE
December 3, 1972

In the fourth worst air crash up to that time, a Spantax Airlines Charter Convair 990-A Coronados lost an engine over Santa Cruz de Tenerife, in the Canary Islands, and plunged to earth. All 155 aboard perished.

SPAIN – CANARY ISLANDS, SANTA CRUZ DE TENERIFE
March 27, 1977

In the worst accident in the history of civil aviation, two charter Boeing 747s, one belonging to KLM, the other to Pan Am, collided on the ground in a fog at Los Rodeos Airport on Santa Cruz de Tenerife, on March 27, 1977. A combination of delays caused by a terrorist incident and the misunderstanding of the Spanish-speaking airport controllers by the Dutch crew of the KLM jet culminated in the death of all 249 aboard the KLM plane and 321 aboard the Pan Am 747.

Ironically, the deadliest accident in civil aviation history took place on the ground. And it involved two Boeing 747s that never would have been there in the first place had it not been for a small, fanatical group of militant separatists who had set off a small bomb near the florist's shop in the Las Palmas Airport earlier that day.

A Pan American Airways charter jet from Los Angeles via New York was taking passengers to Las

Palmas to hook up with a Mediterranean cruise, and a KLM charter jet loaded with Dutch tourists had been diverted to Santa Cruz de Tenerife because the Las Palmas Airport had been shut down. Santa Cruz de Tenerife is ill equipped and unsuited for jumbo jets, or for most aircraft, for that matter. It is noted for the sudden fogs that close in on it at various times of the day and the year and for the dearth of equipment it possesses.

Still, it was probably the difficulty the Dutch crew of the KLM 747 had in understanding the Spanish-accented English of the control tower that was ultimately responsible for this terrible tragedy, which ultimately claimed the lives of 570 people.

The planes had been delayed on the ground nearly two hours when both were finally cleared for takeoff. There was one main runway at the airport and a small holding area at the end of the runway.

Finally, at 4:40 P.M., the KLM jet was given clearance to taxi to the end of the runway first, with the Pan Am jet behind it. When the Dutch craft reached the end of the runway, it would turn around and take off, while the Pan Am jet would taxi off and wait in the small side space. There would be plenty of time for both maneuvers.

It was extremely foggy, and the Pan Am jet had difficulty keeping the KLM jet in sight. Eventually, its tail-lights disappeared entirely into the mist. The Pan Am pilot reached the turnoff when suddenly he saw the lights of the KLM bearing down on him, at full throttle, in a takeoff. 'What's he doing? He'll kill us all!' shouted the Pan Am pilot, as he frantically tried to pull his plane off the runway and into a field of high grass.

It was too late. The KLM jet smashed full force into the Pan Am 747 and then went on to tear through it. Both planes exploded in a giant roar of igniting jet fuel. Black clouds rose in the air, and the cries of the dying pierced the blackness like knives. Blood was everywhere.

Every single person on the KLM died. Because the Pan Am craft had partially left the runway, those in the front of the plane survived. 'It exploded from the back,' said Lynda Daniel, a 20-year-old Los Angeles college student. 'We were sitting next to the emergency exit and it blew off. Most of the people sitting in the first six seats made it. People started climbing over me, and I saw flames, so I decided to get out.'

Fire consumed most of both of the jets, and some of the bodies were burned beyond recognition. All 249 aboard the KLM jet were dead. Three hundred twenty-one died on the Pan Am 747, in a tragedy that never should have occurred.

SPAIN – GRANADA
October 2, 1964

No explanation has been found for the mysterious plunge into the Mediterranean near Granada of a Union Transports Africain Douglas DC-6 on October 2, 1964. All 80 aboard perished.

SPAIN – IBIZA
January 7, 1972

Pilot error was blamed for the smashing of an Iberia Airlines Caravelle into a mountainside on the island of Ibiza on January 7, 1972. One hundred seven died.

SWITZERLAND – BASEL
April 10, 1973

Pilot error caused the crash of a BEA Vanguard charter jet into a mountainside south of Basel, Switzerland on April 10, 1973. One hundred seven died; 39 survived.

THAILAND – SUPHAN BURI
May 26, 1991

A faulty thrust reverser caused the twelfth worst crash in commercial aviation history, when an Austrian Lauda Air Boeing 767–300, bound from Hong Kong to Vienna, exploded and crashed into the jungle near Suphan Buri, Thailand, 16 minutes after takeoff from Bangkok's Don Muang International Airport. All 223 aboard died.

UNITED STATES – ALASKA, ANCHORAGE
June 3, 1963

No official reason was given for the mysterious crash of a Northwest Airlines DC-7 charter carrying U.S. military personnel over the Pacific Ocean near Anchorage, Alaska on June 3, 1963. All 101 aboard died.

UNITED STATES – ALASKA, JUNEAU
September 4, 1971

Alaska Airlines Flight 1866, a Boeing 727, crashed into Mount Fairweather, near Juneau Airport, during a heavy storm at midnight, September 4, 1971. All 109 passengers and crew aboard died.

UNITED STATES – ARIZONA, GRAND CANYON
June 30, 1956

Human error on the part of an air controller caused the first midair collision in U.S. commercial airliner history and the worst air disaster to date when a United Airlines DC-7 collided with a TWA Super Constellation over the Grand Canyon on June 30, 1956. All 128 aboard both planes died.

UNITED STATES – ILLINOIS, CHICAGO
May 25, 1979

Faulty maintenance by American Airlines mechanics caused the worst disaster in U.S. aviation history. Mishandling of engine repair caused the left engine of an American Airlines DC-10 to fall off in flight near Chicago on May 25, 1979, and the plane lunged to earth, killing all 277 aboard and two on the ground.

UNITED STATES – INDIANA, SHELBYVILLE
August 9, 1969

Student pilot error and the lack of a transponder were responsible for the midair collision of an Allegheny Airlines DC-9 and a Piper Cherokee over Shelbyville, Indiana on August 9, 1969. Eighty-three were killed.

UNITED STATES – MARYLAND, ELKTON
December 8, 1963

A combination of lightning and jet fuel with a high flash point caused the explosion of a Pan Am Boeing 707 in the skies over Elkton, Maryland on December 8, 1963. Seventy-three people died.

UNITED STATES – MASSACHUSETTS, BOSTON
October 4, 1960

A flock of birds sucked into the turbines of the engines of an Eastern Airlines Electra caused it to lose control and crash into Boston Harbor on October 4, 1960. Sixty-one died; 10 were rescued.

Flocks of birds are a recurrent and unexpected danger to jets. Groups of birds soaring around airports can be, and frequently are, ingested into the engines of jetliners. In jet travel's early years, this occurrence would bring an engine to a complete stop, thus threatening takeoffs and landings. Modern jet engines, manufactured after the mid-1970s, are designed to handle 'bird strike,' as the phenomenon is now called, without failing.

But jet travel was in its infancy on October 4, 1960, when Eastern Airlines Flight 375, a propjet Electra flying to Philadelphia, took off from Boston's Logan Airport. It was a clear late afternoon, and the plane lifted off at 5:48 P.M., all four of its engines in prime working order. Its takeoff pattern took it over Boston Harbor, where it began a slow turn.

And at that moment, Flight 375 encountered a flock of starlings. The birds were sucked up by the turbines of the engines, stopping the port inboard engine and causing it to catch fire. The aircraft, out of control, dropped like a punctured parachute into the waters of Boston Harbor at the Pleasant Park Channel.

The waters were choppy that evening, with a strong set, but there were five yachts anchored nearby. Divers from these boats went into the water and managed to rescue 10 passengers, still strapped in their floating seats. None of the other 61 passengers and crew members survived.

At first, FAA investigation focused on the Lockheed Electra, a trouble-plagued plane, but close scrutiny of the wreckage revealed one of the first examples of 'bird strike' as a hazard to safe jet travel.

UNITED STATES – MASSACHUSETTS, BOSTON
July 31, 1973

Malfunctioning instruments and delayed rescue attempts may have accounted for the deaths in the otherwise unexplained crash of a Delta Airlines DC-9 on landing at Boston's Logan Airport on July 31, 1973. Eighty-eight died.

UNITED STATES – MICHIGAN, SOUTH HAVEN
June 24, 1950

The cause of the crash of a Northwest Airlines DC-4 into Lake Michigan on June 24, 1950, in heavy weather, has never been determined. All 58 aboard died.

UNITED STATES – NEW JERSEY COAST
April 14, 1933

Human error in piloting and design caused the airship Akron to crash in a thunderstorm off the coast of New Jersey on April 14, 1933. Seventy-three were killed; three were rescued.

UNITED STATES – NEW JERSEY, LAKEHURST
May 6, 1937

Exhaust sparks igniting escaping gas, static electricity caused by a sudden rainstorm or sabotage caused the fiery crash of the giant dirigible Hindenburg as it floated near its mooring mast in Lakehurst, New Jersey after a triumphant transatlantic voyage. Thirty-one died; 61 survived.

UNITED STATES – NEW YORK, BROOKLYN
December 16, 1960

Human error on the part of both flight crews and controllers was deemed responsible for the midair collision of a United Airlines DC-8 and a TWA Super Constellation over New York City on December 16, 1960. One hundred twenty-eight aboard the two liners and eight on the ground in Brooklyn died.

UNITED STATES – NEW YORK, COVE NECK, LONG ISLAND
January 25, 1990

A Federal Transportation Board inquiry determined that faulty judgments by the crew were responsible when an Avianca Boeing 707 ran out of gas and crashed into the residential area of Cove Neck, Long Island on January 25, 1990. But a series of factors were involved in the tragedy, which resulted in the death of 73 aboard the jet. Eighty-five survived.

UNITED STATES – NEW YORK, NEW YORK
July 28, 1945

Pilot misjudgment was responsible for a B-25 Mitchell bomber crashing into New York's Empire State Building on July 28, 1945 in a heavy fog. The crew of three and 11 workers in the building were killed.

One of the more bizarre airplane crashes in the history of aviation occurred on a foggy Saturday morning in July 1945. It involved the collision of a U.S. Army Air Corps B-25 Mitchell bomber with New York City's Empire State Building. The experts at the time said the odds of this sort of accident happening at all were 10,000 to 1. But it happened.

The morning of July 28, 1945 was a murky one in New York City. A heavy fog had rolled in from the Atlantic Ocean overnight, and the sun had not yet burned it away.

Twenty-seven-year-old Lieutenant Colonel William F. Smith Jr., a highly decorated West Point graduate, was flying a B-25 on a short trip from New Bedford, Massachusetts to New York's LaGuardia Airport. The plane was carrying a crew of three and one passenger. At approximately 9:30 A.M., LaGuardia ground control redirected him to Newark, New Jersey. LaGuardia was socked in with fog, ceiling zero and forward visibility about three miles. 'The Empire State Building is not visible,' added the ground controller, in an unconsciously prophetic afterthought.

Smith and his crew headed for Newark in a path that would take them squarely over the island of Manhattan. Fifteen minutes after receiving his wave-off from LaGuardia, Smith found himself a mere 500 feet above Rockefeller Center's towers, more than 40 stories high. According to observers on the ground, he climbed abruptly out of that danger and disappeared into the mist.

But apparently Smith did not climb high enough. Two minutes later, the bomber, flying at 225 miles per hour, smashed squarely into the north side of the 78th and 79th floors of the Empire State Building – the highest building in the world at the time. The fuel in the engines exploded on impact, and the plane's two propeller-driven engines scissored their way through the concrete walls of the building. One engine emerged on the south side of the skyscraper, became airborne for a brief moment over 33rd Street and descended in a long loop through the skylight of the penthouse sculpture studio of Henry Hering. The other flaming engine demolished the elevator door on the 79th floor, snapping the cable of the elevator car. One woman was riding in it, and she began the long plunge to the bottom. Fortunately the elevator's automatic braking device engaged, and she was saved from a plummet to the basement. But just as she stopped, part of the engine hit the top of the car, caving it in.

The plane broke into several pieces. Part of a wing careened a block east onto Madison Avenue. Pieces of the fuselage dug into the walls of nearby skyscrapers as if they had been shot through a high-powered machine gun.

If this had happened on a weekday, the Empire State Building would have been thickly populated with close to 50,000 office workers and tourists. But it was Saturday, and only a handful of workers were at their desks in the 79th-floor offices of the War Relief Services of the National Catholic Welfare Conference. Eleven of them were killed; some of them burned to death; others were crushed. One man was flung through a window. His charred body would be discovered on a 72nd-story ledge of the Empire State Building. Twenty-five were badly injured. All three servicemen on the plane died violently.

Firemen appeared on the scene quickly and doused the blaze. For weeks, until war-appropriated material could be secured for repairs, a gaping hole 18 by 20 feet would exist in the side of the Empire State Building. A tarpaulin was used to cover it, but it was continually blown loose.

The woman who fell 79 stories in the elevator shaft survived, thanks to the quick thinking of Coast Guard hospital apprentice Donald Maloney, who just happened to be strolling by the Empire State Building. He ran to a drugstore and commandeered syringes, hypodermics and other medical necessities. He then dashed into the building, climbed down through the crumpled roof of the elevator cab, and administered a shot of morphine to the injured woman and saved her life.

UNITED STATES – NEW YORK, QUEENS
February 3, 1959

Failure to read new instrumentation correctly resulted in the crash, during an instrument landing, of an American Airlines Lockheed Electra at New York's LaGuardia Airport on February 3, 1959. Sixty-six died; seven survived.

UNITED STATES – NORTH CAROLINA, HENDERSONVILLE
July 19, 1967

Failure to heed instructions by the pilot of a small plane was blamed for the midair collision of a Cessna 310 and a Piedmont Boeing 727 over Hendersonville, North Carolina on July 19, 1967. Eighty-two died.

UNITED STATES – OHIO, AVA
September 3, 1925

Political considerations apparently outweighed weather and safety factors when the Shenandoah, America's proudest lighter-than-air ship, was forced by local vote-getters to fly in bad weather over Ohio. On September 3, 1925 the ship went down in a pasture and broke apart, killing 14 crew members. Twenty-eight survived.

UNITED STATES – TEXAS, DAWSON
May 3, 1968

No explanation has been given for the explosion and crash of a Braniff Lockheed Electra near Dawson, Texas on May 3, 1968. All 88 aboard died.

UNITED STATES – UTAH, BRYCE CANYON
October 24, 1947

Faulty design was determined to be the culprit in the crash of a United Airlines DC-6 on October 24, 1947 as it was descending for a landing at Bryce Canyon Airport, Utah. Fifty-two died.

UNITED STATES – VIRGINIA, RICHMOND
November 8, 1961

Ancient equipment and a failure to profit from the past were the almost certain causes of a catastrophic crash of an Imperial Airlines Lockheed Constellation near Richmond, Virginia on November 8, 1961. Seventy-seven died. Two survived.

UNITED STATES – WASHINGTON, MOSES LAKE
December 20, 1952

Pilot error was blamed for the crash, on takeoff, of a US Air Force C-124 over Moses Lake, Washington on December 20, 1952. Eighty-seven were killed; 44 survived.

USSR – KRANAYA POLYANA
October 14, 1972

Pilot error was responsible for the crash of a Soviet Aeroflot Ilyushin-62 on approach, in bad weather, to the Kranaya Polyana Airport on October 14, 1972. One hundred seventy-six were killed.

The weather was abominable over Moscow on October 14, 1972. A heavy mist broken by intermittent periods of rain reduced visibility to practically nothing. Not only that, the instrument-landing apparatus at Sheremetevo International Airport was temporarily inoperative. The following afternoon, a British European Airways flight would be diverted to Stockholm when the pilot decided that the combination of bad visibility and an out-of-order landing system was a situation he was unwilling to battle.

The same decision should have been made the night before by the pilot of an Ilyushin-62 reportedly chartered from the Soviet airline Aeroflot by the state travel agency Intourist. At 9:00 P.M. that night, he approached the airport and requested clearance for landing. He was granted it but reminded that there were no instrument-landing capabilities.

The flight had left Paris at noon that day with a full passenger load that included 102 French citizens. Early that evening, all but one of these French passengers had disembarked at a stop in Leningrad. Thirty-eight Chileans, five Algerians, three Italians, two Lebanese, a Frenchman, a Briton and 111 Russians were still aboard when it departed for the last leg of its flight to Moscow.

The pilot circled the field and came in for a landing. It was impossible to see the runway. He circled twice more and aborted each time. Finally, on the fourth try, he apparently felt that he had the runway in sight. But he was tragically wrong. He was three miles away from the airport, on the outskirts of the small village of Kranaya Polyana. The plane struck the ground with enough force to explode and send fiery sparks 100 feet into the misty night sky.

Everyone aboard – 176 passengers and crew members – died, making this the worse commercial airline crash in the world to that date. The Soviet news agency Tass stubbornly refused to release details of the crash at first. Soviet authorities even tried to misdirect Western newspeople to the village of Chernaya Gryaz, seven miles from the site of the crash.

But because there were foreign nationals killed in the crash, the Soviets finally released the statistics and a terse story about the disaster.

VENEZUELA – LA CORUBA
March 16, 1969

Pilot error was blamed for the crash, on takeoff, of a VIASA DC-9 at La Coruba, Venezuela on March 16, 1969. Eighty-four died in the airplane; 76 were killed on the ground.

WEST INDIES – GUADALOUPE
June 22, 1962

An Air France Boeing 707 crashed on landing at Guadaloupe on June 22, 1962. The cause of the crash was never ascertained. All 113 aboard died.

YUGOSLAVIA – LJUBLJANA
September 1, 1966

Pilot error was the reason given for the crash on landing at Ljubljana, Yugoslavia of a charter Britannia Airways 102 on September 1, 1966. Ninety-seven died; 20 survived.

One hundred twelve British tourists chartered a turbo-prop airliner from Britannia Airways in September 1966 for a vacation in Yugoslavia. But because of pilot error, only 20 of them would survive the trip.

The aircraft made the journey from London's Heathrow Airport without trouble. The weather and the approach to the airport in Ljubljana, a city of 200,000 north and west of Zagreb and Belgrade, were clear. But the flight was obviously off course when it approached the landing field, and controllers advised the pilot of his error. He was 110 yards off course and 600 feet too low.

The crew apparently received this information and failed to act on it. The plane descended on the wrong path and at the wrong altitude. Then, according to one of the survivors, Arthur Rowcliff, 'The plane slowed down. Then it started to vibrate. A few seconds later we crashed, bounced back in the air and finally fell down. We were thrown clear with our seats.'

The aircraft had plowed into a ridge full of fir trees, leaped into the air and then plummeted to earth, where it burst into flames. Those who, like Rowcliff and his family, were thrown clear survived. The others perished in the inferno that erupted when the plane struck the ground. The ultimate death toll would be 97.

Civil Unrest
and Terrorism

The Worst Recorded Civil Unrest and Terrorism

* Detailed in text

CIVIL UNREST

Armenia/Turkey
  * Armenian massacres by Turks (1895–1922)

Austria
  Vienna
  General strike following Nazi acquittal for political murder (1927)

Burundi
  Marangara
  * Tribal confrontation (1988)

China
  Beijing
  * Massacre in Tiananmen Square (1989)
  Northern Provinces
  * Boxer Uprising (1900)

Czechoslovakia
  Uprising crushed (1977)

Egypt
  Insurrections over exorbitant taxes (189 B.C.)

Europe
  * The Holocaust – attempted genocide of European Jews by Nazis (1939–45)

France
  Paris
  * St. Bartholomew's Day massacre of 2,000 Huguenots (1572)
  Massacre of Champs de Mars (1791)
  * Reign of Terror and White Terror (1793–95)
  Rouen
  Burning of Joan of Arc at stake (1431)
  Vassy
  1,200 French Huguenots slain (1562)

Germany
  Alsace
  First *Bundschuh*, or peasants' revolt (1493)

Great Britain
  England
  Nationalist uprisings in north and west crushed by William I (1068)
  London
  Evil May Day riots – 60 hanged on Cardinal Wolsey's orders (1517)
  * Gunpowder Plot – Guy Fawkes arrested in cellars of Parliament (1605)
  Manchester
  Peterloo massacre (1819)
  Sheffield
  * Hillsborough Stadium crush (1989)

Hungary
  * Uprising crushed (1956)

India
  Amritsar
  * Massacre (1919)

Riot between Sikhs and
 Hindus (1984)
Bombay
* Hindu–Muslim riots
 (1993)
Mandai, Tripura; Assam
* Tribal massacre (1980)
Ethnic violence (1983)
Ireland
Irish railway strike (1920)
Japan
Edo
Yetuna, new shogun,
 overcomes two
 rebellions (1651)
Satsuma
Revolt crushed (1877)
Northern Ireland
Violence begins (1971–72);
 467 Irish killed in 1972
Poland
Warsaw
Massacre when Russian
 troops fire on
 demonstrators (1861)
Rome
Gaius Gracchus killed in
 riot; his reforms
 abolished (121 B.C.)
* Revolt of slaves and
 gladiators under
 Spartacus; crushed by
 Pompey and Crassus
 (71 B.C.)
Russia
St. Petersburg
* Decembrist Revolt
 crushed (1825)
Saudi Arabia
Mecca
* Stampede in pilgrim
 tunnel (1990)
South Africa
Matabele
Revolt against British

South Africa Company;
 crushed by Starr
 Jameson (1893)
United States
California
Los Angeles
* Race riots in Watts (1965)
* Rodney King riots (1991)
Colorado
Sand Creek
* Massacre of Cheyenne
 and Arapaho Indians
 (1864)
Illinois
Chicago
* Race riots (1919)
Strike against Republic
 Steel (1937)
* Police riot at Democratic
 National convention
 (1968)
Massachusetts
Boston
Boston Massacre between
 civilians and troops
 (1770)
New York
New York
* Draft riots (1863)
Ohio
Kent
* Killing of Kent State
 students by Ohio
 National Guard (1970)
Texas
Waco
* Branch Davidian cult
 compound storming
 and fire (1993)
Virginia
Southampton
Revolt of slaves led by
 Nat Turner (1831)
Washington, D.C.
* Bonus Army march (1932)

TERRORISM

Belgium
> Red Brigades try to kidnap and kill Alexander Haig, NATO commander (1979)

Brazil
> Rio de Janeiro
> * First of diplomatic kidnappings: Charles Elbrick, U.S. ambassador to Brazil (1969)

France
> Paris
> Orly Airport bombed by Armenians (ASALA) (1983)

Germany
> Lufthansa hijacking (1977)
> Munich
> * Olympic Games massacre (1972)
> Neo-Nazi plants bomb at Bierfest (1980)
> West Berlin
> La Belle discotheque bombing (1986)

Great Britain
> England
> Birmingham
> Provisional IRA sets series of bombs (1974)
> Brighton
> IRA bomb almost wipes out Margaret Thatcher and entire British cabinet (1984)
> London
> * Harrods attacked by car bomb planted by Provisional IRA (1983)

> Scotland
> * Pan Am jet blown up over Lockerbie (1988)

Greece
> Athens
> TWA plane from Tel Aviv attacked by National Arab Youth for the Liberation of Palestine (Libyan sponsored) (1973)

India
> Bombay
> Airliner explodes; Sikh terrorists suspected (1985)
> JAL hijacking (1977)

Iran
> Tehran
> * U.S. Embassy held hostage (1979–81)

Ireland
> Irish Sea
> * Air India Boeing 747 from Toronto to London blown up and crashes into Irish Sea (1985)

Israel
> Entebbe Airport; first defeat for international terrorism (1976)
> Sinai Desert
> * Israeli Phantoms shoot down Libyan Boeing 707 (1973)
> Tel Aviv
> * Lod (Lydda) Airport; first transnational terrorist attack, between Palestine Liberation Front and Japanese Red Army (1972)

Italy
Bologna
* Neo-fascist terrorists
bomb central train
station (1980)
Rome
First Palestinian hijacking
(1968)
NAYLP bombing and
hijacking of Pan Am
Airliner (1973)
Rome and Vienna,
Austria
Coordinated attacks on El
Al check-in desks
(1985)
Vatican City
Pope John Paul II
severely wounded by
Turkish Grey Wolves;
Bulgarian Secret
Service charged with
complicity (1981)

Japan
Tokyo
First of Japanese Red
Army's international
actions
Hijacking of JAL plane to
North Korea (1970)

Jordan
* Dawson's field
Five planes hijacked;
leads to Black
September formation
(1970)

Lebanon
Beirut
U.S. Embassy destroyed
by car bomb (1983)
* Marine barracks bombed
(1983)
* TWA Flight 847 hijacked
(1985)

Malta
Hijacking; 58 killed after
Israeli commandos rush
plane (1985)

Mediterranean Sea
* *Achille Lauro* hijacking
(1985)

Netherlands
Rotterdam
Fatah blows up fuel tanks
(1971)

Saudi Arabia
Mecca
Muslim extremists kill 150
in Grand Mosque (1979)

Spain
Majorca
Lufthansa flight hijacked
by PFLP/Baader-
Meinhof (1977)

Sweden
Stockholm
West German Embassy
blown up by Rote
Armee Fraktion (1975)

Syria
Damascus
* Bombing (1981)

United States
California
Berkeley
Patricia Hearst kidnapped
by SLA (1974)
New York
New York
FLN bomb exploded in
Fraunces Tavern (1975)
LaGuardia Airport
bombing (1975)
* World Trade Center
bombing (1993)
Washington, D.C.
* Muslim hostage taking
(1977)

Chronology

* Detailed in text

CIVIL UNREST

189 B.C.
Insurrections; Egypt

121 B.C.
Gaius Gracchus killed in riot; Rome

71 B.C.
* Revolt of slaves and gladiators; Rome

1068
Nationalist uprisings; England

1431
Burning of Joan of Arc; Rouen, France

1493
First peasants' revolt; Alsace, Germany

1517
May 1
Evil May Day riots; London

1562
Slaying of French Huguenots; Vassy, France

1572
Aug. 24
* St. Bartholomew's Day massacre; Paris

1605
Nov. 5
* Gunpowder Plot; London

1651
Shogun overcomes two rebellions; Edo, Japan

1770
Boston Massacre; Boston

1791
Massacre of Champs de Mars; Paris

1793–95
* Reign of Terror and White Terror; Paris

1819
Peterloo massacre; Manchester, England

1825
Dec. 14
* Decembrist Revolt; St. Petersburg, Russia

1831
Revolt of slaves led by Nat Turner; Southampton, Virginia

1861
Massacre of demonstrators; Warsaw, Poland

1863
July 13–15
* Draft riots; New York City

1864
Nov. 29
* Massacre of Cheyenne and Arapaho Indians; Colorado

1877
Revolt; Satsuma, Japan

1893
Revolt against British South Africa Company; Matabele, South Africa

1895–1922
* Armenian massacres; Armenia/Turkey

1900
June
* Boxer Rebellion; Northern Provinces, China

1919
April 13
   * Amritsar massacre;
      Amritsar, India
July 27–Aug. 3
   * Race riots; Chicago,
      Illinois
1920
      Irish railway strike;
      Ireland
1927
      General strike; Vienna,
      Austria
1932
May 20–July 28
   * Bonus Army march;
      Washington, D.C.
1937
      Republic Steel strike;
      Chicago, Illinois
1939–45
   * The Holocaust;
      Europe
1956
Nov. 4
   * Hungarian uprising;
      Hungary
1965
Aug. 11–29
   * Race riots; Los Angeles,
      California
1968
Aug. 25–30
   * Police riot at Democratic
      National Convention;
      Chicago, Illinois
1970
May 4
   * Killing of Kent State
      students by Ohio
      National Guard; Kent,
      Ohio
1971
      Violence begins;
      Northern Ireland

1977
      General uprising;
      Czechoslovakia
1980
June 7–8
   * Ethnic violence; Mandai,
      Tripura, India
1983
Feb. 18
   * Ethnic violence; Mandai,
      Assam, India
1984
      Riot between Sikhs and
      Hindus; Amritsar, India
1988
Aug. 14–21
   * Tribal confrontation;
      Burundi, Africa
1989
April 15
   * Hillsborough Stadium
      crush; Sheffield,
      England
April 18–June 4
   * Massacre in Tiananmen
      Square; Beijing, China
1990
July 2
   * Stampede in pilgrim
      tunnel; Mecca, Saudi
      Arabia
1992
April 29–May 2
   * Rodney King riots; Los
      Angeles, California,
      USA
1993
Jan. 6–14
   * Hindu–Muslim riots;
      Bombay, India
Feb. 28–April 19
   * Branch Davidian cult
      compound storming and
      fire; Waco, Texas, USA

TERRORISM

1968
July 22
  First Palestinian
    hijacking; Rome, Italy
1969
Sept. 9
  * First diplomatic
    kidnapping; Rio de
    Janeiro, Brazil
1970
Sept. 6–8
  * Five planes hijacked;
    Dawson's Field, Jordan
1971
Mar. 4
  Fuel tanks blown up;
    Rotterdam, the
    Netherlands
1972
May 3
  * First transnational terrorist
    attack; Tel Aviv, Israel
Sept. 5
  * Olympic Games
    massacre; Munich,
    Germany
1973
Feb. 21
  * Israeli jets down Libyan
    707 airliner; Sinai
    Desert, Israel
Sept. 5
  Pan Am airliner bombed;
    Rome, Italy
Sept. 7
  TWA airliner blown up;
    Athens, Greece
1974
Feb. 5
  Patricia Hearst kidnapped
    by SLA; Berkeley,
    California

Nov. 21
  IRA bombings;
    Birmingham, England
1975
Dec. 24
  FLN bomb explodes in
    Fraunces Tavern; New
    York, N.Y.
1976
June 27
  First defeat for terrorists;
    Entebbe Airport,
    Uganda
1977
Mar. 9–11
  * Muslims take hostages;
    Washington, D.C.
Sept. 28
  JAL hijacking; Bombay,
    India
Oct. 13
  Lufthansa hijacking;
    Majorca, Spain
1979
June 29
  Red Brigades attempt on
    Alexander Haig;
    Belgium
Nov. 4
  * U.S. Embassy held
    hostage until 1981;
    Tehran, Iran
1980
Aug. 1
  * Neo-fascist bombing of
    train station; Bologna,
    Italy
Aug. 1
  Neo-Nazi bomb at
    Bierfest; Munich,
    Germany

1981

May 13
    Attempt on Pope John
      Paul II's life; Vatican
      City, Italy

Nov. 29
  * Bombing; Damascus,
     Syria

1983

April 18
    U.S. Embassy bombed;
      Beirut, Lebanon

July 15
    Orly Airport bombing;
      Paris, France

Oct. 23
  * Marine barracks
     bombed; Beirut,
     Lebanon

Dec. 17
  * IRA Christmas bombing
     of Harrods; London

1984

Oct. 12
    IRA attempt on
      Margaret Thatcher;
      Brighton, England

1985

June 14–18
  * TWA Flight 847 hijacked;
     Beirut, Lebanon

June 22
  * Air India 747 blown up;
     Irish Sea

Oct. 7–9
  * *Achille Lauro* hijacking;
     Mediterranean Sea

Nov. 23
    Egyptair hijacking; Malta

1986

April 15
    La Belle discotheque
      bombing; West Berlin,
      Germany

April 15
    U.S. aircraft attack Libya;
      Libya

1988

Dec. 21
  * Pan Am flight bombed;
     Lockerbie, Scotland

1993

Feb. 26
  * World Trade Center
     bombing; New York,
     N.Y.

Civil Unrest and Terrorism

There is a single, dark thread that runs through and binds together the two categories of this section, and the name of it is motivation. Each of these similar undertakings – civil unrest and terrorism – is motivated by a belief.

That belief may be as simple as a fancied slight or as complex as a philosophy; as closely held as a catechism or as widely held as a form of government, a system of laws or an ordering of ideas. The point of the matter is that in nearly all of the incidents described or listed in this section, the action taken was done so with the purpose of either *overthrowing* a particular ideology or political system or *promulgating* a particular ideology or political system.

What qualifies these events as disasters is that, no matter the purpose, nothing was achieved through them. They were either failures, or they brought about the reverse of their intention. The world, or *their* world, was made worse for their actions.

Political and civil unrest often results in mass assassination. It either involves large groups of people who have been whipped into a fanatic frenzy by leaders who appeal to their dedication to a cause, or it is the massing of the forces of a particular *government* with a particular point of view against a mass of people with an opposing viewpoint. Extended to an international status, it becomes war. Confined to a specific location, it is defined as riot. Extended within the borders of one specific country, it becomes civil war.

The events in this section are largely confined to riots. However, there are two notable exceptions which have been included because they are of such horrific dimensions that they cannot be denied space. These are two attempts at genocide: the Armenian Massacres and the Nazi Holocaust.

Civil Unrest

ARMENIA/TURKEY
1895–1922

Religious intolerance was the core cause for the 27-year attempt by Turkey to commit genocide upon Armenia and its populace. Two million Armenians were massacred, and Armenia as a country was eliminated from the map of the world.

Genocide is one of humankind's lower forms of activity, and one of the most dramatic exemplifications of this was the horrendous massacre, from 1895 to 1922, of Armenians by the Turkish government. During those 27 years, two million Armenian men, women and children were murdered, often after prolonged and barbaric torture. Others were driven across deserts or to ports of debarkation. The purpose was to totally annihilate the Armenian minority in Turkey as a holy necessity. Armenians were Christians; Turks were Muslims, and it became a holy war – traditionally the most savage sort of conflict.

Founded by Haik, a descendant of Noah, Armenia originally occupied the land at the source of the Tigris and Euphrates rivers in Asia Minor. Eventually, it became known as an incorporation of northeast Turkey, the Armenian Soviet Socialist Republic, and parts of Iranian Azerbaijan.

Long a disputed territory that was fought over by Persia, Russia and Turkey, Armenia became the scene of turmoil and oppression for centuries. The Turkish Ottoman Empire invaded Armenia in the 15th century and held all of it by the 16th century.

Although Armenians became successful merchants in Turkey, they were always an oppressed minority because of their religion. Saint Gregory the Illuminator established Christianity in Armenia in the third century, and the autonomous Gregorian church became the centerpiece of Armenian culture and belief. Thus, this country without a portfolio was also an island of Christianity in a vast sea of Muslims, and it was this religious identity that the Ottoman Empire, under Sultan Abd al-Hamid II, used as its reason for launching the first volley in an attempt to exterminate all Armenian infidels from what once was the Armenian Empire.

The Sassoun massacres in January 1895 were merely the first steps in a 27-year-long genocidal campaign. Over three years, 300,000 Armenians perished either by the efforts of government troops, starvation or disease. Troops would swoop down on Armenian settlements with the orders 'Exterminate, root and branch. Whoever spares man, woman, or child is disloyal.'

Thus, when the troops entered a town, they butchered all Armenians without discrimination. Women were raped and then killed. According to the *New York Times* on January 1, 1895, a priest in one village was taken to the roof of his church, hacked to pieces and then set afire. A large group of women and girls was herded into the church, raped and then locked in as soldiers set fire to the church.

In Moosh, Alyan and 14 other villages in the Sassoun district, 7,500 Armenians were butchered in the grisliest of ways. Some escaped into the hills, but starvation eventually drove them back to the villages, where they were set upon by waiting soldiers. Fires were built, and three- and four-year-old children were tossed, alive, into them.

The priests of the church were particular targets for the soldiers. In Ashpig, Der Bedrase, the priest of Geliguson, was stabbed by 40 soldiers wielding bayonets, and his eyes were dug out before he was tossed into a shallow grave he himself was forced to dig. Der

Hohannes, the priest of Senmal, faced an even more gruesome ordeal. According to an eyewitness: 'The soldiers took out Der Hohannes's eyes, seized his hands, and compelled him to dance. Not only was he deprived of his beard, the insignia of his priestly office, but the cruel creatures took along with the razor some of the skin and flesh as well. Having pierced his throat, they forced him to drink water . . . It flowed from the ghastly cut, down on either side. His head was kicked this way and that, as if a football. Human flesh taken from some of his mangled people was put into his mouth. He, too, was pitched into the ditch with more than two score of men that had the promise of safety if they would cease resistance and surrender.'

This was only the beginning. In April 1909, hundreds of thousands of Armenians were butchered in the Massacre of Adana.

By 1913, mass deportations were organized, and tens of thousands of men, women and children were made to march across deserts without food or water. Along the way, they were whipped, bludgeoned, bayoneted and torn limb from limb. Women were raped in front of their husbands and children and then murdered and tossed by the side of the road.

In Marash and in Zeytoon, there were uprisings of Armenian youths, but they were summarily crushed. If soldiers did not kill the Armenians, mobs did, with shovels, axes and blacksmith tools.

In 1915, the deportations increased. Tens of thousands of Armenians were driven ruthlessly from one city to another and back again. On August 7, the prisons in Zeytoon and Fundajak were thrown open, and Armenian prisoners, chained together, were led through the streets to their slaughter. Some were hanged from scaffolds in the center of various villages; the rest were marched to the foot of Mount Aghur and shot.

Not all Armenians were slaughtered or deported. Some were saved for slave labor. Twelve thousand of them worked on the beds of various railroad lines around northeastern Turkey. Overseen by German officers (World War I was now in progress, and Turkey was Germany's ally), these men, women and children were rationed a loaf of bread a day and some water and counted themselves lucky. They were, at least, alive.

Concentration camps of Armenians living in tents sprang up on the countryside, and on June 14, 1916, another mass deportation imprisoned or killed thousands more. Hungry, thirsty, naked, dirty and near death, these Armenians were relentlessly tortured and then killed. When the survivors were led on a deportation march, they were frequently separated from their families. Those who became exhausted fell by the side of the road, where shooting had come to be a kind fate.

Abraham Hartunian, a pastor who survived despite having an eye gouged out and being shot twice in the hip, wrote of this deportation:

> Corpses! Corpses! Murdered! Mutilated! . . . Stepping over them like ghosts of the dead, we walked and walked . . . Armenians were being massacred on the way between Baghtche and Marash . . . Here were the bodies of those driven out before us and shot, stabbed, savagely slaughtered [but] the previous convoys had experienced more.
>
> The men in our group who struck the eyes of the *zaptiye* [Turkish police] were separated, taken a little distance away, and shot. Everyone expected his turn to come next. The old man whose young son had died in Baghtche was walking along beside me with his daughter-in-law and two small grandchildren . . . But now, unable to walk, he was getting in the way of those behind. A *zaptiye* saw him. He came and kicked him and, dragging him out of the group, tripped him into a ditch nearby and emptied his gun into his breast.

At various places along the march, Muslim mobs from

nearby villages waited with guns, axes and sacks. Told they would be blessed by Allah if they robbed and killed Armenians, they did.

'Night fell,' wrote Hartunian in his memoir, *Neither to laugh nor to weep*,

and the prettier women were taken aside and raped. Among them was an extremely beautiful girl, about twenty-five years of age . . . one after the other, the *zaptiye* . . . raped [her] and then, killing her, threw her mutilated corpse to one side because they could not agree who should have her.

Many women were stripped naked and lined up, and their abdomens slashed one by one, were thrown into ditches and wells to die in infinite agony. The *kaymakum* of Der-el-Zor, holding a fifteen-year-old girl before him, directed his words to a murderous band and then, throwing her to the ground, clubbed her to death with the order, 'So you must kill all Armenians, without remorse.'

Convoy after convoy was driven night and day unceasingly, robbed, raped, then brought to the edge of streams and forbidden to drink at the point of the gun. Under the burning sun, thousands perished from hunger and thirst.

Many were gathered in one place and burned alive. One of these, left half dead and later rescued, told me that for days she had remained with the corpses and had lived eating their flesh.

The chronicle of horror was endless. Finally, in 1919, when British troops entered Armenia, an end to the massacres seemed to be in sight. But in one final genocidal sweep, the Turks massacred thousands of Armenians as the British troops were landing. British forces did little to stop these raids, and the remaining Armenians began to lose hope again.

In 1920, the French occupied Turkey. Even so, in that year alone 15,000 Armenians were annihilated in

Marash; 160 Armenian girls were taken from an American girls' seminary in Hadjin, raped in the Turkish harems and then massacred; 3,000 Armenians on the road from Marash to Adana were buried in snow and died and further massacres were planned under the eyes of the French.

The 1920 massacres were as brutal as any that had gone before. According to Hartunian, 'Children were ripped open before their parents, their hearts taken out and stuffed down their mothers' throats. Mothers were crucified naked to doors, and before their very eyes their small ones were fixed to the floor with swords and left writhing.'

By the middle of 1920, the Turks were in full revolt against the French and massacred Armenians at will. Open warfare erupted. Turks burned Armenian homes and businesses; Armenians burned Turkish mosques. The Armenians were eventually overcome, and the Turkish government confiscated the houses, vineyards and fields of dead or fugitive Armenians.

At the end of the year, the Treaty of Sevres was signed, restoring Armenia as a sovereign state. Most Armenians who could, left. There was no guarantee that the massacres that had raged for nearly 27 years would not begin again.

BURUNDI – MARANGARA
August 14–21, 1988

Long-standing animosity between the central African tribes of the Tutsis and Hutus resulted in mass slaughters between August 14 and 21, 1988. Five thousand people, mostly women and children, were killed; thousands were wounded, many seriously. Forty-seven thousand refugees crossed into neighboring Rwanda; nearly 150,000 were made homeless.

For three centuries, highly charged, emotional confrontation has existed between the central African tribes of the Tutsis and the Hutus. The Tutsis arrived from Somalia and Ethiopia in the 16th and 17th centuries and established themselves as a kind of feudal aristocracy over the Hutus. Tall, cattle-raising people, they set up a ruling regime that denied the short-statured Hutu farmers equal rights. Belgium, which later ruled Burundi as a colony, exacerbated the problem by allowing the Tutsis to dominate education, government and the army. When Burundi achieved independence in 1972, war broke out between the two tribes.

Between August 14 and 21, 1988, the Hutus, armed with rocks and knives, attacked Tutsi villages. The reprisals by the Tutsi army were swift and devastating. Hutu villages were burned to the ground. Women and children were shot, mutilated and beaten. Five thousand victims on both sides of the conflict were killed.

As a result of the violence, 47,000 refugees poured across the border into neighboring Rwanda, and the government of Burundi estimated that nearly 150,000 were made homeless by the slaughter. Hospitals were filled with the wounded, most of whom were suffering from infections resulting from wounds that went untreated for weeks while they hid from soldiers in the underbrush. The result was a multitude of amputations, some of them on children only two years old.

The government of Burundi applied to the United Nations for $15 million in aid, but with the government's own army responsible for the massacres, the world body took a negative view of the request.

CHINA – BEIJING
April 18–June 4, 1989

Pro-democracy demonstrations begun by several thousand students in Tiananmen Square, Beijing on April 18, 1989 swelled to one million in mid-May, during a visit by Mikhail Gorbachev. On June 3–4, army troops sent by the government massacred over 1,000 students and workers, injured more than 10,000 and crushed the uprising.

CHINA – NORTHERN PROVINCES
June 1900

Long-festering hostility between Chinese conservatives and foreign partitioners climaxed in the disastrous Boxer Rebellion of June 1900. Thousands of Western missionaries and residents were killed; hundreds more were injured, and China was left vulnerable to Western powers.

EUROPE
1939–45

Adolf Hitler's determination to exterminate 'inferior' races and establish a master race resulted in the six-year-long 'Final Solution,' or Holocaust, as it was eventually called. Between 1939 and 1945, Nazis systematically murdered five million European Jews, three million Russians and two million Slavs.

FRANCE – PARIS
August 24, 1572

The continuing confrontation between Catholics and Protestants in France in the 16th century culminated in a massacre of 2,000 French Huguenots, gathered in Paris on August 24, 1572 to celebrate both St. Bartholomew's Day and the wedding of Henry of Navarre and Margaret of Valois.

One of the bloodiest and most barbaric incidents in the so-called Wars of Religion which raged through France from 1562 to 1598, took place on St. Bartholomew's Day, August 24, 1572 in Paris and later throughout France. Ostensibly it was an attack upon Huguenots for practicing their Protestantism. But palace intrigue and politics were also involved that day.

The Protestant reform movement began in France at the start of the 16th century, but it was given a tangible symbol in 1559, when the first French national synod was held and the Presbyterian church, modeled after John Calvin's reform in Geneva, was founded. The adherents of Protestantism in France were then known as Huguenots – from the German word *Eidgenossen*, meaning sworn companions or confederates. The confederacy extended across class lines but failed to mute the persecution of the Huguenots in France.

In 1560, the Conspiracy of Amboise brought about a fierce confrontation and heavy toll upon the Huguenots. The object of the plot was to allow the House of Bourbon to usurp the power of the Guse family, represented on the throne by Francis II. The plan was to march on the royal castle, abduct the king, and arrest Francois, duc de Guse, and his brother Charles, who was also cardinal of Lorraine.

The cardinal, however, got wind of the plot before it could be put into motion, and the rebel forces were set upon before they could organize themselves. A brutal slaughter followed, and for weeks the bodies of conspirators were hung from the castle and from every tree in sight. The Huguenots were enraged, and the first of the Wars of Religion, in 1562, was a direct result of this slaughter and its grisly aftermath.

By 1572, two of these civil wars had been fought, each ending in reconciliation. But in August 1572 the peace ended violently. That month, the Huguenot nobility was gathered in Paris to attend the wedding of Henry of Navarre (he would later become King Henry IV) and Catherine de' Medici's daughter, Margaret of Valois.

Catherine de' Medici and the duc d'Anjou (later King Henry III), with the reluctant help of King Charles IX, tried, on August 22, to capture the duc de Coligny, the commander of the Huguenots in the second War of Religion and their most respected representative. The attempt failed, and Catherine and her cohorts then determined to kill Coligny and as many Huguenots as they could.

On August 24, St. Bartholomew's Day, while French Huguenots gathered in Paris to celebrate the day and the wedding, the soldiers of the king swooped down on them, massacring every Huguenot in sight. Leaders and ordinary citizens were cut down ruthlessly, and before the day was over, 2,000 Huguenots lay dead in the streets of Paris.

During the next few days, the massacre spread to the countryside and to other cities in France, and within days, the Huguenots regrouped, and the Third War of Religion began. Two more wars would be fought after this, and though the wars themselves would end in 1598, true freedom from oppression for Protestants in France would not come until 1905, when church and state were finally declared separate.

FRANCE – PARIS
1793–95

Between 23,000 and 40,000 were executed during the double reign of terror that followed the French Revolution in 1793–95.

GREAT BRITAIN – ENGLAND, LONDON
November 5, 1605

The presence of harsh penal laws against English Catholics in 1605 led to the ill-fated Gunpowder Plot to blow up Parliament on November 5, 1605. It failed; all of the conspirators were executed.

Anti-Catholic sentiment ran deep in England at the beginning of the 17th century, and it had official and royal sanction. There were harsh penal laws designed to all but prohibit the practice of Catholicism, and in protest against them, a plot was originated in 1605 to blow up both Parliament and King James I. It would take place on November 5, the opening day of Parliament, which was normally given over to ceremony. The king would be in attendance.

Three young men, Robert Catesby, John Wright and Thomas Winter, originated the plan. They were soon joined by Christopher Wright, Robert Winter, Robert Keyes, Thomas Percy, John Grant, Sir Evirard Digby, Francis Tresham, Ambrose Rookwood, Thomas Bates and Guy Fawkes – the last a convert to Catholicism who served as a soldier with the Spanish in Flanders.

The plan was straightforward: Blow up the entire government and set in place a Catholic monarchy. Like all grand designs, it was too good to be kept secret. At any rate, by the middle of 1605, when Thomas Percy had rented a subcellar under the House of Lords, and the conspirators had stocked it with 36 barrels of gunpowder, overlaid with steel bars and firewood, the grand design was known throughout much of the Catholic community of London, including Henry Garnett, the superior of the English Jesuits.

Members of Parliament, however, did not know of the Gunpowder Plot until October 26, when Francis Tresham sent a letter to his brother-in-law, Lord Monteague, warning him not to attend Parliament on November 5. The planners might as well have announced it in the middle of Piccadilly. Lord Monteague informed his colleagues, among them the first earl of Salisbury, who, in short order, discovered the cellar and its lethal provinder.

On the night of November 4, Guy Fawkes, who because of his military background had been elected to detonate the dynamite, crept quietly into the cellar, to check the fuses and the powder. Soldiers were waiting for him and arrested him on the spot. He was taken to the Tower of London and under torture revealed the names of his co-conspirators.

Soldiers fanned out throughout London and began to

make arrests. Catesby tried to fight his way through the arresting party and was killed. Percy, the renter of the cellar, was shot and mortally wounded while trying to flee from his captors. The rest were captured and either imprisoned, killed outright or sentenced to be hanged. Among those hanged in November 1606 were Henry Garnett (the superior of English Jesuits), Thomas and Robert Winter and Guy Fawkes.

Rather than making the lot of Catholics in England better, the Gunpowder Plot worsened their lives. Instead of erasing repressive laws against the practice of their religion, the aborted plot caused the enactment of harsher, more repressive ones. And to this day Guy Fawkes Day is celebrated on November 5 with fireworks and bonfires and the image of Guy Fawkes hanged in effigy.

GREAT BRITAIN – ENGLAND, SHEFFIELD
April 15, 1989

In the worst tragedy in the history of British soccer, and one of the worst disasters in the history of sport, 95 soccer fans were crushed to death on the overcrowded terraces of Hillsborough Stadium in Sheffield during the first six minutes of the 1989 FA Cup semi-final tie between Liverpool and Nottingham Forest. Two hundred were injured.

No one would accuse the builders of British soccer stadiums of making them overly comfortable. Most of them are sandwiched into urban neighborhoods. Most of them were built during Victorian or Edwardian times. Many of them have turned ramshackle with age.

British soccer fans are also far from genteel. For five years following the tragic riots during the European Cup final between Liverpool and Juventus at the Heysel Stadium in Brussels, in which 39 fans – 31 of them Italian – were killed and over 400 were injured,

English clubs were banned from European competition.

But, on the afternoon of April 15, 1989, there was no rioting between opposing fans during the opening moments of the FA Cup semi-final between Liverpool and Nottingham Forest in Sheffield's Hillsborough Stadium. There was much pushing and shoving, as there always was. And there was nearly criminally poor judgment on the part of the officials, who allotted 6,000 fewer seats to Liverpool than to Nottingham, despite the undisputed fact that Liverpool had far more supporters.

Nevertheless, the Liverpool fans who were swarming through the gates to the terraces at the Leppings Lane end were willing to endure a little crowding to cheer on their team. As Brian Wolfson, a Liverpool native who runs London's Wembley Stadium, put it: 'You have a culture, the camaraderie of the terraces. It is directly behind the goal, where the action is, where you can throw yourself around and come away drained, as if you had played yourself.'

But when the match began, the Leppings Lane end was dangerously overcrowded. And then, as play heated up, the fans surged forward. Those at the gates shoved ahead, to enter the section. Those in the upper terraces pressed against those in front of them, and a terrifying mounting pressure began to build. The spectators in front were flung forward, against the iron barricades and the perimeter fences. The crush increased, and within moments, despite their screams, 95 fans died of trampling or suffocation. Hundreds suffered painful injuries.

It was the worst tragedy in the history of British soccer, surpassing the death toll of 66 people in 1971, when crowd barriers collapsed during a match in Glasgow, and only surpassed in the history of sport by the catastrophic riots on May 24, 1964 during an Olympic qualifying match between Peru and Argentina. In that horrible debacle, 318 fans died and 500 were injured.

The Hillsborough tragedy brought about increased security, and some improvements in the facilities at UK soccer grounds, including all-seater stadiums.

HUNGARY – BUDAPEST
November 4, 1956

Hungarian Freedom Fighters, fired by the success of the Polish uprising and a Russian-appointed regime, declared independence on October 23, 1956 with a student uprising. On November 4, 1956, Russian tanks reclaimed Budapest and Hungary. Twenty-five thousand Hungarians were killed in the fighting; thousands more were killed in the ensuing executions.

Today it seems almost inconceivable that tens of thousands of Hungarians lost their lives and their hope in one week of fierce fighting against the Stalinist regime that had held Hungary captive since World War II. Nor does it seem possible that both the United Nations and the Western powers – themselves involved in the 'Suez crisis' – could stand by and watch as a bloodbath of staggering proportions took place, while the victims pleaded, over their radio station, for help from the rest of the world.

Yet, it happened, from Tuesday, October 23, 1956, when the first student uprising occurred, until Sunday, November 4, 1956, when Russian tanks reclaimed Budapest.

The world had a chance to help, but did not. Perhaps it was bad timing. Events choose their moments, and this was not the most propitious moment for Hungary to find its freedom.

The impetus for the Hungarian uprising came with the death of Joseph Stalin in March 1953, which was surrounded by a maelstrom of plots and threats. Stalin's tyrannical hold on Russia and the lands it had acquired at the end of World War II was so complete and so ruthless that it carried with it the seeds of an inevitable revolt.

There were demonstrations in East Germany and Czechoslovakia, and in Yugoslavia there was Tito, who preferred his own brand of communism to that of the Stalinist loyalists. So in May 1955, Nikita Khrushchev formed the Warsaw Pact, a treaty of mutual friendship, cooperation and mutual aid, uniting the satellites as an answer to NATO.

But within the Warsaw Pact, there was discontent. In Poznan, Poland on June 28, 1955, a strike occurred. It was put down ruthlessly. Russian tanks and troops arrived, surrounded the city for two days, killed 113 people and broke the strike.

Almost simultaneously, Anastas Mikoyan arrived in Hungary, where a group of intellectuals were already expressing discontent about life under Stalinism. Matyas Rakosi, the head of Hungary's Central Committee, was notoriously repressive, employing the AVH, or Secret Police, to enforce his edicts and intimidate the Politburo. He was opposed by Imre Nagy, a moderate. If Mikoyan had, on that visit to Budapest, replaced Rakosi with Nagy, the Hungarian Revolution might never have taken place. He did not. He replaced Rakosi with Erno Gero, Moscow's handpicked man and one of Rakosi's henchmen.

Meanwhile, crisis erupted in Poland. Riots over the Poznan killings sprang up in Warsaw. The army and Polish students faced each other. To defuse the situation, Khrushchev met with Polish leaders and announced that the Soviet government would allow a form of communism to exist in Poland that was not precisely Russian. The Hungarians thus learned that it was possible to stand up to the Russians and win. They congratulated Poland and made plans for their own revolution.

From October 19 through 21, 1956, Hungarian students and intellectuals escalated their demands for the withdrawal of Soviet troops from Hungary. Meetings were held. A large student demonstration was scheduled for Tuesday, October 23 in Budapest. It was first forbidden; then the prohibition order was withdrawn.

The demonstration took place, and its makeup would have made Lenin smile. It was a spirited alliance of workers and intellectuals – just the mix that Lenin said was indispensable to a revolution.

By that night, the revolution was well under way. The intellectuals, students and workers wanted Nagy; Gero was determined to remain in place. The demonstrators in the streets had created a 16-point manifesto, and they went to the radio station to request that these 16 points be broadcast. According to a UN report filed later, an army major volunteered to present the paper to the head of broadcasting, but as he approached the main entrance to the building, he was gunned down by police.

And so the bloodshed began. Tear gas was lobbed into the crowd, and AVH men, the Hungarian equivalent of the KGB, opened fire, killing a number of people and wounding more. Tanks arrived, but the commander in charge informed everyone that he was a worker and would not participate in a massacre.

The crowd was now armed with machine guns and rifles, driving vans and trucks taken from factories. On Dozsa Gyorgy Street, an immense bronze statue of Stalin was hauled down, with the help of metalworkers using blowtorches. Red stars and other Communist emblems were shot off buildings, and Russian bookshops were looted.

By the next day, Nagy had been installed as prime minister, but the Russians were still in control. Russian tanks reinforced the AVH, which had taken up positions around the city.

The Hungarian Army soon joined the street demonstrators. Most important, a heavily decorated war hero, Colonel Pal Maleter, ordered to lead a formation of five tanks against the insurgents, made a fateful decision. 'Once I arrived there,' he later said, 'it quickly became clear to me that those who were fighting for their freedom were not bandits, but loyal sons of Hungary. As a result I informed the Minister of Defense that I was going over to the insurgents.'

On the 25th, a huge group of demonstrators advanced on Parliament Square, demanding Gero's resignation. They were unarmed. Russian tanks and AVH men opened fire on them, killing an estimated 600 unarmed civilians. It was a ghastly massacre, and the Russians replaced Gero as first secretary of the party with Janos Kadar.

The fighting in the streets increased. After the Parliament Square massacre, AVH men were hunted down and strung up on trees. Sometimes they were found to be carrying their pay – 10 times that of a worker – and the money was then pinned to their bodies.

A revolutionary cabinet was now formed, with Nagy at its head. By Sunday, October 28, a cease-fire was negotiated, and the Russians appeared to be allowing Nagy and his followers to assume control. It was, to the jubilant insurgents, Poland all over again.

On Monday, according to the United Press, 'Soviet tanks crunched out of this war-battered capital [Budapest] . . . carrying their dead with them. They left a wrecked city where the stench of death already [rose] from the smoking ruins.' An announcement was made that the AVH would be abolished. Nagy set about tying the various strands of the revolution together. Hungary was free, despite the fighting in the streets.

Meanwhile, in the outside world, Great Britain and France were making plans to take the Suez Canal by force. On the morning of October 31, the news reached Hungary. Nagy fell into a mild depression. 'God damn them!' one of the ministers exploded. 'Aren't we going to put out feelers to the Western Powers *even now*?'

'Certainly not *now*,' Nagy replied.

The Russian withdrawal from Hungary seemed to be inexplicably stalled. Reports from the countryside told of tanks stopping and soldiers grouping. Communications circulated that trainloads of soldiers estimated at more than 75,000 men accompanied by 2,500 tanks were moving across the frontiers from Russia, Romania and Czechoslovakia. The new, free government of Hungary sent telegrams to the Kremlin questioning this apparent violation of the October 28 agreement of conditions for a cease-fire. By Saturday, November 3, a Russian military delegation arrived at Parliament to negotiate the withdrawal of Soviet troops.

Joseph Cardinal Mindszenty, who had been arrested and convicted of conspiracy in December 1945, was freed, and he gave a radio address. At 8 o'clock that evening, General Maleter drove to Tokol, outside Budapest, to renew negotiations at the Russian military headquarters.

He would never return. Shortly after midnight, General Serov, chief of the Soviet Security Police, would arrest the entire Hungarian delegation.

At 5 A.M. on November 4, 1956, Imre Nagy went on Hungarian radio. He was broadcasting from the Parliament building, where he had spent the night. His words contained a heartrending urgency:

'Attention! Attention! Attention! Attention!

'. . . This is Imre Nagy speaking, the president of the Council of Ministers of the Hungarian People's Republic. Today at daybreak Soviet forces started an attack against our capital, obviously with the intention to overthrow the legal Hungarian democratic government.

'Our troops are fighting.

'The government is in its place.

'I notify the people of our country and the entire world of this fact.'

Free Radio Kossuth would continue to broadcast bulletins to the world throughout the day. The reports would increase in intensity and despair. Gyula Hay, the playwright and friend of Nagy, broadcast the most impassioned one:

'This is the Hungarian Writers' Association speaking

to all writers, scientists, writers' associations, academies and scientific organizations of the world. We appeal for help to all intellectuals in all countries. Our time is limited. You know the facts. There is no need to review them. Help Hungary! Help the writers, scientists, workers, peasants and all Hungarian intellectuals. Help! Help! Help!'

Kadar had gone over to the Russians and now announced a breakaway government. Nagy took refuge in the Yugoslavian embassy, with his other cabinet ministers.

Heavy artillery opened up on the city. Soviet tanks rolled into Budapest and rumbled through its streets. When sniper fire came from a building, they blasted the entire building to oblivion. The Hungarian News Agency painted the picture: 'People are jumping up at the tanks, throwing hand-grenades inside and then slamming the driver's windows. The Hungarian people are not afraid of death. It is only a pity that we can't stand for long.'

The fighting roared on for three days and nights, sputtered and then died. The Soviet tanks had completely retaken Hungary, and all of the cries for help had gone unanswered. At exactly the moment that Soviet tanks entered Budapest, British and French paratroopers were dropped at Port Said, Egypt, and America and the United Nations were busy bringing about a cease fire there.

In a later interview on television, President Dwight Eisenhower said, 'The thing started in such a way, you know, that everybody was a little bit fooled, I think, and when suddenly the Soviets came in strength with their tank divisions, and it was a *fait accompli*, it was a great tragedy and disaster.'

It certainly was for the Hungarians. The government of Janos Kadar took over and negotiated amnesty for Nagy and his associates. They were loaded into a bus that was to take them to their homes. But before it could leave the Yugoslavian embassy, the bus was boarded by Soviet military personnel, who commandeered it and took it to the headquarters of the Soviet Military Command. The two Yugoslavian diplomats who were to accompany the former Hungarian officials to safety were ordered to return to the embassy, and Nagy and his associates were arrested and imprisoned outside the country at Sinaia in Romania.

In June 1958, those who had not died in captivity were executed: Nagy, General Pal Maleter, the journalist Miklos Gimes and Nagy's secretary, Jozsef Szilagyi. In total, 2,000 were executed and 20,000 were imprisoned after the uprising. An estimated 25,000 died in the street fighting.

The border with Austria remained open for a few weeks after the revolution, and 200,000 refugees streamed across it. Housed in camps and shelters in Austria, they moved on to whatever countries in the West would accept them. Among the refugees were some of the finest minds in Hungary.

Shortly after this, barbed-wire enclosures went up, and the Iron Curtain was firmly redrawn around Hungary. It would be 35 years before it would be torn down again, this time through diplomacy.

INDIA – AMRITSAR
April 13, 1919

Several thousand Indians, gathering in defiance of a British ban on public meetings, were fired upon in the Sikh Holy Shrine of Jalianwala Bagh on April 13, 1919 by soldiers under the direction of Brigadier General R. E. H. Dyer. Three hundred seventy nine Indians died in the barrage; 1,200 were wounded. None was armed.

INDIA – BOMBAY
January 6–14, 1993

For nine days and nights, from January 6th through 14th, 1993, Hindu mobs rampaged through the streets of

Bombay, India, hunting down, killing and burning Muslims. The orgy of self-righteous, religious cleansing, a pogrom that ranked in horror with the Nazi Holocaust and the atrocities of Bosnia, left 1,800 dead and 2,000 injured.

INDIA – MANDAI, TRIPURA; ASSAM
June 7–8, 1980; Feb. 18, 1983

Driven by Hindu–Muslim hatred, tribal youth organizations conducted raids on Indian villages, massacring Muslims. In the two worst incidents on June 7–8, 1980 and February 18, 1983, 5,500 Bengali immigrants were massacred; 1,000 were wounded; 300,000 were made homeless.

The most savage and disastrous confrontations between people have been ethnic and religious ones. When a cause is perceived to be a religious one, cruelty can apparently be justified and swallowed up in the cause. 'Men never do evil so fully and so happily as when they do it for conscience's sake,' said Pascal, and this has never seemed so true as in the confrontations between those driven by differing beliefs.

When Great Britain partitioned India in 1946, isolating its Muslim population in Pakistan and its Hindu population in India, it sowed the seeds of religious confrontation. Hindus in Pakistan were driven out by Muslims and settled in the northeastern provinces of West Bengal and Bangladesh, which was, until 1971, East Bengal. The Bengalis, concentrated mostly in the adjoining states of Tripura and Assam, were predominantly Hindus. The native tribal people who lived there were mostly Muslims.

Thus, the Bengalis were looked upon as foreigners, immigrants and Hindus, a combination the tribespeople regarded with bigoted distaste. In 1980, the situation erupted when tribal youth organizations, dedicated to the expulsion of 'foreigners,' began systematic massacres.

The first such massacre to reach the attention of the

world occurred in Mandai, in Tripura state. Adjoining the border of Bangladesh, the village had long been a Bengali dwelling place; some of its inhabitants had lived there a generation, ever since the partition. Others were new immigrants.

On June 7 and 8, tribal gangs swooped down on the village and laid waste to it. Armed with guns, spears, swords, scythes and bows and arrows, they emptied houses, chased men, women and children out into the flatlands around the village and slaughtered them, crushing their heads and severing their limbs. Children were run through with spears. Three hundred fifty people were killed in this massacre, which left not one person alive in the village of Mandai.

As news of the massacre began to emerge from India, officials in Tripura admitted that nearly 700 people had died in the past year after similar raids, which had rendered 200,000 homeless and had necessitated the setting up of 100 camps to house them.

The Communist-led government of Tripura, which had displaced Prime Minister Indira Gandhi's Congress Party in the 1977 elections, was charged with incompetence and blamed for not controlling the situation. The Tripura government countercharged the New Delhi government with indifference.

Two weeks later, on June 22, Tarun Basu, a reporter for the New Delhi weekly current affairs journal *Contour*, uncovered a staggering fact: Four thousand Bengalis had been slaughtered by tribesmen during the month of June, and the government of Tripura had burned many of the bodies to cover up the slayings.

This resulted in an immediate tightening of security for the Bengalis which lasted for three years. Then, an important state election was scheduled to elect a 126-member state legislature and 12 members of the national parliament from the neighboring state of Assam. In this case, the settlements were Muslim, and the tribespeople Hindus. This time, an added political dimension, a motive to prevent Muslims from electing

Muslims to the legislature and parliament, was added.

The village of Bhagduba Habi in the center of the state was typical. There, Bengali-speaking Muslims who went to vote found themselves surrounded by hostile Assamese tribespeople who turned them back from the polling places. Those who did manage to vote were found murdered the next day.

And then the worst massacres occurred. On Friday, February 18, the violence was particularly vicious. In Bhagduba Habi, old people, women and children were chased into the outlying fields, tortured and killed. Reporters arriving the next day counted 157 bodies, mostly those of children, lined up in rice fields, being readied for mass burial.

On that same day, 17 Muslim villages were attacked in a 20-square-mile area about 50 miles northeast of Gauhati, the state capital. Out of a population of 12,000, 1,200 were slaughtered. Retaliatory attacks against Hindu villages swelled the figure to 1,500. Police, trying to restore order, killed 127. Eight hundred wounded were treated in hastily set up camps.

Once again, the government of India stepped in. In Gauhati, the capital of Assam, the High Court released four prominent leaders of the anti-immigrant movement, hoping to defuse the situation.

With thousands of voters boycotting the voting and thousands more prevented from voting, the Congress Party of Prime Minister Indira Gandhi swept to a landslide victory in the state legislature. Troops would maintain peace. But Indira Gandhi's term in office would be short. One year later, she would be assassinated.

ROME
71 B.C.

The gathering of freed slaves and gladiators, attempting to sever themselves from Roman rule and escape to the Alps, was crushed by the Roman generals Crassus and

Pompey in 71 B.C. *Six thousand slaves and gladiators were crucified.*

In Ancient Rome, slaves were usually enemy soldiers who had been defeated and captured in battle. One of these was Spartacus, a Thracian captured when Rome defeated and annexed Thrace during the first century B.C.

Taken to Capua, Spartacus was installed in the gladiator school there. But in 73 B.C., leading 78 men armed with kitchen knives, he escaped from Capua and established an army of runaway slaves that would eventually number 100,000.

Their first attacks were ragtag ones, made with makeshift swords. Compensating for a lack of organization and skill, they excelled in fierce resolve. As time went on, they defeated more and more Roman legions, appropriating their weaponry and improving their organization. Slave prisons were invaded, and their inmates joined the swelling ranks.

The Roman Senate first sent small armies headed by praetors into the field. They were roundly defeated. The Senate then dispatched consular armies, and they too were beaten. It was time to unite several armies under one consul. Pompey was abroad, fighting in Spain. The second choice was Marcus Crassus, better known for his real estate astuteness than his fighting skills. But Crassus was ambitious, and he brought a strong organizational hand to his resolve to crush the slave revolt. This was a distinct advantage over Spartacus's command. His army was effective but unruly.

It had been Spartacus's aim to fight his way north from Capua and then leave Italy and strike out for the Alps. He wanted nothing more than to return to Thrace. His army laid waste to southern Italy and Campania and developed a taste for plundering. They were in no hurry to leave.

It would be a fatal error. The Roman army under Crassus was given time to organize and arm itself and to force the slave army into a formal battle, a situation both Crassus and Spartacus knew the slave army could not win.

The battle took place near Rhegium, in the toe of Italy, where Crassus trapped the slave army. It was a rout. A heavy snowstorm provided cover for a third of the slaves, who managed to flee from this battle. The remaining two-thirds broke into two fleeing armies, and Spartacus met Crassus on the field near Lucania. He died in a hand-to-hand battle with the Roman consul.

Meanwhile, Pompey had returned from Spain and caught the rest of the escaping slave army. His troops annihilated them, and those they did not kill in battle they crucified. Six thousand slaves on crosses lined the highway from Capua to Rome.

Ironically, the armies of Pompey and Crassus found 3,000 Roman prisoners in the abandoned camp of the rebels. They were unharmed.

RUSSIA – ST. PETERSBURG
December 14, 1825

The Decembrists, a secret society of army officers who had served in Europe and were influenced by Western liberal ideals, revolted against Czar Nicholas I on December 14, 1825. The coup failed, and several hundred officers were killed.

There is a certain mystical fascination about the reign and life of Czar Alexander I. It was he who defeated Napoleon in 1812. It was he who advocated a benign, liberal treaty with France afterward. It was he who then, after 1812, began to subscribe to a sort of general Christian ideal but, in contradiction to its teachings, began to suppress any liberal movements in Russia, calling them 'threats to Christian morality.' He supported Metternich in crushing all national movements and, under the influence of Juliana Krudenar, created the Holy Alliance to uphold Christian morality in Europe.

In Russia, he established military colonies and paraded them as Christian enclaves. They were actually little serfdoms, in which the common soldiers were treated like chattel.

Alexander I died in 1825. Or possibly he didn't. Rumors maintain that he actually went to Siberia and became a hermit. In 1926 his grave was opened, and it was found to be empty. The mystery remains unsolved to this day.

When Alexander disappeared in 1825, the throne passed unexpectedly to his brother Nicholas I. Nicholas inherited all of the problems set in place by the repressive measures of Alexander. One of these was the formation of secret societies challenging Alexander and his fervent repressions.

One of the secret societies was called the Decembrists, and they were a unique group. Composed of army officers and aristocrats who had fought Napoleon and had thus spent time in the rest of Europe, they were consumed by new, liberal ideas of existence and government. They advocated the establishment of representative democracy but disagreed about the form it should take in Russia. Some supported a constitutional monarchy; others wanted a democratic republic.

They were not the ideal group to stage a rebellion, but the disappearance of Alexander I and the ensuing confusion offered them an opportunity they chose not to refuse.

It seemed that the assumed death of Alexander, who had remained childless, would necessarily result in the assumption of the throne by the next in line, Constantine. But, unbeknownst to all but a very few, he had renounced the throne in 1822. The confusion led the Decembrists to think that they could challenge the unpopular younger brother, Nicholas I, overwhelm him and demand that Constantine grant a constitution.

Ill organized but determined, they advanced upon

Senate Square in St. Petersburg on December 14, 1825, the first day of Nicholas's reign. Fully armed and riding horses, the Decembrists formed themselves into a fighting force.

Nicholas attempted to negotiate. They refused. Artillery opened up on them, and the czar's cavalry charged. Improperly shod, the Decembrists' horses slipped and fell on the icy pavement of Senate Square. The artillery cut down more of them.

Within a short time, the revolt was crushed. Five of the leaders were later executed; hundreds more were killed in Senate Square.

It had been an unsuccessful revolt, but its effects would be felt for years. There was an immediate police repression, ordered by Nicholas I and inherited by his heirs. This inspired considerable revolutionary fever and activity. For a small effort, the Decembrist revolt of December 14, 1825 accomplished much and precipitated more.

SAUDI ARABIA – MECCA
July 2, 1990

One thousand, four hundred twenty-six Muslim pilgrims were trampled to death in a stampede on July 2, 1990 in a tunnel connecting Mecca and Mina, Saudi Arabia during the Muslim celebration of hajj.

Every year, between one and two million Muslims travel to the holy city of Mecca, in Saudi Arabia, to celebrate *hajj*, or the holiday *Eid Al-Adha* (the Feast of Sacrifice). The rituals of the holiday commemorate the Prophet Abraham's offering of his son in sacrifice to God, and sheep are slaughtered to emulate Abraham's oblation. The Islamic faith requires that each worshipper try to attend the pilgrimage, and in the early summer of 1990, over two million pilgrims crowded into Mecca and the nearby tent city of Mina.

In previous years, terrorism, attributed to Iran or to

radical Shiite Muslims, marred the deeply religious celebration. In 1986, Saudis confiscated large quantities of explosives from Iranian worshippers. In 1987, Iranians engaged in pitched battles with security forces, and 402 Iranian pilgrims died in the conflict. Following that tragedy, the Saudis set a quota of 1,000 pilgrims per million of population for each Islamic nation, and the Iranians angrily boycotted the pilgrimage.

And so, by June and July of 1990, terrorism, except for an occasional bomb planted or thrown by Shiite Muslims, had dissipated. But the crowds had not.

The concluding days of the 1990 *hajj* were blisteringly hot. The temperature climbed to 112°F (44°C) on the morning of July 2, the day that pilgrims would trek to Jamarat al Akaba in Mina, one of the three 'Satan's stoning points.' Each pilgrim would cast pebbles at the rock pillar in a ritual that symbolized the faithful's struggle against evil.

At 10 A.M., thousands of pilgrims, in traditional attire, began the short journey from Mecca to Mina. They had a choice: either cross a pedestrian bridge, or enter an air-conditioned tunnel, 1500 feet long and 60 feet wide, cut through a mountain. Most chose the tunnel, but some trudged across the bridge.

Shortly after 10 o'clock, a railing gave way on the bridge just above the exit of the tunnel in Mina. Seven worshippers, leaning on the railing, plunged 26 feet to their deaths among the slow-moving crowd of pilgrims exiting from the tunnel.

Foot traffic came to an immediate standstill around the seven bodies. But at the other end of the tunnel, and in it, unaware pilgrims still pressed forward. Within a few minutes, 50,000 of them entered a space that was built for a maximum of 10,000.

And then, a power failure abruptly plunged the tunnel into total blackness, and the air-conditioning stopped. In the sudden, eerie stillness, the air seemed to drain away. Panic set in, and the crowd pressed forward mindlessly. The wave of humanity increased its speed and force, and individuals in it began to faint from the heat, or lose their footing. More and more were trampled as thousands slammed against each other in a mindless stampede. Hundreds were crushed against the walls or each other. 'It was terrible,' a survivor later told Saudi television. 'When one stumbled, scores trampled him and hundreds fell on top of them.'

Before the screaming, writhing mass of terrified and dying pilgrims could be calmed and led out of the tunnel, an astonishing 1,426 Muslims were trampled to death or died of suffocation.

To Western ears, the statement by Saudi King Fahd that, 'It was God's will, which is above everything. It was fate,' sounded peremptorily heartless and needlessly cruel. He amended it for world consumption shortly thereafter, adding that he would work for better safety measures so that, 'God willing, we will see no tragedies in the coming years.'

According to Islamic teachings, to die while on the *hajj* ensures immediate ascension to heaven. One thousand, four hundred twenty-six Muslims made the ascent that fetid and horrible morning.

UNITED STATES – CALIFORNIA, LOS ANGELES
August 11–29, 1965

Festering racial resentments, poverty and sultry summer weather converged to cause the racial riots of August 11–29, 1965 in Watts. Thirty-four died; 874 were injured; 3,800 were arrested; and there was $20 million in property damage.

There can be no doubt that the 1960s, remembered in retrospect as the age of the flower children, was also a decade of extreme violence – Vietnam; the assassinations of President John F. Kennedy, Robert Kennedy and Dr. Martin Luther King Jr.; and civil unrest.

The summer of 1965 was a hot and sultry one in Los

Angeles, and in the Watts neighborhood, an outwardly neat and well-kept suburban section of Los Angeles, it was seemingly serene. Roughly 20 square miles in area, Watts held about a sixth of Los Angeles County's 523,000 blacks.

Shortly before 8 o'clock on the night of August 11, 1965, at the corner of Imperial and Avalon streets, a white California Highway Patrol officer stopped Marquette Frye, who, with his brother Ronald, was driving erratically. Some 25 people watched while their mother, Mrs. Rena Frye, entered the scene and began to berate her son, who in turn began to berate the police.

The crowd grew and became involved. Stones were thrown. The police radioed for help. By 10 P.M., crowds were stoning city buses, and 80 police officers sealed off the 16-block area in an effort to contain the violence.

It was fruitless. Looters had already moved beyond the sealed-off area, and the Watts riots of 1965 had begun.

By the next night, black youths had acquired firearms and were firing on police from the tops of buildings. Anarchy ruled the streets. Fires were started and fire fighters fired upon. White television crews were mauled and their equipment destroyed.

As the fever mounted over the next two days, roving bands of black teenagers assaulted cars containing whites. By August 13, four people had died, 33 police officers had been injured and 249 rioters had been arrested. And the fierceness and tempo of the riot were increasing.

No whites were safe anywhere near the Watts section of Los Angeles. Whenever a car containing whites entered the area, gangs of teenagers, egged on by shouts of 'Kill Kill!' descended upon it. Black police officers who tried to contain the crowds were jeered, called traitors and then stoned.

Robert Richardson, a black advertising salesman for

the *Los Angeles Times* who had entered the area, wrote, 'Light skinned Negroes such as myself were targets of rocks and bottles until someone standing nearby would shout, "He's blood. He's a brother – lay off."

'As some areas were blockaded during the night, the mobs would move outside, looking for more cars with whites. When there were no whites, they started throwing rocks and bottles at Negro cars. Then, near midnight, they began looting stores owned by whites.

'Everybody got in the looting – children, grownups, old men and women, breaking windows and going into stores.

'Then everybody started drinking – even little kids 8 and 9 years old.'

And it was then that teenagers started to fan out, into white neighborhoods, up to 20 miles from the riot scene. One group of 25 blacks tossed rocks in San Pedro, in the harbor area; another appeared in Pecoima, a black community in the San Fernando Valley.

Los Angeles Police Chief William Parker did nothing to try to bring peace. His public statements, comparing the rock throwers to 'monkeys in a zoo,' only fanned the flames.

On the morning of August 13, 2,000 heavily armed National Guard troops converged on Los Angeles. Moving in with machine guns, they fired at rioters, who fled and then regrouped elsewhere. At one point, a group of rioters charged Oak Park Hospital, where those who were injured and wounded in the riots were being treated.

The next day, 20,000 National Guardsman were called up and began to penetrate the riot area. A curfew from 8 P.M. to sunrise was imposed on a 35-square-mile area surrounding the riot scene. Snipers shot from rooftops. Fires began to break out with increasing frequency. There was hardly an unlooted store in Watts or the surrounding area. Twenty-one people had been killed. Nineteen were rioters, one was a sheriff's deputy and one was a fireman. Six hundred had been injured.

Chief Parker appeared on television to assail black leaders in the community, calling them 'demagogic . . . pseudo leaders of the Negro community who can't lead at all.' There was some evidence that Black Muslims were encouraging the riot and egging teenagers on, but by and large, black civil rights leaders from all over the country issued pleas for the violence to end.

There were not enough fire fighters and equipment to stop the continuing string of fires that blazed through the area. But 2,500 of the 15,000 National Guard troops in Los Angeles began to secure the riot area, and by late on August 14, the rioting had begun to subside.

The death toll rose that day from 22 to 31. One victim was a 14-year-old girl killed in a traffic accident while fleeing the scene of a looting; one was a five-year-old child shot by a sniper. Bricks, rocks and bullets continued to rain down from rooftops, some striking guardsmen and police, some striking black residents. The guardsmen used rifle fire, tear gas, machine guns and bayonets, and Governor Edmund G. Brown widened the curfew area to 50 square miles.

Meanwhile, violence broke out in Long Beach, south of Los Angeles. One policeman was killed and another wounded when they were ambushed by snipers. Troops were ordered into that city.

Governor Brown came to Watts, surrounded by guardsmen, and met with black leaders, trying to calm the atmosphere and effect a reconciliation. Gradually, an embittered calm descended over Los Angeles, and the gasoline bombs, rifles and rocks began to disappear.

A score of relief agencies entered the battle-scarred, smoldering area to begin rehabilitation after five days of riots. Slowly the troops were withdrawn, but the curfew remained in place. Racial tension throughout the city remained for a long time.

Two hundred businesses were totally destroyed; 500 were damaged; $200 million in property damage was estimated. Nearly $2 million in federal funds were allocated to aid in the rebuilding of a 45-square-mile area of Los Angeles. One thousand six hundred people were hired under the antipoverty program of Los Angeles County to aid in the cleanup.

In the last hours of the riots, a black woman was killed by a Guardsman, bringing the death toll to 34.

It would be a long path back for Watts.

UNITED STATES – CALIFORNIA, LOS ANGELES
April 26–May 2, 1992

The beating of Rodney King by four white Los Angeles police officers on the night of March 3, 1991 was caught on television, and the jury decision on July 26, 1992, to acquit all of the police officers on state charges sparked a wave of deadly riots across the country. The most extensive occurred in Los Angeles, California, where 53 lost their lives. In a subsequent federal trial, two of the policemen were convicted of violating King's civil rights.

UNITED STATES – COLORADO, SAND CREEK
November 29, 1864

Colonel John M. Chivington's disdain for both Indians and treaties manifested itself in the massacre on November 29, 1864 of peaceful Cheyenne and Arapaho Indians. One hundred forty-eight Indians, mostly women and children, were killed, among them nine Indian chiefs; hundreds of Indians were wounded or mutilated; nine soldiers were killed; 38 soldiers were wounded.

UNITED STATES – ILLINOIS, CHICAGO
July 27–August 3, 1919

The famous Chicago race riots of July 27–August 3, 1919 were caused by ill feeling between blacks and whites after World War I, a small altercation on a Chicago beach and hot summer weather. By their end, 35 were dead and more than 500 were injured.

UNITED STATES – ILLINOIS, CHICAGO
August 25–30, 1968

Antiwar demonstrators who had gathered outside the Democratic National Convention on August 25–30, 1968 to protest the Vietnam policies of the Johnson administration were beaten and gassed by a police force that had gone momentarily berserk and had been ordered to enforce excessive repression measures by Mayor Richard J. Daley. Hundreds of demonstrators, scores of newspeople and bystanders and some delegates were injured.

In 1968, embittered and discouraged by public reaction to his Vietnam policies, Lyndon Johnson announced that he would not run for reelection. It had been a terrible year for him and for the country. The nation was sharply and irrevocably divided over American involvement in Southeast Asia. In April, Dr. Martin Luther King Jr., an advocate of civil rights, had been assassinated. In June, Robert Kennedy, openly challenging President Johnson's Vietnam stance, and an announced candidate for the Democratic nomination for president, had been assassinated.

Eugene R. McCarthy, a solid opponent of the Vietnam War, was the voice of anti-war youth in the country, but it was generally agreed that the powers in the Democratic Party did not feel that he could challenge Richard Nixon for the presidency in 1968. They favored Hubert Humphrey, vice president under Lyndon Johnson, and therefore an advocate of the Vietnam strategy that had divided the country so bitterly.

Thus, a large contingent of anti-war protesters journeyed to Chicago in August 1968 to make their voices heard and, it was hoped, influence the floor votes at the Democratic Convention.

Fearful of violence, Mayor Richard Daley, who was also the political boss of the Cook County Democratic Committee, ordered a mobilization of police forces to contain the demonstrators and prevent possible riots. In addition, he requested and received from Governor Samuel Shapiro 5,649 Illinois National Guardsmen, to be stationed on round-the-clock duty. On top of this, 6,000 regular army troops received riot control training at Fort Hood, Texas in an exercise called Operation Jackson Park, after the park in Chicago that was expected to be the gathering point for the student demonstrators. On August 25, 5,000 of these troops were flown to Chicago, where they were quartered at the Glenview Naval Air Station and the Great Lakes Naval Training Center outside the city. It was an awesome array of power for a peaceful nation to set up against a portion of its own citizenry.

Meanwhile, approximately 1,000 student protesters gathered, in a carnival mood, in Lincoln Park, on the fringes of one of the posher areas of Chicago. On Sunday night, August 25, at 11 P.M., the curfew hour on all public parks in Chicago, they were ordered out of the park by 400 policemen carrying tear gas launchers and rifles and wearing riot gear. The police drove the crowd into the downtown area of Clark Street and LaSalle Street. Traffic was disrupted, and the police waded into the mob of demonstrators, clubbing them with their nightsticks.

Claude Lewis, a black reporter for the *Philadelphia Bulletin*, was scribbling notes when a policeman approached him and demanded that he hand over his notebook. 'He snatched the notebook out of my hand and started swinging away,' Mr. Lewis later wrote. The first of many newspeople to be worked over by Chicago police, Mr. Lewis was treated for head lacerations at the Henrotin Hospital that evening.

By the next night, 27 newspaper and television reporters had been roughed up by police despite the fact that they had displayed their press credentials. Delos Hall, a cameraman for the Columbia Broadcasting System, reported to the *New York Times* that he was filming police action when he was clubbed from behind, knocked down and then attacked by several more policemen. He was treated for a blow on the mouth and a cut forehead. James Strickland, a cameraman for the National Broadcasting Company, was struck in the face when he photographed Mr. Hall lying in the street.

At 12:20 on the night of August 26, in Lincoln Park, 300 policemen wearing Plexiglas shields fired tear gas into a crowd of nearly 3,000 youths who had erected a barricade of overturned picnic tables, upon which they had affixed Viet Cong, black anarchist and peace flags. In the crowd was poet Allen Ginsberg, who led 300 protesters in a gentle chanting of 'Om,' the mystic Sanskrit sound of peace and love.

This apparently deflected most of the police force. They waited to make arrests. Finally, Tom Hayden, one of the protest coordinators, was arrested for the second night in a row. All in all, some 150 protesters had been booked so far, and nearly 60 had been injured.

On August 27, at 12:30, in Lincoln Park, the police again moved into the mob of demonstrators that now numbered 2,000 and began to fire tear gas into it. A group of clergymen and demonstrators, gathered around a 12-foot cross that they had set up in the hope of conducting an all-night prayer vigil, were routed and clubbed.

The 2,000 made their way toward Michigan Avenue

to Grant Park, where they merged with some 3,000
Yippies, New Leftists and adherents of the National
Mobilization Committee to End the War in Vietnam.
Grant Park was directly across the street from the
Conrad Hilton Hotel, a center of activity for the
Democratic National Convention and the headquarters
of all of the major nominees.

August 28 was the climactic – and most brutal – day
and night. Police were joined by National Guardsmen
in the streets. The Democratic National Convention
was nearing its most important business, and Hubert
Humphrey was expected to win the nomination. A
huge march was planned on the Amphitheatre that
housed the convention. Already, news from the streets
and some of the violence had invaded the floor of the
convention itself.

Alex J. Rosenberg, a delegate from New York, was
wrestled from the floor by an orange-arm-banded security guard when he refused to show his credentials.
Once in the entryway, he was struck by a policeman
and hauled away. Paul O'Dwyer, the Democratic candidate for the U.S. Senate, was roughed up by police
when he attempted to intercede, as was Mike Wallace,
the CBS television reporter, who was also struck on the
chin and hauled from the hall.

Later that night, Robert Maytag, a delegate from
Colorado, interrupted the seconding of Hubert Humphrey's nomination for president by shouting into a
microphone, 'Is there any rule under which Mayor
Daley can be compelled to end the police state of terror
being perpetrated?' Cheers greeted the interruption
while Mayor Daley sat impassively, and no move was
made by the Democratic National Convention to deter
the attempts to control demonstrators on the streets of
Chicago.

Later, in his nomination speech putting George
McGovern's name in contention for Democratic nomi-
nee for president, Senator Abraham M. Ribicoff of
Connecticut said, 'If Senator George McGovern were

President, we would not have these Gestapo tactics in the streets of Chicago.'

Impassive no longer, Mayor Daley and his supporters rose angrily to their feet and tried to shout down Senator Ribicoff, who turned to them and added, 'How hard it is to accept the truth.'

Outside the convention hall, a steady crescendo of activity had been accumulating all day. That afternoon, a gathering of approximately 15,000 young people had filled Grant Park and gathered around its band shell in a rally designed both to protest the violence in the streets and to prepare the demonstrators to march on the Amphitheatre.

There were skirmishes between police and protesters at the exterior of the gathering. At the band shell, poet Allen Ginsberg again led the group chanting 'Om,' though his voice by now was cracked from chanting and swallowing tear gas; French author Jean Genet spoke to the crowd through a translator; authors William Burroughs and Norman Mailer exhorted them; comedian Dick Gregory, mounting the platform, said, 'You just have to look around you at all the police and soldiers to know you must be doing something right.' Entertainers Judy Collins and Peter, Paul and Mary led the crowd in folk songs of the resistance movement, and leaders of the protest led the mob out of the park.

Some groups, such as the Poor People's March, had permits, but more purposely did not. There was manipulation by the more militant leaders of more naive and young and marijuana-smoking youngsters.

At the Congress Street Bridge leading from the park to Michigan Avenue, police and Guardsmen opened up with tear gas and mace, attempting to hold the demonstrators within the park. But the numbers were overwhelming, and between 2,000 and 5,000 youths, led by David Dellinger, the national chairman of the Mobilization Committee to End the War in Vietnam, and poet Allen Ginsberg, headed south on Michigan Avenue toward the Amphitheatre.

The police, moving in in phalanxes and using their clubs as prods, broke up the march, sending protesters fleeing up side streets. Those who escaped the police charges faced a tank and National Guardsmen with machine guns. Newspeople were again clubbed to the ground as demonstrators chanted, 'The whole world is watching.'

Reverend John Boyles, the Presbyterian chaplain at Yale and a staff worker for candidate Eugene McCarthy, was hauled off to a patrol wagon and charged with breach of the peace. Speaking to a *New York Times* reporter afterward, Mr. Boyles said, 'It's an unfounded charge. I was protesting the clubbing of a girl I knew from the McCarthy staff. They were beating her on her head with clubs and I yelled at them "Don't hit a woman." At that point I was slugged in the stomach and grabbed by a cop who arrested me.'

There were 178 arrests that night alone, and 100 persons, including 25 policemen, were injured.

Shortly after midnight, an uneasy calm settled over the city, as 1,000 National Guardsmen arranged themselves in front of the Conrad Hilton Hotel and 5,000 demonstrators drifted back into Grant Park. A field piece was poised in the lobby; officials had prevented the National Guard from bringing bazookas onto the premises.

Blue police barricades were lined up on the streets, and several dozen people, many of them elderly, watched quietly as protesters and police, illuminated by television lights, chased one another in and out of the park. Suddenly, 'for no apparent reason,' according to reporters on the scene, the police turned on the spectators and charged the barriers, crushing the spectators against the windows of the Haymarket Inn, a restaurant in the hotel. The plate glass windows gave way, sending screaming women and children backward through the broken shards of glass. The police then ran into the restaurant and beat some of the victims who had fallen through the windows. As they were clubbing them, they arrested some of these bewildered and bleeding citizens.

'Outside,' wrote Nora Sayre, who was caught in the crush, 'people sobbed with pain as their ribs snapped from being crushed against each other . . . Soon, a line of stick-whipping cops swung in on us. Voiceless from gas, I feebly waved my credentials, and the warrior who was about to hit me said, "oops, press." He let me limp into the hotel, where people were being pummelled into the red carpet, while free Pepsi was timidly offered on the sidelines.'

In St. Chrysostrom's Church and the sixth-floor offices of the Church Federation of Greater Chicago, volunteer doctors treated the gassed, maced and injured demonstrators. A specially equipped van manned by students of Yale Medical School and the Columbia College of Physicians and Surgeons roamed the riot area to dispense first aid, but police harassed first aid teams and forced the van away by threatening to confiscate it. Dr. Albert S. Braverman, an internist from Manhattan who was helping the wounded, was himself a victim. 'I was hit and pushed by a cop while I was coming back from dinner and while wearing my white coat and red cross,' he told reporters for the *Times*. 'When a friend said I was a doctor, the cop replied, "I don't give a damn." '

On the next night, August 29, another march was planned to the Amphitheatre. This time, several delegates joined the 3,000 marchers led by Dick Gregory (Dellinger was in jail, and Rennie Davis, his second, had had his arm broken the night before).

'Such blood . . .' wrote Nora Sayre.

Broad bloodstreaks on the pavements showed where bodies had been dragged . . . Each day, scores staggered bleeding through the streets and parks, reeling or dropping, their faces glistening with vaseline – for Mace . . . With two doctors, I walk[ed] five blocks ahead of . . . Dick Gregory . . . to the Amphitheatre; we [saw] the tank with the machine guns that await[ed] them. We turn[ed] back to tell them, discovering that the empty alleys – where we'd planned to disappear if necessary – [were] now crammed with police and Guardsmen.

Armored personnel carriers and jeeps with barbed-wire barriers mounted on their hoods further blocked the way. The marchers were ordered to stop at 18th Street and Michigan Avenue, on the advice of the Secret Service. Dick Gregory argued that he had invited the demonstrators to his home on 55th Street and wished to pass. He was denied his request, as were others behind him. He pushed past the barricades and was arrested, as were 422 others, including nine delegates. A steady shuttle of police vans ran between the street corner and a specially convened night court.

Ms. Sayre returned to McCarthy headquarters on the second floor of the Conrad Hilton Hotel. 'As I watched the beatings and gassings from a second-floor McCarthy room,' she wrote, 'twelve policemen surged in, slamming down the windows, drew the curtains, and told us to turn away and watch the TV set, where Humphrey was starting to speak – "And that's an order." '

Earlier, in the Convention Hall, Mayor Daley had mounted the podium to defend his police and his tactics. He mentioned that 51 police had been injured but failed to note that 300 demonstrators had also been injured. 'The people of Chicago,' he said, 'will never permit a lawless, violent group of terrorists to menace the lives of millions of people, destroy the purpose of a national political convention and take over the streets.'

At dawn, police raided the headquarters of Senator Eugene McCarthy, on the 15th floor of the Conrad Hilton Hotel, herded 30 McCarthy aides from several rooms into elevators and took them to the lobby. In the scuffle, three McCarthy workers were injured seriously enough to require hospital treatment. One required 10 stitches in his head, another, six. The police reported four injuries to their ranks. No arrests were made and no charges filed, but Senator McCarthy postponed his departure to call a news conference to protest the police action, which was, authorities said, in response to complaints that objects were being thrown from the windows of McCarthy headquarters – a charge the aides denied.

That same morning, Frank J. Sullivan, the Chicago Police Department's director of public information, called a news conference. He described the demonstrators as 'revolutionaries' and called some of their leaders, including Tom Hayden and Rennie Davis, 'Communists who are the allies of the men who are killing American soldiers.

'The intellectuals of America hate Richard J. Daley,' he continued, 'because he was elected by the people – unlike Walter Cronkite [the CBS anchor man at the convention].'

By August 1, the demonstrators had dispersed, as had the National Guard and police. The army personnel had never been called up, and they quietly boarded planes and returned to their camps. More than 71% of the Chicago citizens polled by local papers approved of the police handling of the demonstrators; many replied that they were certain the protesters were Communists, and J. Edgar Hoover announced an FBI investigation. Nevertheless, the rest of the nation and the world looked upon the riots differently. 'The Chicago cops taught us that we were rubble with no protection or defense,' wrote Nora Sayre. 'In future, we can understand the ghettos' rage.'

In September 1969, eight radicals and antiwar activists – David Dellinger, Rennie Davis, Tom Hayden, Abbie Hoffman, Jerry Rubin, Bobby Seale, John Froines and Lee Weiner – were tried in Chicago for conspiracy to riot. Bobby Seale, the head of the Black Panthers, was chained and gagged for outbursts in the courtroom. His case was separated from that of the others. Five of the remaining seven defendants were convicted of intent to riot and sentenced to five years in prison and fines of $5,000 each, the maximum penalties permitted. The riot convictions were eventually overturned on appeal because of improper rulings and conduct by the trial judge, Julius Hoffman. Contempt charges stemming from the trial were also dropped.

UNITED STATES – NEW YORK, NEW YORK
July 13–15, 1863

The July 11, 1863 Conscription Act, designed to replenish a depleted Union Army during the Civil War, allowed wealthy draftees to buy their way out of the draft for $300. It produced three days of rioting in New York City, from July 13–15, in which 2,000 rioters died, 10,000 rioters were wounded; 60 soldiers died, 300 soldiers were wounded; 76 blacks, turned on by the rioters, were reported 'missing'; 18 blacks were hanged; and 5 blacks were drowned.

UNITED STATES – OHIO, KENT
May 4, 1970

Three days of demonstrations by students of Kent State University protesting the U.S. invasion of Cambodia climaxed, on May 4, 1970, in the killing of four students by Ohio National Guardsmen. Nine students were wounded, and the protest movement of college students in the United States lost its momentum.

UNITED STATES – TEXAS, WACO
Feb. 28–April 19, 1993

Four agents of the United States Bureau of Alcohol, Tobacco, and Firearms were killed and 16 injured in a fierce gun battle that was ignited when officers tried to serve warrants for firearms violations at the Branch Davidian compound outside Waco, Texas on February

28, 1993. After a 51-day standoff, a fire thought to have been started by the followers of cult leader David Koresh destroyed the compound, killing at least 80 people.

UNITED STATES – WASHINGTON, D.C.
May 20–July 28, 1932

World War I veterans, out of work during the Great Depression, marched on Washington, D.C. in May 1932 to demand that a bonus due them in 1945 be paid immediately. On July 28, an army unit led by General Douglas MacArthur cleared the veterans out and set fire to their encampments. One veteran was killed; scores were injured.

Terrorism

BRAZIL – RIO DE JANEIRO
September 9, 1969

Members of Brazil's ALN and MR-8, demanding the release of 15 political prisoners, kidnapped U.S. ambassador Charles Elbrick on September 9, 1969. The prisoners were freed, and so was Ambassador Elbrick.

GERMANY – MUNICH
September 5, 1972

Israel's Olympic team was captured in Munich's Olympic Village on September 5, 1972 by Black September terrorists seeking to free political prisoners. A bungled rescue attempt by German authorities ended in the deaths of all 11 athletes and three terrorists.

There will hopefully never be another session of the Olympic Games remotely like that which occurred in September 1972 in Munich, Bavaria.

One of the objects of the Games was to contrast the Nazi Germany of 1936 – the last time the Games were held there – with the prosperous, democratized West Germany of the 1970s. Instead, they would be interrupted by the horrible massacre of 11 of Israel's top athletes.

Until the fearful events of September 5, the XX Olympiad had been an enormous success. More records had toppled than in any other Olympiad to date.

But while this was occurring, Black September, a fanatical splinter group in Fatah, the PLO fighting unit that drew its recruits from other Palestinian groups working under the PLO umbrella, was planning a dramatic kidnapping plot that would publicize its cause to the world. The week before the Olympics began, several Black September members, bearing a veritable arsenal of Russian-built Kalashnikov submachine guns, pistols and hand grenades, set out for Munich.

Once in Munich, they spread out, and a number of them got jobs among the 30,000 temporary employees of the Olympic Village.

At 4:20 A.M. on the morning of September 5, 1972, two terrorists, wearing sports warm-up suits and carrying athletic equipment, scaled the six-and-one-half-foot fence surrounding the village. Two telephone linemen saw them but thought little of it. They were, as far as they knew, a couple of Olympic athletes who had broken the curfew and were sneaking back to their quarters.

In total, there were eight Black September members within the compound. Pausing momentarily outside the athletic quarters, they either blackened their faces with charcoal or pulled on ski masks and made their way to the Olympic Village apartments that housed 22 Israeli athletes, coaches and officials. Two of them knocked on one door, inquiring, in German, 'Is this the Israeli team?' Wrestling coach Moshe Weinberg opened the door a crack, saw the masked gunmen, flung himself against the door and shouted to his roommates to flee. Immediately, Weinberg was riddled by a burst of submachine gunfire through the door. He died on the spot.

Simultaneously, in the other apartments, similar scenarios were being played out. In one, Yosef Gottfreund, an impressively tall wrestling referee, tried to hold off invading terrorists and was knifed to death.

Altogether, 18 Israeli athletes scrambled through windows to safety. Nine who did not make it were bound hand and foot in groups of three and pushed together onto a bed in one of the apartments. As hostages, they would be the bartering chips for the terrorists.

By 6 A.M., Munich police had been alerted, and 600 of them surrounded the area. An ambulance removed

The German naval dirigible LZ-18 plunged to earth in a fiery crash on October 17, 1913, killing 28 — the highest death toll in an air crash to that date. (*Library of Congress*)

Rescuers comb the wreckage of Japan Airlines Flight 123 after it crashed into Mount Ogura, north of Tokyo, on August 12, 1985. Five hundred twenty died in the crash of the Boeing 747 en route from Tokyo to Osaka. (*National Transportation Safety Board*)

The death of all 310 passengers aboard this Saudi Airlines Lockheed-1011 at Riyadh was a result of the Saudi custom of allowing passengers to cook on board and a failure of airline personnel to follow proper evacuation procedures. (*National Transportation Safety Board*)

The worst disaster in United States aviation history in the making. American Airlines Flight 191 rolls sharply to the left moments after losing its left engine over Chicago's O'Hare Airport. (*National Transportation Safety Board*)

Pieces of a Delta Airlines DC-9 dot the landscape following the unexplained crash of the liner on its approach to Logan Airport in Boston, on July 31, 1973. (*National Transportation Safety Board*)

The German dirigible *Hindenburg* burns at its mooring ⁀st in Lakehurst, New Jersey on May 6, 1937. This spectacular finale to the age of lighter-than-air transportation was blamed on exhaust sparks igniting escaping gas, static electricity caused by a sudden rainstorm or sabotage. (*Smithsonian Institution*)

Wreckage is strewn over Sterling Place, Brooklyn after the mid-air collision of a United Airlines DC-8 and a TWA Super Constellation on December 16, 1960. One hundred twenty-eight aboard the two liners and eight on the ground died. (*National Transportation Safety Board*)

The wreckage of the Avianca Boeing 707 that crashed in Cove Neck, Long Island on January 25, 1990 is flung over a large part of this thickly populated suburban community. Fortunately no one on the ground was killed. (*National Transportation Safety Board*)

Political considerations forced the *Shenandoah* to fly in bad weather and thus crash on September 3, 1925 near Ava, Ohio. The wrecked carcass of the once-proud airship was picked clean by souvenir hunters the following day. (*Smithsonian Institution*)

A mother grieves over her dead child in a field near Aleppo, in the midst of the Armenian massacres. Two million Armenians were killed over a period of 27 years by Turks, who eventually erased Armenia from the map of the world. (*Library of Congress*)

A contemporary Chinese print depicts the Boxer Rebellion of 1900. (*Library of Congress*)

Dismembered bodies are grisly evidence of executions in Canton during the Boxer Rebellion, a grim conflict between Chinese conservatives and Western partitioners. (*Illustrated London News*)

The brutal slaughter of French Huguenots in the streets of Paris, the famous St. Bartholomew's Day Massacre of August 24, 1572, is depicted in a period drawing. (*New York Public Library*)

The crushing of the uprising of the slaves and gladiators and the death of their leader, Spartacus, are depicted in a 19th-century drawing. (*New York Public Library* (*H. Vogel*))

Frontier art depicting the slaughter of Cheyenne and Arapaho Indians during the Sand Creek, Colorado massacre on November 29, 1864. (*Currier and Ives*)

The confrontation between police and rioters in front of Horace Greeley's *Tribune* during the draft riots in New York City, July 13–15, 1863. (*Harper's Weekly*)

Members of the 'bonus army' of World War I veterans gather outside one of their makeshift dwellings in Washington, D.C. in the summer of 1932. Shortly afterward, a U.S. Army unit led by General Douglas MacArthur routed the protesters and set fire to their encampment. (*Library of Congress*)

The three leaders of the Hanafi Muslim siege of Washington, D.C. from March 9 to 11, 1977 are transported to jail in a Red Cross ambulance. (*American Red Cross*)

Rescued miners wait to be lifted to the surface after the gigantic mine explosion in the Courrieres Colliery, France, in which 1,060 miners died. (*Illustrated London News*)

Rescuers inside the Courrieres Colliery. (*Illustrated London News*)

The giant explosion in the Oaks Colliery in Barnsley, England on December 12, 1866 is graphically portrayed in a contemporary lithograph. Three hundred forty men and boys died in the tragedy. (*Illustrated London News*)

An anxious crowd gathers outside the ruined Universal Colliery in Sengenhydd, Wales following the worst mine disaster in the history of Great Britain, on October 14, 1913. (*Illustrated London News*)

A graphic re-creation of the first discovery of the victims of the explosion in the Lackawanna and Western Railroad's Avondale coal mine in Plymouth, Pennsylvania on September 6, 1869. (*Frank Leslie's Illustrated Newspaper*)

The horrendous explosion of the steamship *Sultana* near Memphis, Tennessee on April 27, 1865. An appalling 1,547 died in one of the worst tragedies in American history. (*Frank Leslie's Illustrated Newspaper*)

Heavy clouds of acrid smoke hang over Texas City, Texas following the cataclysmic explosion of April 16, 1947. (*American Red Cross*)

A young wife discovers the body of her husband, blown from the mouth of the Laurel Mine of the Southwest Virginia Improvement Company in Pocahontas, Virginia on March 13, 1884. One hundred twelve were killed and two were injured in the blast. (*Frank Leslie's Illustrated Newspaper*)

Wreckage in the Monongah Mine in Monongah, West Virginia on December 6, 1907. Expectant families and rescuers line the hill that encloses the mine. Three hundred sixty-two miners died in an explosion caused by a runaway rail car. (*Frank Leslie's Illustrated Newspaper*)

A spectacular fire interrupted a performance of Massenet's *Mignon* at Paris's Opera-Comique on the evening of May 25, 1887. Two hundred died, and the opera house was gutted. (*Illustrated London News*)

A molten roof collapsed on hundreds of society patrons attending Paris's Grand Bazar de Charite at the end of a flash fire on the night of May 4, 1897. Here, the grim job of identifying their remains is conducted. (*Illustrated London News*)

Survivors prepare a mass grave for the dead following the firebombing of Dresden, Germany on February 13, 1945. Some 135,000 died, hundreds of thousands were injured and the so-called Florence of Germany was leveled. (*Library of Congress*)

The fire which engulfed the main stand at Bradford City's Valley Parade ground during a match on May 11, 1985 was responsible for 56 deaths and over 200 injuries. The disaster remains one of the worst in British soccer history. (*Rex Features*)

The Exeter Theatre fire in progress on the night of September 4, 1887. The theater, one of the prides of Exeter, England, was totally destroyed; 200 died and hundreds were injured. (*Illustrated London News*)

The Great 1666 Fire of London is depicted in a period painting. Thirteen thousand homes and 87 churches were destroyed; eight people died, and the black plague was thought to be incinerated in the flames. (*New York Public Library*)

The grisly aftermath of the King's Cross fire in which 31 people died on November 18, 1987. It is the worst fire in the history of the London Underground. (*Rex Features*)

A fire brigade rushes down a Constantinople street during the consuming fire of June 5, 1870. (*Illustrated London News*)

Terrified audience members flee the Barnum and Bailey Circus fire in Hartford, Connecticut on July 6, 1944. (*American Red Cross*)

Weinberg's body, which had been dragged to a terrace and left by the gunmen.

Police Chief Manfred Schreiber attempted to brazen his way into the apartments. He was met by the group's leader, wearing a white tennis hat and sunglasses. For a moment, it seemed possible for Schreiber to take him hostage, and then, according to Schreiber, the man asked, 'Do you want to take me?' He opened his hand and showed a hand grenade to the police chief. The terrorist's thumb was on the grenade's pin.

At 9 A.M., a message in English was tossed from a window. On it was a list of 200 prisoners currently held in Israeli jails. They included Ulrike Meinhof and Andreas Baader, the leaders of a gang of German terrorists who had robbed eight banks, bombed U.S. Army posts and killed three policemen before they were captured the previous June, and Kozo Okamoto, a Japanese Red Army terrorist who took part in the massacre at Tel Aviv's Lod Airport in which 26 people died (see p. 129). All were to be freed, according to the note, before the Israeli athletes would be released.

Furthermore, the Palestinians demanded that they and their prisoners be flown out of West Germany to any Arab nation except Lebanon or Jordan, aboard three airplanes that would leave at agreed upon intervals. Officials had three hours to comply. If they did not, the hostages would be executed at the rate of two every thirty minutes.

International phone lines hummed. West German Interior Minister Hans Dietrich Genscher took personal charge of the negotiations, first offering an unlimited sum of money for the release of the hostages and then offering himself and other West German officials as hostages in place of the athletes. Although he was turned down, he was able to stall for time by stating that he was in touch with Israeli authorities. There were two extensions of the deadline, the first to 3 P.M., the next to 5 P.M.

Meanwhile, 15 volunteer police sharpshooters were

brought into the area, and worldwide television coverage showed them crouching in readiness until German authorities realized that the terrorists could also tune them in, at which point they ceased the TV coverage.

The games were suspended at 3:45 P.M. that afternoon, after a request from Israel. By that time, Willie Brandt, West Germany's chancellor, had made the decision to permit the terrorists to fly out of West Germany with the hostages. Speaking of the athletes, Brandt said to newspeople later, 'We are responsible for the fate of these people.'

By 6 P.M., Genscher had run out of stalling tactics. He was told by Brandt that the Palestinians and their hostages would be taken to Munich's airport and flown out on a Lufthansa 727 jet to any place they named. The terrorists selected Cairo, and a 7 P.M. deadline was set.

In actuality, the Germans were moving their sharpshooters to Furstenfeldbruck Field, and the Arabs were planning a destination other than Cairo.

At 10 P.M., 18 hours after the initial assault, the terrorists herded their prisoners, tied together in single file and blindfolded, out of the building and into a German army bus, which drove them through a tunnel under the village to a lawn 275 yards away.

The green expanse had been converted into a helicopter pad. There were three helicopters there; two took the terrorists and their hostages on the 25-minute ride to Furstenfeldbruck Airport; the third went ahead, carrying German officials and Israeli intelligence officers.

The airport was ringed by 500 soldiers. But there were only five sharpshooters to pick off eight terrorists. The rest had unexplainably been left behind at the Olympic Village.

The helicopters landed. The terrorists leaped out and took the German crews hostage. They arranged them in front of their helicopters and proceeded to inspect the 727.

As they walked toward it, the police sharpshooters opened fire. The two Arabs guarding the helicopter crews were killed, and one of the pilots was wounded. One more guerrilla on the tarmac died. The leader dove under a helicopter, fired back and knocked out the floodlights on the field and the radio in the control tower. A Munich police sergeant was gunned down.

The battle would rage for an hour more. Five guerrillas, including their leader, would be killed, and three would surrender. And every one of the hostages would be killed. One group of four was burned to death when a terrorist tossed a grenade into the helicopter in which they were being held. The remaining five would be machine-gunned by their captors.

It would be four hours before the horrendous results of the failed ambush would reach the outside world. Reaction from the Arab world would be divided. Lebanon would offer condolences to Israel. Egypt would charge that German bullets killed them all.

In coming days, Israeli retaliation was swift and fierce. On the eve of Rosh Hashanah, Israeli jets struck Lebanon and Syria with the heaviest strikes since the 1967 war. Arab sources later said that 66 were killed in the raids by 75 jets. Israeli ground troops crossed the Lebanese border to battle commandos who had been mining roads in Israel. Syria put its army on alert. Meanwhile, in Libya, Colonel Qaddafi conducted a martyr's funeral for the dead terrorists.

The three surviving Arabs would be tried and imprisoned, but in November they would be released in exchange for a Lufthansa airliner hijacked in Beirut by other Black September terrorists. In Tripoli, Colonel Qadaffi would give the three a hero's welcome and parade.

GREAT BRITAIN – ENGLAND, LONDON
December 17, 1983

Continuing IRA terrorism attacks on British citizens

resulted in the explosion of a car bomb planted by the Provisional IRA during the Christmas shopping season, on December 17, 1983. Six were killed; 94 were wounded.

It was Dalthi O'Connell, one of the founders of the Irish Republican Army, who is credited with inventing the car bomb, the stock-in-trade of terrorists world-wide. By 1983, the Provisional IRA had much experience with setting car bombs, and it was one such device that accounted for the Christmas carnage of Harrods department store in London on December 17, 1983.

There had been warnings issued, via radio, television and newspapers, of possible IRA bombings during the holiday season. Scotland Yard intelligence reports from Northern Ireland had warned of 'a Christmas blitz.'

At approximately 12:40 P.M. on December 17, the phone rang at the Samaritans, a voluntary charity organization in London. A distinctly Irish-accented voice announced, 'Car bomb outside Harrods. Two bombs in Harrods.'

The Samaritans called Scotland Yard, and at 1:15 a team of police, including animal handlers and trained dogs, arrived on the scene. They went to work in the store first, trying to trace down the interior bombs, while other police conducted a search of cars on the streets surrounding the giant store. The last Saturday before Christmas, thousands of shoppers jammed the store and the sidewalks surrounding it.

At exactly 1:20, a car not checked by the police suddenly exploded with a thunderous, earsplitting roar. Black smoke and shrapnel erupted as if they had been launched from a volcano. The concussion shattered windows for blocks and instantly killed five shoppers and a policeman. Other unsuspecting pedestrians and shoppers were injured, some horribly, by rainstorms of glass and metal.

Ninety-four would be injured; six would die. Those responsible for the bomb would never be captured.

GREAT BRITAIN – SCOTLAND, LOCKERBIE
December 21, 1988

No clear-cut responsibility was established for the midair terrorist bomb explosion aboard Pan Am Flight 103 from London to New York on December 21, 1988. Two hundred fifty-six people on board the plane and 11 on the ground were killed in the fiery crash.

Pan Am Flight 103, a Boeing 747, took off from London's Heathrow Airport 25 minutes behind schedule, at 6:25 P.M., on December 21, 1988. Aboard were 246 passengers and 10 crew members, among them 35 of 38 Syracuse University students who had been studying abroad and were returning home for Christmas, and Brent Carisson of Sweden, the chief administrative officer of the United Nations' Council for Namibia. Carisson was flying to New York for the signing of an accord on Namibian independence.

Fifty-two minutes later, while Flight 103 was flying at an altitude of 31,000 feet over the small village of Lockerbie, in the extreme southern end of Scotland, a bomb, planted in a tape recorder and radio in the plane's luggage compartment, exploded. The main part of the airplane dropped like a flaming missile, landing near a gas station on the outskirts of Lockerbie, setting fire to the station, a dozen row houses and several cars that were on the A74 highway to Glasgow.

Other pieces of the liner and some bodies were strewn over the countryside in an 80-mile-long arc. It was the worst airline crash in British history, and the worst single plane crash in Pan Am's history. The BBC broadcast horrendous pictures of raging fires, devastated houses and cars and shreds of aircraft wreckage. 'The plane came down 400 yards from my house,' said Bob Glaster, a retired policeman, to reporters. 'There was a ball of fire 300 feet into the air, and debris was falling from the sky. When the smoke cleared a little, I could see bodies lying on the road. At least one dozen houses were destroyed.'

The terrible part of the tragedy was that Pan Am and government agencies had been warned of the possibility of the bombing in ample time to prevent it and had been unable to accomplish this. One week before the bombing, the American Embassy in Finland had received a notice saying that an unidentified caller had warned that 'there would be a bombing attempt against a Pan American aircraft flying from Frankfurt to the United States.' Flight 103 had originated in Frankfurt, on a 727 with the same flight number. In London, at Heathrow Airport, passengers and baggage had been transferred to the larger 747 for the longer leg of the journey to New York.

Later investigation revealed that there was, indeed, increased surveillance of passengers boarding the craft and that embassy personnel scheduled to board the flight were warned of the threat, and many canceled their reservations. The general public was *not* warned, and this would make headlines in the United States, particularly in light of later disclosures (see below).

For many months, because of the plastic nature of the explosive, blame was directed toward two anti-Arafat Palestinian terrorist groups, the PFLP General Command, led by Ahmed Jabril, and the Fatah Revolutionary Council, led by Abu Nidal. Later investigation by Scotland Yard, however, led to the conclusion that the initial investigation linked the bombing to the Iranian callers, or, some speculated, at least a terrorist group sympathetic to Iran.

In November 1990 it was revealed that the US Drug Enforcement Agency regularly used Pan Am Flight 103 to fly informants and suitcases of heroin from the Middle East to Detroit. Nazir Khalid Jafaar, of Detroit, was aboard this flight and involved in this operation.

Pan Am's baggage operation in Frankfurt, it was further revealed, was used to put suitcases of heroin on planes, apparently without the usual security checks, under an arrangement between the drug agency and German authorities. Thus, it was eminently possible that Jafaar, who was either an agent or an informer for the DEA, was the unwitting carrier of the bomb that destroyed Flight 103 and killed 256 people in the air and 11 on the ground on the night of December 21, 1988.

Later information refuted this and intimated that the bomb was planted by Libyan terrorists in retaliation for the 1986 attack on Colonel Muammer el-Qaddafi by American jets. This line of investigation ultimately led to the demand, by Great Britain and the United States, for the extradition for trial of two Libyans, Lamen Khalifa Fhimah and Abdel Basset Ali al-Megrahi. The two, the investigation concluded, had planted the bomb responsible for the crash of Pan Am 103.

The two powers took the charges to the United Nations Security Council in early 1992, asking for sanctions against Libya if Colonel Qaddafi did not turn over the two agents. In March 1992, the Security Council passed Resolution 731, ordering Libya to surrender the two men for prosecution in Britain and the United States and also surrender evidence that could be used against them.

Colonel Qaddafi refused, then agreed to turn them over to representatives of the Arab League, then changed his mind again. In late March, the United Nations Security Council gave the colonel two weeks to conform to Resolution 731 or face sanctions that would cease air travel into and out of that country and severely reduce Libya's diplomatic presence in the rest of the world. As this is written, Colonel Qaddafi's reply was to threaten to cut back on oil exports to various countries sympathetic to the UN resolution.

Even if the two terrorists were handed over, experts and family members of those who perished in the crash announced that this would be settling only a small part of the crime. International politics – specifically, the role of Syria in the Persian Gulf War – were preventing investigators from acting on what they knew about the entire operation, these critics and family members charged. President George Bush's statement that Syria had received a 'bum rap' simply did not square with the facts, they noted.

In a statement to *New York Times* columnist A.M. Rosenthal, on March 30, 1992, Steven Emerson, the Washington journalist who, with Brian Duffy, wrote *The Fall of Pan Am 103* in 1990, said:

> The undisputed intelligence shows that Syria-based and -supported terrorists, led by Ahmed Jabril, head of the Popular Front for the Liberation of Palestine – General Command, planned and organized multiple airplane bombings against U.S., European and Israeli airlines in October 1988.
>
> The money and orders for the operation came from Iran, seeking revenge for the shooting down of the Iranian airbus that summer by the U.S. According to intelligence officials, Iranian officials traveled to Germany to oversee the operation and to personally witness the transfer of explosives and bombs.
>
> But the plan went awry when Syrian-based terrorists were arrested by German police in late October 1988. Jabril, who had received funding from Libya for at least the previous two years, handed off the operation to Libya, which had its own terrorist infrastructure in place.

Thus the sequence of events as reconstructed by international investigators: Iran bankrolled it. Syrian-based terrorists planned it. Libyans executed it.

The reason that Pan Am 103 was chosen? According to Vincent Cannistraro, who headed the CIA investigation of the crash until he left the agency in 1990, the Jabril group settled on Pan Am because its surveillance indicated that in Frankfurt the airline was not 'reconciling' baggage fully. That is, it was not making sure that every piece of luggage 'was identified directly with a passenger before being taken on board.'

As this goes to press, nobody has been brought to trial or held accountable in a court of law for the bombing of Pan Am Flight 103.

IRAN – TEHRAN
November 4, 1979–January 20, 1981

The need for the Ayatollah Khomeini to galvanize anti-Western, pro-Islamic loyalty was the root cause of the taking of the U.S. Embassy in Tehran and the imprisonment of 52 hostages for 444 days.

At a few minutes before 11 A.M. on November 4, 1979, 400 young Iranian 'students,' later learned to be members of the Revolutionary Guard, cut through chains that joined together the gates of the American Embassy in Tehran, Iran. The Iranian guards stationed at the gates offered no resistance, and the invading crowd soon swarmed over the embassy compound.

It seemed at first to be a mirror image of other temporary embassy takeovers that had occurred in the world in the previous months, and President Jimmy Carter, spending Sunday at Camp David, Maryland, did not even return to Washington when informed of the break-in.

But by the next day, it became apparent to the president and the world that this was a move without precedent. Bound and blindfolded hostages were paraded before angry crowds chanting death to the Great Satan, America.

A year earlier, Shah Mohammad Reza Pahlavi had been deposed by revolutionary forces spurred on by Iran's spiritual leader, the Ayatollah Khomeini. The shah had fled to Mexico, and two weeks before the break-in at the American Embassy in Tehran he had flown to New York, where he was undergoing treatment for cancer. The 'students' demanded that the deposed shah be returned to Iran for trial.

The United States refused, and thus began one of the longest standoffs in history. For the next 444 days, a tug of war would pit Iran against the United States, with the hostages as the pawns in the game.

Two weeks after the takeover of the embassy, the militants released 13 hostages – eight black men and five women – who returned to the United States in time for Thanksgiving of that year. The shah's health improved, and Mexico, not wishing to become involved in the U.S.-Iran standoff, refused to let him return. He fled to Panama, where he remained in exile, despite Iran's demands.

That Christmas, the White House tree remained dark out of respect for the hostages, and Americans, using the words of a popular song as their cue, began to tie yellow ribbons around trees, where they would shred and fade until the hostages would finally be set free.

At year's end, 1979, three American clergymen were permitted to hold Christmas services for most of the hostages. The International Court of Justice at The Hague unanimously called for their immediate release, and the secretary general of the United Nations, Kurt Waldheim, went to Tehran to try to mediate the standoff. He was denied meetings with either the hostages or the ayatollah, and his car was mobbed and beaten on by demonstrators.

In mid-January, American television crews and correspondents were expelled from Iran, but by late that month, some hope was held out by the newly elected president of Iran, Abolhassan Bani-Sadr, who criticized the militants and promised to try to calm the situation.

Later that month, six American diplomats who had been hidden in the Canadian Embassy escaped using forged Canadian passports. It was the first good news from Iran in three months.

In February, Bani-Sadr announced that the hostages might be released without the return of the shah, but this hope was dashed quickly by the ayatollah, who refused to allow a United Nations commission to see the hostages.

As winter gave way to spring, President Carter's approval rating began to drop. He was up for reelection the following November, and the hostage crisis was eroding the president's chances for a second term in office. Something had to be done to break the deadlock.

On the day after Easter, President Carter formally broke off diplomatic relations with Iran, ordered all Iranian diplomats out of the United States within 24 hours, asked Congress to allow Americans to settle claims against Iran on the $8 billion in Iranian assets that the government had frozen following the embassy takeover, and announced a trade embargo on Iran. Later that month, he also banned travel to Iran by all Americans except journalists, who had been recently readmitted.

On April 25, the United States government launched a dramatic attempt to rescue the hostages. But in a tangle of confusion and mismanagement, the raid dissolved in ignominious failure. Three of the eight helicopters assigned to the mission dropped out with mechanical failure (they were the wrong kind of machine for the Iranian desert). Without them, the mission was canceled, but not before one of the remaining helicopters collided on the ground with a C-130 transport plane, sending both up in flames. Eight servicemen died in the fire, and the rest fled, leaving the charred bodies of their comrades in the sand of the Iranian desert, 250 miles short of Tehran, their destination.

It was the worst fiasco since the CIA-bungled Bay of Pigs invasion of Cuba in 1961. President Carter would be permanently damaged by the incident. Secretary of State Cyrus Vance, who had opposed the raid from the very first, resigned and was replaced by Edmund Muskie.

In early July 1980, Richard I. Queen, one of the hostages who was suffering from multiple sclerosis, was released. This left 54 still in captivity.

On July 27, the shah died in Egypt of the final effects of his cancer. Now the ayatollah went on Iranian radio and read off a new list of conditions: return of the shah's wealth, cancellation of U.S. claims against Iran, unblocking of Iranian assets frozen in America and a pledge by Washington not to interfere in Iranian affairs. It was a list designed to humble a major power before the resolve and strength of the ayatollah.

But the events of history blunted even the power of the spiritual leader of Iran. A full-scale war broke out between Iran and Iraq as the U.S. elections drew near. The hostages faded from the front pages of the world's newspapers. Behind the scenes, the United States knew that Iran was strapped for spare parts and ammunition. It was also aware that Iran felt that it might be able to gain concessions from a president fighting for reelection.

The United States pledged neutrality in the Iran-Iraq war and hinted that if the hostages were freed, some Iranian assets would be unfrozen and more than $500 million worth of spare parts already purchased by Iran would be delivered.

There was a flurry of rumors, climaxing in the week before the election, that an agreement was imminent. But the ayatollah, as was his pattern, again dashed hopes on the eve of election day, 1980, which was the first anniversary of the hostage seizure.

Jimmy Carter lost the election by a landslide to Ronald Reagan, and the day after, President Carter asserted that the 11th-hour developments in the hostage crisis had been the primary cause of his defeat.

During his final weeks in office, President Carter and his administration, using Algeria as an intermediary, haggled with Iran over the hostages. For the second year, he ordered the Christmas tree at the White House to remain dark, but, responding to a request from the hostages' families, he lit it on Christmas Eve for 417 seconds, one for each day of their captivity.

On Christmas Day, three Iranian Christian clergymen and the papal nuncio held religious services for the hostages, and negotiations resumed. Iran conceded that its claim of $14 billion in frozen assets was high and accepted the U.S. figure of $9.5 billion, of which approximately $2.5 billion was subject to legal claims.

Iran's minister for executive affairs, in a speech to the Iranian parliament, probably put his finger on the real reason for the agreement. 'The hostages are like a fruit from which all the juice has been squeezed out,' he said. 'Let us let them all go.'

Thus, at 12:25 P.M. on January 20, 1981, just as the newly elected president, Ronald Reagan, was finishing his inaugural address, an Algerian Airlines 727 lifted off from Mehrabad Airport in Tehran with 54 hostages aboard. 'God is Great! Death to America!' chanted the men who had brought the hostages to the airport. As the plane left Iranian airspace, nearly $3 billion of Iranian assets were unfrozen by the United States, and more was made available for Iranian repayment loans. The next day, $8 billion of Iranian assets would be funneled into the Bank of England in a special Algerian account accessible to Iran.

The purpose of the ayatollah had been served. He had humbled a great Western power and had arguably sent an American president down to defeat at the polls.

'With thanks to Almighty God,' said Ronald Reagan at an inaugural luncheon, 'I have been given a tag line, the get-off line, that everyone wants for the end of a toast or a speech, or anything else.'

'I doubt that at any time in our history,' said Jimmy

Carter from his home in Georgia, 'more prayers have reached heaven for any Americans than have those given to God in the last 14 months.'

IRELAND – IRISH SEA
June 22, 1985

On June 22, 1985, a bomb planted by Sikh extremists exploded in an Air India 747 over the Irish Sea. All 329 aboard died in this, the first downing of a jumbo jet by a terrorist bomb.

On June 6, 1984, a violent confrontation took place between Sikhs and Hindus at the Golden Temple in Amritsar, in the Punjab region of India. One thousand two hundred were killed that day when the Indian Army raided the temple, among them Bhai Amrik Singh, a former president of the Sikh Student Federation, a militant terrorist organization that had been outlawed by the Indian government. Leaders vowed revenge, and although a lack of physical evidence precluded positive proof, it is generally accepted that it was the Sikh Student Federation that was responsible for the planting of a bomb that blew an Air India 747 to pieces over the Irish Sea on June 22, 1985.

The flight, bound for London, took off uneventfully from Toronto on the evening of June 21. At 8 A.M. the following morning, air controllers at Shannon Airport made contact with the crew of the flight as it entered Irish airspace. Clearance was given to proceed to London.

And then, at 8:15, the airplane disappeared from Shannon's radar screens. No distress signal was radioed by the jet's captain, Commander Narendra. The flight merely disappeared in an instant.

Rescue boats and helicopters were dispatched immediately. It was a bone-chilling morning, with clouds at 500 feet and heavy rain, and at first it was thought that perhaps a freak of weather had caused the crash. But this was rejected summarily by rescuers, who noted that pieces of the airplane were scattered over a five-square-mile area, indicating that the plane had exploded long before it hit the sea.

None of the bodies recovered from the water were wearing life jackets, indicating that the explosion occurred without warning, and no piece of wreckage was larger than 30 square feet, indicating that the detonation must have been enormous.

That very day, the *New York Times* received a telephone call from a member of the 10th Regiment of the Sikh Student Federation, who claimed responsibility for the bombing. Their purpose was in his words, to 'protest Hindu imperialism.' Similar calls were placed to other newspapers in Europe and India.

There were no survivors; all 329 aboard the jetliner were killed. It was the first jumbo jet downed by a terrorist bomb. No arrests were made, and no incendiary device was discovered.

ISRAEL – SINAI DESERT
February 21, 1973

Fear that a Libyan jetliner had been hijacked and was flying a bomb aimed at Tel Aviv was the reason given for the downing of the jetliner by Israeli Phantoms on February 21, 1973. All 106 aboard died.

ISRAEL – TEL AVIV
May 31, 1972

An agreement between the PFLP and the Red Army to continue terrorist attacks on Israel resulted in the first transnational terrorist incident at Lod (Lydda) Airport on May 31, 1972. Twenty-six unsuspecting travelers were killed; 76 were wounded.

'How does it happen,' asked one dazed and bloodied survivor of the Lydda Airport Massacre of May 31,

1972, 'that Japanese kill Puerto Ricans because Arabs hate Israelis?'

It was a microcosmic question that had no reason to be asked until that horrible day. Until that time, each terrorist organization seemed to be autonomous. But some time in late 1971, members of Japan's United Red Army made contact with George Habbash, the leader of the Popular Front for the Liberation of Palestine, PFLP, and met with him in Pyongyang, North Korea. From there, they traveled to Jordan, where, along with members of West Germany's Baader-Meinhof Gang, they underwent guerrilla training.

The Japanese Red Army, an ultra-leftist group, had lost support in Japan earlier that year when, after police had arrested hundreds of its adherents, including five of its leaders, the bodies of 14 young people were discovered. The 14 had been tortured to death for deviating from the Red Army's revolutionary line. Thus, the Japanese terrorist group sought to gain credibility and approval in the terrorist world by aligning itself with the PFLP.

Three of its members, trained in Lebanon, boarded an Air France jet in Paris on May 31, 1973. Passengers aboard Air France jets in 1973 felt safe. France practiced a friendly relationship with Arab countries, and at the beginning of May, although Asher Ben Nathan, Israel's ambassador to France, had called on Herve Alphand, secretary-general of the French Foreign Ministry, to plead for increased security measures on flights to Israel, Alphand had refused him, noting that France and the Arab countries were not enemies.

Air France Flight 132 arrived on time and without incident at Tel Aviv's Lydda, or Lod, Airport on May 31. Passengers debarked and proceeded to luggage conveyor belt number 3.

Three young Japanese tourists claimed their bags from the belt and then began to behave strangely. They removed their jackets and crouched to open their suitcases. When they straightened up, they were all holding Czech-made VZT-58 automatic rifles, which they immediately began firing, rapidly and indiscriminately. They fanned their weapons in wide arcs, mowing down the passengers near them, and then raised the barrels of the rifles to shoot those farther away.

Two of the gunmen then dashed for the tarmac, firing at two parked planes. One killed the other, nearly decapitating him with a brutal burst of automatic gunfire. The third terrorist leaped on the now blood-slick baggage conveyor belt, holding a grenade. He pulled the pin, slipped, fell on the grenade and was blown to bits by its explosion.

The one surviving gunman continued to shoot into the crowd until he ran out of ammunition. As he stopped to reload, an El Al traffic controller, Hanan Zaiton, leaped on him and beat him to the ground. Guards rushed to his aid, and then hauled the terrorist, a 24-year-old college dropout named Kozo Okamoto, into a nearby office.

The airport was strewn with the dead, the dying and the wounded. Twenty-six people, including Dr. Aharon Katchalsky, one of Israel's leading scientists, and 14 Puerto Ricans making a pilgrimage to the Holy Land, were killed. Seventy-six others were injured.

An hour after the killings, a spokesperson for the PFLP announced to local papers that it had recruited the Japanese fanatics 'to kill as many people as possible.'

It was barbaric and senseless, but it proved that there was no safe haven for the innocent who hoped to escape terrorism in the 1970s.

ITALY – BOLOGNA
August 1, 1980

To 'honor' an accused neo-fascist bomber, neo-fascist terrorists detonated a bomb in the Bologna train station on August 1, 1980 at the beginning of the holiday season. Eighty-four died; 200 were injured.

August is the traditional holiday month in Italy and France, and on August 1, 1980 the Bologna train station was packed to capacity with vacationers and tourists. That morning, a judge in Bologna announced that eight neo-fascists, among them, Mario Tuti, had been indicted and would be tried.

Amid unsuspecting travelers in the Bologna train station, a group of terrorists planted a bomb equivalent in power to 90 pounds of TNT in a corner of the second-class waiting room.

Shortly after 1 P.M., the bomb exploded with a thunderous roar, totally demolishing one wing of the massive train station. A restaurant, two waiting rooms and a train platform were flattened as the roof collapsed on them.

Mayhem followed. The screams of the injured and the shouts of rescuers and survivors ricocheted off the columns and walls of the ruins. It was the worst terrorist disaster in Italy's history, eclipsing the 1968 bombing of a Milan bank, in which 16 people were killed and 16 injured. The toll in Bologna would be 84 dead and 200 injured.

On August 2, while smoke still filtered upward from a wing of the station that now had only two iron girders standing, 10,000 Bolognans turned a left-wing rally into a demonstration against terrorism, and labor unions held a rally in Rome's Colosseum, in which they announced a four-hour strike.

That same day, two calls from terrorist groups were received by police. One claimed responsibility for the blast by the Red Brigades, the far left wing terrorist organization that had kidnapped and killed former Prime Minister Aldo Moro. But the caller incorrectly described the time and location of the bomb.

The other caller claimed to represent the Armed Revolutionary Cells, a neo-fascist organization, eight of whose members were to be tried for the railroad bombing of the Bologna-Florence train six years before. The bombing, it was stated, was to honor Mario Tuti, one of the accused.

Police believed this caller and began an exhaustive investigation that would end a little over a year later, on September 12, 1981, in London, with the arrest of the terrorists who planted the bomb.

JORDAN – DAWSON'S FIELD
September 6–8, 1970

A PFLP guerrilla group's demands for the release of Palestinian prisoners culminated in the 1970s' most spectacular terrorist incident, at Dawson's Field in Jordan. Five civilian jetliners were hijacked; four were flown to Jordan and blown up. One hijacker was killed in the explosion, and 300 passengers were taken hostage.

In what began as the largest, most spectacular hijacking operation of the 1970s, four airliners from four countries were hijacked in one morning and early afternoon. The day was September 6, 1970, and all four hijackings took place shortly after each plane took off from its home airport. All were headed for New York.

The first of these, El Al's Flight 219 from Tel Aviv, a Boeing 707 with 148 passengers and 10 crew members aboard, took off from Amsterdam in the morning. Shortly after takeoff, two hijackers, Patrick Arguello, a Nicaraguan working for the PFLP, and Leila Khaled, a Palestinian, sprang to their feet, shouting. Arguello dashed toward the cockpit door. Schlomo Vider, an El Al steward, pounced on him but was shot in the stomach.

The plane was thrown into a steep dive by its pilot, which flung the hijackers off balance and allowed one of the two Israeli security guards aboard to shoot and kill one hijacker, Arguello. Meanwhile, a passenger overpowered Khaled, and she was tied hand and foot with string and a necktie.

The jet diverted to London's Heathrow Airport, where it made an emergency landing. Vider, with three bullets in his stomach, was taken by ambulance to a hospital, and Khaled was led off to jail. The plane was cleaned up, the passengers reloaded and the flight proceeded to New York.

The other three hijackings were considerably more successful for the hijackers.

Pan Am Flight 93, a Boeing 747 on the last leg of a flight from Brussels to New York, with 152 passengers and a crew of 17 aboard, was hijacked shortly after it left Amsterdam. Apparently confused, the hijackers allowed the plane to land in Beirut, Lebanon and then, after they conferred with PFLP 'brothers' at the airport, allowed the plane to take off again and eventually land in Cairo. There the hijackers unloaded passengers and crew and blew up the $23 million craft. The passengers were evacuated the following day to New York and Rome.

Meanwhile, TWA Flight 741, a Boeing 707 on an around-the-world voyage, with 141 passengers and a crew of 10, was commandeered shortly after it took off from Frankfurt and diverted to Dawson's Field, a former World War II RAF base in the Jordanian desert. Dawson's Field had been taken over as a 'revolutionary airfield' by the PFLP.

Finally, Swissair Flight 100, a DC-8 with 143 passengers and 12 crew members, was hijacked 10 minutes after it took off from Zurich and was ordered to change its course to the Middle East. It set down at Dawson's Field shortly after the other jet.

A spokesman for the PFLP, speaking from Beirut, announced the reasons for the multiple hijacking: The American planes had been seized, he said, 'to give the Americans a lesson after they have supported Israel all these years' and in retaliation for the U.S. involvement in peace negotiations in the Middle East between Israel and the Arabs.

The Swiss plane was captured and held in ransom for

the release of three Arab commandos convicted by a Swiss court for an attack on an Israeli airliner at the Zurich airport the previous December.

The spokesman also gave the reason for the hijacking of the El Al jet: 'We are fighting Israel; they are our enemy and we will fight them everywhere.'

The morning of September 7, the scene was an ominous one. The two planes were poised on the old runways, shimmering with heat. In between was a tent, the hijackers' field headquarters. Nearby was a water truck with a sign in Arabic reading 'The Popular Front at your service.' Around the periphery of the field were PFLP guerrillas armed with Russian Kalashnikov submachine guns, Katyusha rockets and jeeps with heavy-caliber machine guns.

And 250 yards away was the Jordanian Army, ringing the field in an impenetrable circle of tanks, armored personnel carriers, anti-aircraft guns, communications jeeps, ambulances and fire trucks. Each was pointed directly at the planes. King Hussein of Jordan wanted nothing to do with the hijackers, nor did he want the world to feel that he was in complicity with them.

By noon, the hijackers threatened to blow up the planes and their hostages unless the armor was withdrawn. The Jordanian Army backed off two miles and reformed its circle.

As the days passed and deadlines were made and then extended, the hijackers released women and children, conducted press conferences with appearances by hostages and eventually allowed the International Red Cross to fly in a planeload of relief supplies, and a Jordanian Airlines toilet-cleaning vehicle to service the parked planes.

At midweek, on September 8, the PFLP hijacked another jetliner, a British Overseas Airways Corporation VC-10 carrying 117 passengers and crew. The plane was diverted to Beirut, where it refueled, and then flown to Dawson's Field, where it was forced to land and take up its position with the other two jets. It and its occupants would be held, the PFLP announced, until Leila Khaled was released.

By this time, five governments and the United Nations were involved in negotiations. As the days drifted on, token numbers of hostages were released. Sixty-eight were taken to Amman, Jordan and flown to Nicosia, Cyprus and London; 23 more were transferred to a hotel in Amman; 20 were allowed to fly to Beirut. The hijackers now demanded the release of an unspecified number of Arab guerrillas in Israel.

The parent of the PFLP, the PLO, was growing increasingly restive with the extremist tactics of the guerrillas and began to withdraw its support. Eventually, it would disassociate itself completely from the group, which continued to fire off demands including the release of six Arab guerrillas imprisoned in Germany, the return of two Algerians taken from a BOAC flight by Israelis and the release of 2,000 guerrillas held in Israel.

As the relationship with the PLO continued to deteriorate, the hijackers decided on a dramatic action: They freed 260 passengers and kept 40 and blew up all three jetliners. The hostages, some from each of the negotiating countries – the United States, Britain, West Germany, Switzerland and Israel – were to be held until prisoner exchanges could be arranged with each country.

Eventually, all hostages would be released, but not all Palestinian hostages. Leila Khaled would be returned; the Swiss and West German hostages would be traded, but that would be all.

Foreseeing the consequences of violating Jordanian sovereignty by the actions of George Habbash and his PFLP, PLO leader Yassir Arafat expelled the organization from the PLO for lack of discipline.

King Hussein would eventually drive the PLO from its base in Jordan as a result of the incident, and Black September would be formed.

LEBANON – BEIRUT
October 23, 1983

A suicide bomber representing the Islamic Jihad drove an explosive-filled truck into the U.S. Marine compound in Beirut, Lebanon on October 23, 1983. Two hundred forty-one U.S. Marines were killed; 58 French soldiers were also killed in a related attack.

Lebanon was a bloody battlefield in 1983. Beirut, formerly one of the most beautiful cities in the world, was on the way to becoming the demolished, smoking shell it is today. Rival religious factions roared back and forth across it and the rest of Lebanon, and both Syria and Iran financed and supplied some of these groups.

The Islamic Jihad, one of the most fanatical of terrorist groups, was founded at this time, and its chief support came from Syria and Iran, though it was headquartered in Lebanon. Its enemies were the United States, Western Europe, Iraq, Jordan and Egypt. A supercharged religious energy, as much as money and arms, fueled this fledgling terrorist organization. Some Middle East observers, among them correspondents Christopher Dobson and Ronald Payne in their study of terrorism, *The Never Ending War*, assert that it was the Israelis who invaded Lebanon in June 1982. This they say, gave the Islamic terrorists in Lebanon their 'launching pad.'

After a terrorist attack on its ambassador to Britain in London, the Israeli government ordered its armed forces into Lebanon ostensibly to root out the Palestinians. The attack worked, but it also strengthened the resolve of terrorist groups in that country.

Shortly after the Israeli invasion, and while Israeli troops were surrounding Beirut, President Ronald Reagan sent U.S. Marines into that city to try to restore peace through a forceful presence. Aided by small contingents of French, British and Italian troops, they managed to maintain an uneasy truce.

But Shiite organizations, and particularly the newly formed Jihad, were planning the use of a new and gruesome weapon in the continuing escalation of terrorist attacks against the West and Arab enemies. On Monday, April 18, 1983, a truck loaded with explosives was driven onto the U.S. Embassy grounds and detonated. Forty-five people were killed, including 16 Americans. It was the first such suicide bombing in the Middle East, but it would not be the last; nor would it be the most devastating.

That would come at 6:20 A.M., Sunday, October 23, when a pickup truck approached the south gate of U.S. Marine headquarters in Beirut. It was coming from the direction of Beirut International Airport and was noticed by the sergeant on guard duty. Inside the barracks, some 200 marines were sleeping.

Suddenly, the driver of the truck gunned his motor, sending the truck barreling through a sandbag barrier and into the interior courtyard of the compound. Seconds later, the driver tripped a switch and blew himself and the truck and most of the barracks into small slivers of metal, wood and flesh. The crater left by the bomb was 30 feet deep and 40 feet across, and the explosion had the force of a ton of TNT.

'I haven't seen carnage like this since Vietnam,' said Marine Major Robert Jordan, who, with other officers who were quartered elsewhere, rushed to the scene to begin the grisly business of rescue and recovery of bodies.

A few minutes after the initial blast, another car bomb driven by a suicidal terrorist rammed into a building housing a company of French troops and exploded.

Machinery was moved into place to lift girders and concrete from wounded survivors. Lebanese and Italian soldiers aided in the rescue effort. Ships of the U.S. Sixth Fleet went on alert. Helicopters airlifted the wounded to the amphibious assault ship *Iwo Jima* and the battleship *New Jersey*, poised offshore near Beirut harbor. Muslim snipers on rooftops shot at the helicopters.

Two hundred forty-one marines were killed, nearly 100 were wounded, and 58 French soldiers were killed in the related bombing of their quarters.

Retaliation consisted of shells lobbed from the *New Jersey* into known terrorist strongholds. Israeli jets bombed the same targets. Intelligence forces from Israel, the United States, France and Lebanon sifted through the rubble. The 12,000 pounds of TNT and PETN, a plastic explosive that was used in the marine barracks bombing, and hexogen, which was involved in the explosion at the French barracks, plus a $50,000 money order to local mercenaries that was traced to Iranian diplomats clearly implicated both Syria and Iran.

Fourteen terrorists were finally named. They included Palestinians, renegade PLO members, professional terrorists and a fundamentalist mullah. The organization was being financed and supported by Shiite, Syrian and Iranian forces, but its network of supply and its operations were Byzantine in their complexity.

On December 12, the suicide bombers struck again, this time in eight locations in Kuwait. One was the American Embassy, which was destroyed through the same method used in Beirut. The other seven locations included the headquarters of the Raytheon Company, an American outfit that was installing Hawk missiles in Kuwait, and the French Embassy.

The peacekeeping force of American, French and Italian armed forces withdrew from Lebanon, leaving it to be destroyed by warring factions. Special barricades would be erected in front of the White House in Washington to guard against possible suicidal drivers of trucks loaded with explosives. Other government buildings would be provided with concrete pylons.

Apparently because of a dwindling supply of terrorists willing to commit suicide for their cause, this type of terrorist bombing stopped after this incident. But it had made its psychological point and had weakened the West in the Middle East.

LEBANON – BEIRUT
June 14–18, 1985

The Islamic Jihad was responsible for the hijacking of TWA Flight 847 from June 14 to 18, 1985. Hundreds of passengers were terrorized, 39 men were held hostage and then released, and one U.S. Navy man was killed.

MEDITERRANEAN SEA
October 7–9, 1985

A perceived need by the PLO to call world attention to itself led to the bungled, improvised hijacking of the Italian cruise ship Achille Lauro *in the Mediterranean from October 7 to 9, 1985.*

SYRIA – DAMASCUS
November 29, 1981

Anti-Assad Muslims continuing terrorist attacks on Syrian installations were responsible for the detonation of a car bomb on the crowded streets of Damascus on November 29, 1981. Seventy bystanders and police were killed; scores were wounded.

UNITED STATES – NEW YORK, NEW YORK
February 26, 1993

Shortly before noon on February 26, 1993, an enormous car bomb, planted in the underground parking garage of Number One World Trade Center, in the heart of New York City's financial district, exploded. Seven people were killed, 600 were injured, and 50,000 workers spent

*most of the day being evacuated through smoke-filled
staircases in the huge, twin tower complex. Six men, all
Islamic Fundamentalists and followers of Sheik Omar
Abdel Rohmon, were arrested and charged in the terror-
ist plot. The apparent reason for the bomb: a protest of
U.S. policies in the Middle East.*

UNITED STATES – WASHINGTON, D.C.
March 9–11, 1977

*The assassination by Black Muslims of the family of
Hanafi Muslim Hamaas Abdul Khaalis led to a three-
day occupation of three Washington, D.C. sites by
Khaalis and his followers from March 9 to 11, 1977.
One person died; 19 were wounded; 134 were taken
hostage.*

Explosions

The Worst Recorded Explosions

Durham (Feb. 16, 1909)
Mine explosion

Haydock (June 7, 1878)
Mine explosion

* Hulton (Dec. 21, 1910)
Mine explosion

Lancashire (June 18,
1885) Mine explosion

Northumberland (Jan. 16,
1862) Mine explosion

Podmore Hall (Jan. 12,
1918) Mine explosion

* Sunderland (Aug. 17,
1880) Mine explosion

Yorkshire (Feb. 19, 1857)
Mine explosion

Scotland
Lanarkshire (Oct. 22,
1877) Mine explosion

* North Sea (July 5, 1988)
Piper Alpha oil-rig
explosion

Wales
* Abercane (Sept. 11, 1878)
Mine explosion

Clyfnydd (June 23, 1894)
Mine explosion

Glamorgan (July 15,
1856) Mine explosion

Monmouthshire (Feb. 6,
1890) Mine explosion

Pontypridd (Nov. 8, 1867)
Mine explosion

Risca
(Dec. 1, 1860) Mine
explosion
(July 15, 1880) Mine
explosion

* Sengenhydd (Oct. 14,
1913) Mine explosion

Wrexham (Sept. 22, 1934)
Mine explosion

India
* Asansol (Feb. 19, 1958)
Mine explosion

* Bombay (April 14, 1944)
Steamship explosion

Chasnala (Dec. 27, 1975)
Mine explosion

* Dharbad (May 28, 1965)
Mine explosion

Japan
* Fukuoka (June 1, 1965)
Mine explosion

Nagasaki (Mar. 29, 1906)
Mine explosion

Otaru (Dec. 27, 1924)
Harbor explosion

Sapporo (July 16, 1920)
Mine explosion

Shimonoseki (April 13,
1915) Mine explosion

Mexico
Barrotean (Mar. 31, 1969)
Mine explosion

* Guadalajara (April 22,
1992) Sewer explosion

Mexico City (Nov. 19,
1984) Gas storage area

Prussia
Rhenish (Jan. 28, 1907)
Mine explosion

Upper Silesia (June 10,
1895) Mine explosion

Rhodesia
* Wankie (June 6, 1972)
Mine explosion

Russia
Jusovka (July 1, 1908)
Mine explosion

Spain
Cadiz (Aug. 18, 1947)
Naval mine and
torpedo factory

Switzerland
Berne (June 20, 1921)
Mine explosion

Turkey
Kharput (Mar. 1, 1925)
Munitions plant

* Kozlu (Mar. 9, 1992)
    Mine explosion
United States
    California
* Port Chicago (July 17,
    1944) Harbor explosion
    Illinois
* Cherry (Nov. 13, 1909)
    Mine explosion
    New Mexico
* Dawson (Oct. 22, 1913)
    Mine explosion
    Pennsylvania
    Cheswick (Jan. 24, 1904)
    Mine explosion
* Jacob's Creek (Dec. 19,
    1907) Mine explosion
* Mather (May 19, 1928)
    Mine explosion
* Plymouth (Sept. 6, 1869)
    Mine explosion
    Tennessee
    Coal Creek (May 19,
    1902) Mine explosion
* Memphis (April 27,
    1865) Steamship
    Sultana
    Texas

* New London (Mar. 18,
    1937) Gas explosion:
    school
* Texas City (April 16–18,
    1947) Liner *Grandcamp*
    Utah
* Castle Gate (Mar. 8,
    1924) Mine explosion
* Scofield (May 1, 1900)
    Mine explosion
    Virginia
* Pocahontas (Mar. 13,
    1884) Mine explosion
    West Virginia
* Eccles (April 28, 1914)
    Mine explosion
* Monongah (Dec. 6, 1907)
    Mine explosion
    Wyoming
* Hanna (June 30, 1903)
    Mine explosion
USSR
* Ufa (June 3, 1989) Gas
    pipeline; passenger
    trains
Yugoslavia
* Kakanj (June 7, 1965)
    Mine explosion

Chronology

1867
Nov. 8
    Pontypridd, Wales; mine
    explosion
1869
Sept. 6
  * Plymouth, Pennsylvania;
    mine explosion
1875
Dec. 14
    Mons, France; mine
    explosion
1877
Oct. 22
    Lanarkshire, Scotland;
    mine explosion
1878
June 7
    Haydock, England; mine
    explosion
Sept. 11
  * Abercane, Wales; mine
    explosion
1880
July 15
    Risca, Wales; mine
    explosion
Aug. 17
  * Sunderland, England;
    mine explosion
1884
Mar. 13
  * Pocahontas, Virginia;
    mine explosion
1885
Mar. 17
    Camphausen, Germany;
    mine explosion
June 18
    Lancashire, England;
    mine explosion

1887
May 4
    Vancouver Island, British
    Columbia; mine
    explosion
1889
July 3
    St.-Etienne, France; mine
    explosion
1890
Feb. 6
    Monmouthshire, Wales;
    mine explosion
1892
Sept. 7
    Mons, France; mine
    explosion
1894
June 23
    Clyfnydd, Wales; mine
    explosion
1895
June 10
    Upper Silesia, Prussia;
    mine explosion
1900
May 1
  * Scofield, Utah; mine
    explosion
1902
May 19
    Coal Creek, Tennessee;
    mine explosion
May 23
    Ferme, British Columbia;
    mine explosion
1903
June 30
  * Hanna, Wyoming; mine
    explosion
1904
Jan. 24
    Cheswick, Pennsylvania;
    mine explosion

1906
Mar. 10
  * Courrieres, France; mine
    explosion
Mar. 29
    Nagasaki, Japan; mine
    explosion
1907
Jan. 28
    Rhenish, Prussia; mine
    explosion
Dec. 6
  * Monongah, West
    Virginia; mine
    explosion
Dec. 19
  * Jacob's Creek,
    Pennsylvania; mine
    explosion
1908
July 1
    Jusovka, Russia; mine
    explosion
Nov. 11
    Westphalia, Germany;
    mine explosion
1909
Feb. 16
    Durham, England; mine
    explosion
Nov. 13
  * Cherry, Illinois; mine
    explosion
1910
Dec. 21
  * Hulton, England; mine
    explosion
1913
Oct. 14
  * Sengenhydd, Wales; mine
    explosion
Oct. 22
  * Dawson, New Mexico;
    mine explosion

1914
April 18
  * Eccles, West Virginia;
    mine explosion
June 19
    Lethbridge, Alberta;
    mine explosion
1915
April 13
    Shimonoseki, Japan; mine
    explosion
1916
Feb. 6
    Skoda, Austria; arsenal
    explosion
1917
Dec. 6
  * Halifax, Nova Scotia;
    ammunition ship
1918
Jan. 12
    Podmore Hall, England;
    mine explosion
Aug. 3
    Hamont Station,
    Belgium; ammunition
    train
1920
July 16
    Sapporo, Japan; mine
    explosion
1921
June 20
    Berne, Switzerland; mine
    explosion
Sept. 21
  * Oppau, Germany (See
    NUCLEAR AND
    INDUSTRIAL
    ACCIDENTS)
1924
Mar. 8
  * Castle Gate, Utah; mine
    explosion

Dec. 27
Otaru, Japan; harbor
explosion
1925
Mar. 1
Kharput, Turkey,
munitions plant
May 25
Peking, China; arsenal
explosion
1928
May 19
* Mather, Pennsylvania;
mine explosion
1930
Oct. 21
Alsdorf, Germany; mine
explosion
1931
Feb. 12
* China (Manchuria); mine
explosion
1934
Mar. 14
La Libertad, El Salvador;
explosives warehouse
Sept. 22
Wrexham, Wales; mine
explosion
1935
Oct. 26
* Lanchow, China; arsenal
explosion
1837
Mar. 18
* New London, Texas; gas
explosion: school
1940
Mar. 29
Tsingtsing, China; mine
explosion
1944
April 14
* Bombay, India; steamship
explosion

1947
April 16–18
* Texas City, Texas; liner
Grandcamp
Aug. 18
Cadiz, Spain; naval mine
and torpedo factory
1949
Nov. 29
* Johanngeorgendstadt,
East Germany; mine
explosion
1956
Aug. 7
* Cali, Colombia; dynamite
truck convoy
1958
Feb. 19
* Asansol, India; mine
explosion
1960
Mar. 4
* Havana, Cuba;
munitions ship *La
Coubre*
1962
Feb. 7
* Volklingen, West
Germany; mine
explosion
1965
May 28
* Dharbad, India; mine
explosion
June 1
* Fukuoka, Japan; mine
explosion
June 7
* Kakanj, Yugoslavia; mine
explosion
1969
Mar. 31
Barrotean, Mexico; mine
explosion

1972
June 6
  * Wankie, Rhodesia; mine
    explosion
1975
Dec. 27
    Chasnala, India; mine
    explosion
1982
Nov. 2
  * Salang Tunnel,
    Afghanistan; truck
    collision
1984
Feb. 25
    Cubatao, Brazil; oil
    pipeline

Nov. 19
    Mexico City, Mexico; gas
    storage area
1988
July 5
  * North Sea, Scotland;
    Piper Alpha oil rig
1989
June 3
  * Ufa, USSR; gas pipeline;
    passenger trains
1992
Mar. 9
  * Kozlu, Turkey; mine
    explosion
April 22
  * Guadalajara, Mexico;
    sewer explosion

Explosions

Explosions are the most spectacular and dramatic of man-made disasters. Like volcanic eruptions, they occur instantaneously, usually without warning and always with great disturbance to the atmosphere. And their casualty counts are high. Those who die as a result of the initial explosions die cruelly and quickly. Of the secondary catastrophes set off by the blast, fire is the most obvious and pervasive. Thus, those who are not blown to bits are frequently burned to death. And in the case of mine explosions, those who escape either of these fates often expire by asphyxiation.

Historically, the worst and most widespread explosions have occurred in coal mines. Ever since its beginnings in Shropshire, England near the end of the 17th century, coal mining has been one of the most hazardous of all human occupations. And from the very beginning, the threat of explosions in the mines, which sometimes burrowed two miles beneath the earth's surface, has haunted miners and their families.

Coal is generally mined in two ways. The first, a laboriously slow method, is to chip away at the walls of shafts, breaking up the coal into sizable chunks that are then transported by cart to the surface.

The second method, more dangerous and widespread, is to drill holes in the face of the wall of coal, pack the holes with explosives, detonate the explosives and blast the coal into manageable chunks. The trick is to blast only the coal, not the mine, and the failure to maintain that delicate balance has resulted in a multitude of tragedies.

The hazard of overexploding is further compounded by the usual presence of toxic and ignitable gases. While the need for constant ventilation in the mines has always been apparent, it has not always successfully or diligently been assured. Even the most modern methods of ventilation sometimes fail to remove pockets of noxious and ignitable gases, which are called, in the parlance of mining, 'damps.' These damps come in different varieties, each of them dangerous: *Firedamp*, which consists of methane and other flammable gases, often mixed with air. Explosive mixtures of firedamp with air usually contain from 1% to 14% methane.

Afterdamp, which is the mixture of gases remaining after an explosion of firedamp. It consists chiefly of carbon dioxide and nitrogen.

Chokedamp, which is the general name given to any mixture of oxygen-deficient gases that cause suffocation.

And that last description is important, for it is perhaps the most pervasive cause of fatalities in mine explosions.

The unavoidable presence of damps has always plagued both the operators and workers in mines, and various methods for detecting them have evolved over the ages. Keeping canaries in the depths of the first mines was one way of detecting the presence of damps. The birds have a low tolerance for noxious gases, and their deaths warned miners that damps were present. The Davey safety lamp was one of the first detection devices developed that did not require the deaths of birds. The color and height of the lamp flame indicated the amount of firedamp present. If the flame was extinguished, it was a sign of chokedamp. In modern mines, colorimetric detectors and methanometers are used to detect firedamp.

But no amount or sophistication of detection equipment can overcome human failure, and a quick survey of explosions, both within mines and without, points to human error, miscalculation or carelessness as causes.

The criterion for inclusion in this section is based largely on the number of fatalities. A general low figure of around 200 deaths was used as a cutoff point, and even that seems generous, considering that the high point of fatalities has reached into the thousands.

AFGHANISTAN – SALANG TUNNEL
November 2, 1982

The collision of a Soviet army vehicle with a fuel truck in the Salang Tunnel near Kabul, Afghanistan on November 2, 1982 caused a massive explosion and fire. Three thousand motorists and soldiers trapped in the tunnel died from either the explosion, fire or fumes; hundreds more were injured.

The 1.7-mile-long Salang Tunnel is a gateway between Kabul, Afghanistan and the border of the USSR. Built by the Soviets in the 1970s, it is located 11,100 feet high in the rugged Hindu Kush range, a region in which, in late 1982, there was considerable activity between the Soviet army and Afghan rebels.

On November 2, 1982, a long Soviet army convoy entered the tunnel, which was crowded with civilian buses, cars and trucks. The convoy was traveling from Hairotum, on the Amu Darya, the border stream separating Afghanistan from the Soviet Union. Midway through the tunnel, which is 17 feet wide by 25 feet high, one of the Soviet army vehicles collided with a fuel tanker. With a gigantic roar that echoed from one end of the tunnel to the other, the tanker exploded, sending gouts of flame outward in all directions. Thirty army vehicles containing Soviet soldiers were consumed instantly, their occupants burned to death on the spot.

Flames rocketed along the narrow passage of the tunnel, setting fire to buses and civilian vehicles. Panic spread as quickly as the flames, and those in cars at either end of the tunnel tried to escape. But the Soviet army, thinking the explosion was the beginning of a rebel attack, blocked both ends of the tunnel with tanks, thus killing hundreds more from asphyxiation.

The nightmare was increased by two other factors: It was bitterly cold, and those motorists who were unable to see the cause of the tie-up assumed that it was just another traffic jam and remained in their cars with the engines running. This increased the carbon monoxide level in the tunnel, killing more unwary occupants. And to further complicate the situation, the tunnel's ventilation system had broken down days before and was not operating.

All of these factors combined to kill thousands of trapped and innocent civilians and soldiers alike, either from the blast, fire or asphyxiation. It would take days to retrieve the dead from the tunnel, and reports that inched their way slowly out of Afghanistan (no foreign reporters were allowed into the country in 1982) stated that there was hardly a person in the capital city of Kabul who did not have either a relative or a friend who had died in the disaster. The Soviet dead were taken to Kabul; the Afghan dead and injured had to be transported 70 miles east of Kabul to Jalalabad in Nangathar Province.

The exact number of dead would never be known. Estimates ranged between 2,000 and 3,000, with credence given by eyewitnesses to the higher figure.

CANADA – NOVA SCOTIA, HALIFAX
December 6, 1917

Eight million tons of TNT ignited to set off the worst accidental explosion in the history of the world when the munitions ship Mont Blanc *collided with the* Imo *in Halifax Harbor on December 6, 1917. Twelve hundred were killed; 8, 000 were injured.*

The worst accidental explosion in the history of the world – that of eight million tons of TNT – occurred in Halifax Harbor on the morning of December 6, 1917, at the height of World War I. Commenting to the

Times of London just after the calamity, Lieutenant Colonel Good of Fredericton opined that he had not seen that much carnage on the battlefields of France. 'All that could be seen for a great circumference,' he said, 'were burning buildings, great mounds of iron and brick in the streets, and dead bodies.'

Halifax was, during World War I, a gathering point for transatlantic convoys. Six miles long with a breadth of about one mile, it provided secure deep-water anchorage at times of both high and low tide. There was not a ship afloat that could not be comfortably accommodated at Halifax, and so, on December 7, 1917, a number of ships had gathered there, to be led by the British cruiser HMS *High Flyer* across the U-boat-infested Atlantic to Europe.

A few days earlier, the French freighter *Mont Blanc* had picked up a lethal cargo in New York. The 3,121-ton ship was loaded to the capacity of its hold with TNT, picric acid, gun cotton and barrels of benzene.

The morning of Thursday, December 6 was fog laden in its early hours, making visibility difficult, except for the experienced pilots aboard ships such as the *Mont Blanc*, who were used to the harbor. The *Mont Blanc* arrived at 8:40, and by then the sun had burned off most of the fog. All that was necessary was for the pilot to navigate 'The Narrows,' a portion of the harbor that slimmed down to a half-mile-wide channel. On the south shore lay the Richmond section of Halifax; on the north, the town of Dartmouth. Slightly beyond it was the berth into which the *Mont Blanc* was to ease, temporarily.

Suddenly, from around a bend in the channel, the Belgian relief ship *Imo* appeared, heading out to sea. Its course was carrying it directly toward the *Mont Blanc*. The captain of the *Mont Blanc* described what happened then to the London *Times*:

[Responding to a blast of the *Mont Blanc's* whistle by

pilot Frank Mackie,] the *Imo* signaled that she was coming to port which would bring her to the same side with us. We were keeping to starboard and could not understand what the *Imo* meant, but kept our course, hoping that she would come down as she should on the starboard side, which would keep her on the Halifax side of the harbour.

. . . Then we put the rudder hard aport to try to pass the *Imo* before she should come to us. At the same time the *Imo* reversed engines. As she was light, without cargo, the reverse brought her around slightly to port, her bow towards our starboard. As a collision was then inevitable, we held so that she would be struck forward of the hold where the picric acid substance, which would not explode, was stored, rather than have her strike where the TNT was stored.

It was a correct and safe plan, if it had worked. But it did not. The *Imo* slammed into the *Mont Blanc*, gashing a huge hole in her side and setting fire to the benzene. The fire spread alarmingly. Once it reached the TNT, there would be a cataclysmic explosion. The captain knew this and immediately issued an abandon-ship order.

At pier eight, where the *Mont Blanc* was to dock, two simultaneous activities took place: A fire alarm was set, and Halifax's fire brigade rushed to the scene. At the same time, the captain of the British ammunition ship *Pictou*, moored at pier eight, realized the imminent mortal danger and ordered his ship abandoned too.

The two crews reached shore and began to scramble for the woods, which were only a short distance away, nestled against high cliffs that secured the harbor against winds. Workers in the dockside factories, seeing the running, shouting sailors, swarmed out of their factories and offices and, joining them, scrambled up the cliff toward the Citadel, Halifax's ancient fortress.

Only the captain of the cruiser *High Flyer* thought of

trying to contain the blaze, and his heroic decision proved to be foolhardy and fatal. He ordered 23 men to man a launch and try to sink the *Mont Blanc* before she exploded.

The men had scarcely boarded the ship when, with a roar like a concentrated bombardment, it exploded, sending pieces of metal, balls of fire and white-hot explosive incendiaries sky high. A huge wall of water was forced outward from the explosion. It doubled back upon itself in a tidal wave that ripped huge ships from their moorings and tossed them up on the shore.

In Halifax, William Barton, eating his breakfast at the Halifax hotel, described it: 'In ten seconds it was all over. A low rumbling, an earthquake shock, with everything vibrating, then an indescribable noise, followed by the fall of plaster, and the smashing of glass. A cry went up: "A German bomb." '

Richmond, on the other side of the harbor, was hit by pressure waves roaring through the trough of hills with the speed and force of a hurricane. An area two and a half miles in circumference was totally flattened by the blast and its aftermath. The explosion was felt up to 125 miles away; in the immediate vicinity it laid waste to everything. The Intercolonial Railway Station, a brick and stone structure in downtown Halifax, was flattened, crushing crowds of people waiting within. A hundred workers were killed in a sugar refining plant on the docks. Children were just gathering in the area schools to begin their school day. And sadly, every one of the schools would be torn asunder. Of the 550 school children in the Halifax area, only seven would survive.

Now fire began to spread, but every fireman in Halifax lay dead in the midst of the wreckage of all of Halifax's fire equipment. Twenty-five thousand people would ultimately be rendered homeless by either the explosion or its resultant fire.

It could have been considerably worse, but for the tidal wave, an act of heroism and a change in the weather.

The tidal wave caused by the explosion washed over the naval ammunition works at The Narrows, preventing it from catching fire and exploding.

Marine superintendent J. W. Harrison climbed aboard the abandoned British ammunition ship *Pictou*, tied up at pier eight, opened the sea valves and set the vessel adrift. Within minutes, the *Pictou* sank, along with its lethal cargo.

And finally, an hour after the explosion, the weather suddenly turned cold, and it began to snow furiously. The storm extinguished the fires that had been burning out of control and laying waste to large areas of Halifax.

Despite these modifications of a truly cataclysmic disaster, a large part of the city lay in ruins. By afternoon, the city militia would take charge. Trains with supplies from New York and Boston began to arrive, and public buildings were opened for the homeless and injured. Emergency hospitals set up by the Red Cross bulged.

Estimates of the dead ranged from 1,200 to 4,000. The official tally was 1,200 with over 8,000 injured. Ironically, and in contrast, only 12 soldiers from Halifax would lose their lives on the battlefields of Europe during the entire war.

**CHINA – LANCHOW
October 26, 1935**

Sabotage was suspected but never proved in the explosion of an arsenal in the middle of Lanchow, China on October 26, 1935. Two thousand were killed; thousands were injured.

**CHINA – MANCHURIA
February 12, 1931**

A paucity of information available in Manchuria on February 12, 1931 obscured or erased the reason for the gigantic mine explosion of that date. Three thousand died, and an unknown number were injured.

COLOMBIA – CALI
August 7, 1956

No cause has ever been found for the explosion of seven dynamite trucks parked in the middle of Cali, Colombia on the night of August 7, 1956. Twelve hundred died, and thousands were injured in the blast.

CUBA – HAVANA
March 4, 1960

A broken hoist cable allowed a net full of grenades to plummet to the deck of the Belgian ammunition ship La Coubre *in Havana Harbor on March 4, 1960. One hundred were killed in the explosion; scores more were injured.*

FRANCE – COURRIERES
March 10, 1906

The worst mine explosion in French history, in the Courrieres Colliery in northern France on March 10, 1906, was caused by a combination of a smoldering fire in the pit and trapped gases. One thousand sixty miners died; hundreds were injured.

GERMANY – JOHANNGEORGENDSTADT
November 29, 1949

Soviet security prevented the rest of the world from knowing the cause and details of the explosion in the uranium mine in Johanngeorgendstadt, East Germany on November 29, 1949. Three thousand seven hundred were reportedly killed and an unknown number injured.

GERMANY – OPPAU
September 21, 1921

See NUCLEAR AND INDUSTRIAL ACCIDENTS, p. 302.

GERMANY – VOLKLINGEN
February 7, 1962

Methane gas exploded in the Luisenthal pit in Volklingen, West Germany on February 7, 1962. Two hundred ninety-eight miners were killed; more than 200 were injured.

GREAT BRITAIN – ENGLAND, BARNSLEY
December 12–13, 1866

An overabundance of blasting powder caused the explosion in the Oaks Colliery, in Barnsley, England on December 12, 1866. Three hundred forty died; the number of injured was unreported.

The Oaks Colliery, located at Barnsley, was one of the largest producers of coal in South Yorkshire in the 19th century. Over 430 miners toiled in its depths, whose principal shaft was known as the 'dip' and along which ran a broad roadway. Adjacent to this was the so-called engine plane, a passage that ran for two miles. Underground, the colliery resembled a small city, with horses that pulled the carts of coal upward housed in underground stalls, and an air circulation system facilitated by a large furnace that burned night and day.

Boys worked alongside men in the 19th century. There were no child labor laws to speak of, and the day shift of December 2, 1866 consisted of one-third boys and two-thirds men. Although the mine was worked around the clock, the day shift was the most active, and it was only during this time that coal was removed from the mine.

Three hundred thirty men and boys entered the mine at 6 A.M. on Wednesday morning, December 12. At 1:20 P.M., the ground shook, and a dull, heavy explosion erupted from the mouth of the main shaft of the mine. Dense columns of smoke and dust shot into the air from each of the shafts, and in a few seconds the pit bank was enveloped in a thick black cloud.

The explosion had collapsed all of the air shafts, locking noxious fumes in the tunnels in which the miners worked. Rescuers arrived on the scene almost immediately, and, led by a Mr. T. Diamond, the managing partner in the mine, and Superintendent Greenhalgh, a rescue party immediately lowered itself as far as it could into the main shaft. Eighteen badly injured men were discovered and brought immediately to the surface. That would be the last good news of the day.

The longer they searched, and the more deeply they dug, rescuers found only the bodies of miners, caught by the afterdamp or crushed under falling timbers. The stables were flattened, and 20 horses lay dead there. Many of the miners were frozen in attitudes of prayer; one group of 20 was clustered together in a last gesture of communal protection.

Rescuers worked all day and all night of the 12th, digging out tunnels and transporting an increasing number of bodies to the surface. By 8 A.M. on the morning of the 13th, nearly 800 yards of temporary airways had been constructed, and the searchers had penetrated some of the farthest reaches of the mine's tunnels. Only one level contained fire, and it was minor.

And then, shortly after 8 A.M., some of the 37 rescuers in the mine noticed that the air was being rapidly drawn from them. A miner in the rescue party recognized the signs: Another explosion was in the making. Sixteen of the 37 scrambled to the surface and warned another party that was about to descend that there was danger of another explosion. Incredibly, most of this search party refused to believe the escaped rescuers and descended into the mine anyway.

This second party had just reached the bottom of the shaft, at approximately 9 A.M. on the morning of Thursday, December 13, when a second explosion tore through the tunnels of the Oaks Colliery. Debris and pieces of the rescue party shot out of the newly made openings as if they were part of an artillery barrage.

Forty minutes later, shortly before 10 A.M., a third, lesser explosion rocked the works and made rescuers think twice before resuming their work. By nightfall, the mine had apparently quieted, and search parties resumed their digging. Some miraculous rescues occurred; individual miners, nearly dead from chokedamp, managed to climb through the debris and meet the rescue parties, who then raised them to the surface by means of a wooden tub suspended from a makeshift block-and-tackle system.

Not many lived, however. Three hundred forty men, 28 of them rescuers, died in the three explosions.

The reason for the tragedy had been a long time coming, according to a report in the Sheffield *Independent*: 'It seems that there have been for some time complaints of the heat of the atmosphere from the long distance the air had to travel through the workings,' the newspaper report noted. The engine plane had been the only passage used to ventilate the tunnels, and so Mr. Diamond, the managing partner, had determined that December to dig another ventilating tunnel.

Apparently an impatient man, Diamond ordered a maximum amount of blasting powder to be used to expedite the task. On Wednesday morning, December 12, miners Richard Hunt and John Clayton began to use a long drill. They decided that a large charge of dynamite was needed to drive it through to its destination and thus wired up a large charge. William Wilson, the man in charge of operations, learned of this while he was working at another location; realizing the possible consequences of setting off such a charge at that specific place – which was filled with pockets of methane – he dashed to the site where Hunt and Clayton were by now setting a fuse.

He got there too late. The fuse was set and detonated just as he arrived on the scene, and the dynamite went up in a fearful roar, igniting the gas and causing a cataclysmic explosion. Astonishingly, Wilson lived to tell the story. The other two were killed by the blast they set.

GREAT BRITAIN – ENGLAND, HULTON
December 21, 1910

No cause was determined for the explosion in the Little Hulton Mine in Hulton on December 21, 1910. All 360 miners in the mine were killed.

The Little Hulton Mine, owned by the Hulton Colliery Company and located in the small town of that name some four miles from Bolton, was entirely demolished by a calamitous explosion and fire on the morning of December 21, 1910.

At a little after 7 A.M., shortly after the morning shift descended into the colliery, an ear-shattering explosion rocked the countryside, wrecked the lift mechanism of the shaft and showered the hills with debris. Almost immediately, an inferno of flames spit out of the head of the shaft, preventing rescuers from entering.

When the fire was finally brought under control, rescuers found their way blocked. The shaft had collapsed entirely below the 400-yard level, burying the entire shift of miners.

For a few hours, the fate of 400 other men working in an adjoining mine was in jeopardy when passageways between the two mines collapsed. But all 400 men of that shift were brought to the surface, including several who were injured by the impact of the explosion.

The fate of the workers in the Little Hulton Mine was just the opposite. Rescuers found small groups of bodies of men who were working above the 400-yard level, and that was all. By 9:30 that night, the fate of the entire shift of 360 boys and men was obvious. None could have survived; they were either crushed, blown apart or asphyxiated. Not one person escaped alive from the mine.

GREAT BRITAIN – ENGLAND, SUNDERLAND
August 17, 1880

The ignition of afterdamp was responsible for the explosion in the Seaham Colliery in Sunderland on August 17, 1880. One hundred sixty-one were killed; scores were injured.

Large collieries proliferated throughout Britain and Wales in the 19th century and the first half of the 20th century, and one of the largest of these was the Seaham Colliery near Sunderland. Sixteen hundred miners worked three shifts in this hugely productive mine, churning out coal for the world.

On August 17, 1880, the village of Sunderland had scheduled its annual flower show. Heavily attended, it drew a large percentage of the village and surrounding areas, and it, more than anything else, probably accounted for the saving of hundreds of lives in the early morning tragedy that blasted apart the lowest seams of the mine's main tunnel and killed 161 members of a 'light shift' of only 246. The death toll would have been considerably heavier and the mine certainly more thickly populated had it not been for the flower show. Many miners had decided to sleep in and go to the show rather than work this shift.

The explosion, touched off by the ignition of afterdamp – the highly combustible gas given off by coal, which, when it accumulates in the shafts, becomes lethal to humans – was set off by the lighted lamp of an unsuspecting miner, at 2:30 A.M. It collapsed the walls and ceilings of the shaft, burying many of the miners.

Others, near the blast, were ripped apart and found in pieces later that day.

The other, latent danger in any mine explosion is the spreading of the afterdamp, which, now released, filled the other tunnels, killing the survivors as quickly and effectively as an army's poison gas.

Ralph Markey, a miner who had survived three previous explosions, was trapped, along with 18 other men, in a pocket of space caused by the collapse of a shaft wall. Speaking later to the *Illustrated London News*, Markey recalled feeling a rush of wind an instant before the blast.

Sizing up the situation, Markey led the men in a digging-out exercise that brought them into one of the main shafts. They followed this for a quarter of a mile, stepping over the corpses of their fellow miners. 'A deputy overman named Wardle,' recalled Markey '[was] lying insensible, with his face covered with blood, and here [came] the afterdamp.'

The group pressed cloths to their faces and tried to crawl under the lethal layer of gas.

Eventually, they reached the elevator shaft, but the cage was useless, jammed halfway between tunnels. At last air filtered down to them, and they posted shouters to continually call up the shaft, while the rest of them prepared tea.

It would be two hours before shouted encouragement reached them, assuring them that rescuers were on their way, and another eight hours before a party led by Stratton, the owner of the mine, would reach them. Eighty-five miners would be rescued; 161 would die in the great colliery explosion of 1880.

GREAT BRITAIN – SCOTLAND, NORTH SEA
July 5, 1988

One hundred sixty-six men died and 65 were pulled from the water after the Piper Alpha oil rig exploded in the North Sea, 120 miles off the coast of Scotland on July 5,

1988. It was the worst disaster ever to strike British oil rigs in the North Sea.

In the late 1960s, Britain began to tap the rich and abundant oil reserves beneath the North Sea. The amount of oil under the floor of the sea seemed enormous, and it would provide a healthy economic lift for the United Kingdom from the 1970s onward. By 1988, there were 123 British oil rigs dotting the stormy waters of the North Sea, prominent among them the huge Piper Alpha rig, 120 miles off the shore of Scotland, opposite Aberdeen.

Like all oil rigs, the Piper Alpha performed a number of duties. It not only serviced oil wells under the sea, carrying the oil by pipeline to a terminal in the Orkneys; it was a conduit for natural gas in another pipeline that went to Norway's Frigg field. In addition, it served as a transfer point for gas from Texaco's Tartan field and supplied gas to power the nearby Claymore platform.

It was an immense, 34,000-ton structure of steel and wood, built stronger than the oil rigs of the Gulf of Mexico because of the fierce battering it would take in North Sea weather. It was 649 feet high, but most of this height was sunk, by six huge steel legs, into 440 feet of water. There was a helicopter pad above the water line, and, nestled among the rigging, with the multiple pipes that contained oil and gas running directly through them, were the crew quarters, housing the 230 workers who worked in two shifts aboard the rig.

There had been two minor explosions in the North Sea during that week of July. On Sunday, July 2, the British Petroleum Sullom Voe terminal in the Shetland Islands blew up, causing heavy damage but no casualties. On Tuesday, July 4, the Brent Alpha platform exploded, again with no casualties.

Some of the men aboard the Piper Alpha were uneasy. For three days, beginning on Sunday, July 2, workers had complained of a heavy gas smell. On

Monday, July 3, worker Craig Barclay phoned his fiancée and told her that he had refused to ignite a welding torch that day because of the strong smell of gas. On Tuesday, July 4, Thomas Stirling phoned his fiancée, Janice Stewart, in Glasgow and complained of a sickening gas smell. He went on to tell her how some workers had donned breathing masks to work that day. It was the last either woman would hear from their fiancés.

At dusk on July 5, half of the workers were sleeping in their quarters; half were at work. Beneath the water line, directly under the crew's quarters, a leak had developed in a compression chamber. Natural gas was forcing itself into the chamber, and it ignited. Two cataclysmic explosions geysered up from the chamber, tore through the quarters, and split the rig in two. In seconds, an inferno of fire followed, shooting flames between 300 and 400 feet in the air.

Those in the living quarters had no chance of surviving. They were either blown apart, incinerated, or tossed into the sea, then buried under the collapsing platform. One hundred sixty-six men died, most of them in their quarters, some who were too slow in escaping.

'It was a case of fry and die or jump and try,' Roy Carey, a 45-year-old survivor told reporters from his hospital bed in Aberdeen. 'There was no time to ask – it was over the side or nothing. I just dived – it may have been 60 feet.'

It *was* 60 feet, and the survivors either slid down hoses or dove from the platform into the water, where they dodged missiles of flaming debris.

No lifeboats were launched; there was no time for that. A rescue boat that rushed to the platform caught fire during the second explosion. Two of the three rescue workers in the boat were killed.

Flames could be seen 70 miles away, and helicopters and planes of the RAF flew to the tragic scene. By dawn, all the survivors had been picked up. The rig still burned, and would, for another week.

Investigations were launched, safety improvements were promised, and the Prime Minister and the Queen extended their condolences to the families of the victims of the worst oil-rig explosion in the short history of British oil exploration in the North Sea.

GREAT BRITAIN – WALES, ABERCANE
September 11, 1878

The cause of the explosion in the Ebbw Vale Steel, Iron and Coal Company's Abercane Colliery in Abercane, Wales on September 11, 1878 was and remains unknown. Two hundred sixty-eight miners died in the explosion; 12 were injured.

The Abercane Colliery, owned by the Ebbw Vale Steel, Iron and Coal Company, was one of the largest collieries in South Wales during the end of the 19th century. Situated a few hundred yards from the Abercane railway station, on the Western Valley section of the Monmouthshire Railway, it nestled in a picturesque valley, in the shadow of the Crumlin Viaduct, one of Wales' most charming and well-visited tourist attractions.

It was not unusual to have a working colliery in the midst of town in the 1800s. The Abercane Colliery in its most productive times produced 1,000 tons of bituminous coal daily.

It was also one of the most up-to-date mines in the world. Its winding, pumping and ventilating machinery was the most modern for its day; its use of safety lamps was rigidly enforced.

Thus, the 373 men and boys who entered the mine at 11:00 A.M. on September 12, 1878 felt protected and secure. If there ever was an explosion-proof mine, it was this one. And thus, the reason that the mine exploded with an ear-shattering roar at 12:10 P.M. that day was and would remain an unexplained mystery.

The first explosion was followed by two others of equal force. Within seconds, a huge tongue of flame flew from the main shaft opening, followed by dense clouds of acrid smoke, dust and debris. An enormous fire was obviously burning within the pit, incinerating whoever was there.

The winding gear for the buckets that transported men in and out of the mine was damaged by the explosion and had to be repaired before rescuers could begin their work. When it was back in operation, they brought out 82 men and boys who had been working within a few hundred yards of the shaft opening.

But that would be the extent of the rescue. Descending to the bottom of the 330-yard-deep mine, rescuers found horrible devastation. The underground stables yielded 14 dead horses, 12 terribly burned men and 13 bodies. Most of the ambient tunnels had collapsed, and those that had not were unapproachable. The chokedamp was pervasive and lethal, and rescuers were repeatedly turned back.

Finally, at 2:30 A.M. on September 13, to the despair of hundreds of relatives at the scene, it was decided to flood the mine to prevent further fire and explosions. The bodies of 255 men and boys were buried underground; only the 13 bodies that were discovered near the stables were brought to the surface. It would be one of Wales' worst and most mysterious mine disasters.

GREAT BRITAIN – WALES, SENGENHYDD
October 14, 1913

There is no known cause for the greatest mine disaster in the history of Great Britain, the explosion in the Universal Colliery at Sengenhydd, Wales on October 14, 1913. Three hundred forty-three died; 12 were injured.

The Universal Colliery at Sengenhydd, eight miles from Cardiff consisted of two pits, side by side, the Lancaster and York. At 6:00 A.M. on October 14, 935 men descended into the two mine shafts, beginning the first and most active shift of the day.

At 8:12 A.M., the earth around the mine shafts shook, and an enormous explosion ripped through the Lancaster pit, spewing a fountain of debris and dust skyward and ripping out the pithead gear. Within minutes, plumes of orange flames shot up from the pit opening.

Hundreds of rescuers came on the scene immediately, but they were unable to descend into the Lancaster pit because of the intensity of the fire. Not only was the heat tremendous, but the fire was blocking the only air intake to the shaft. It would be an hour before the fire would be controlled enough to allow the pit gear from the undamaged York pit, 50 yards away, to be set in place so that rescuers could be lowered into the Lancaster shaft.

The teams found a holocaust. The force of the explosion had been enormous. Scores of headless and dismembered bodies were found, but fortunately, so were hundreds of survivors. All in all, 498 men were raised, in groups of 20, to the surface by miners from nearby collieries. Twelve seriously injured men were taken to nearby hospitals.

But that still left nearly 350 men trapped within the collapsed mine shaft. Rescuers attempted to enter these shafts, but the afterdamp threatened to kill them, too, and by nightfall, it was apparent that the only survivors of the explosion were now above ground. By that time, 40,000 people had gathered at the pitheads, hoping for a miracle.

The rescuers dug on into the night, recovering 73 more bodies. Finally, on the morning of October 15, the decision was made to seal the mine. Three hundred forty-three men and boys had lost their lives, and slightly more than 200 of them would be sealed in the mine that morning.

Prince Arthur of Connaught and his bride of only a few weeks sent messages of sympathy to the bereaved

families of the dead miners and announced that the
royal wedding presents would be exhibited in public for
the next month as a means of raising money for relief
funds.

INDIA – ASANSOL
February 19, 1958

*A gas explosion collapsed a mine in Asansol, India on
February 19, 1958. One hundred eighty-three died;
scores were injured.*

INDIA – BOMBAY
April 14, 1944

*No cause was ever discovered for the explosion of the
ammunition ship* Fort Stikine *in Victoria Dock, Bombay, India on April 14, 1944. One thousand three
hundred seventy-six were killed, and more than 3,000
were injured.*

INDIA – DHARBAD
May 28, 1965

*A methane gas ignition was responsible for the explosion
in the coal mine in Dharbad, India on May 28, 1965.
Three hundred seventy-five were killed; hundreds were
injured.*

JAPAN – FUKUOKA
June 1, 1965

*Failure to install safety devices by the management of the
Yamano coal mine, near Fukuoka, Japan, led to an
explosion in the mine on June 1, 1965. Two hundred
thirty-six miners were killed; 37 were injured.*

MEXICO – GUADALAJARA
April 22, 1992

On April 22, 1992, the sewers of Guadalajara, Mexico suddenly erupted, flinging manhole covers into the air, splitting streets apart, killing at least 194 people and injuring 1,500.

RHODESIA – WANKIE
June 6, 1972

A methane gas ignition caused the explosion that decimated the Wankie Colliery in Rhodesia on June 6, 1972. Four hundred twenty-seven miners were killed; 37 escaped unscathed.

TURKEY – KOZLU
March 9, 1992

Portions of the Incirharmani Coal Mine, located in the northern Turkish town of Kozlu, on the Black Sea, collapsed on March 15, 1992. Several explosions of natural methane gas triggered the cave-in, which killed 270 miners. It was the fifth explosion in the mine since 1945, and the most tragic.

UNITED STATES – CALIFORNIA, PORT CHICAGO
July 17, 1944

Unstable, outdated ammunition being loaded on the ammunition ships E. A. Bryan *and* Quinault Victory *exploded in Port Chicago, California on July 17, 1944. Three hundred twenty-one were killed; hundreds were injured.*

UNITED STATES – ILLINOIS, CHERRY
November 13, 1909

The November 13, 1909 explosion in the St. Paul Company mine in Cherry, Illinois was caused by a miner's torch igniting a pile of hay. Two hundred fifty-nine miners died, and an unknown number were injured.

UNITED STATES – NEW MEXICO, DAWSON
October 22, 1913

The blast that destroyed one of the Stag Canyon Fuel Company's coal mines in Dawson, New Mexico was caused by dynamite charges igniting coal dust in the mine. Two hundred sixty-three miners were killed, and 10 were injured in the explosion.

UNITED STATES – PENNSYLVANIA, JACOB'S CREEK
December 19, 1907

No cause was ever discovered for the explosion of the Darr Mine of the Pittsburgh Coal Company in Jacob's Creek, Pennsylvania on December 19, 1907. Two hundred thirty-nine miners were killed, and one was injured.

UNITED STATES – PENNSYLVANIA, MATHER
May 19, 1928

Gas ignition from an electric locomotive caused the explosion in the Mather shafts of the Pittsburgh Coal Company on May 19, 1928. One hundred ninety-five died; six were injured.

UNITED STATES – PENNSYLVANIA, PLYMOUTH
September 6, 1869

Sparks from an underground furnace ignited support

timbers, which caused an explosion that collapsed adjacent tunnels in the Lackawanna and Western Railroad's Avondale coal mine in Plymouth, Pennsylvania on September 6, 1869. One hundred ten miners were killed; 30 were injured.

UNITED STATES – TENNESSEE, MEMPHIS
April 27, 1865

One of the worst tragedies in American history, the boiler explosion aboard the steamboat Sultana *in Memphis, Tennessee on April 27, 1865 was caused by human negligence, overloading and an overstoked boiler. Officially, 1,547 deaths were recorded, but this figure is generally thought by historians to be too low; hundreds were injured.*

The month of April 1865 was an eventful one in the United States. President Abraham Lincoln was assassinated on April 14. Vice President Andrew Johnson assumed the presidency on April 15. General William Sherman accepted the surrender of General Joseph E. Johnston on April 26, thus bringing the armed resistance of the Confederacy to an end. On the same day, John Wilkes Booth was shot to death in a Virginia barn.

Thus, when the steamboat *Sultana* blew up in the Mississippi River just north of Memphis, Tennessee at approximately 2:00 A.M. on April 27, 1865, the horrendous tragedy, one of the worst in U.S. history, went largely unreported and unrecorded. In fact, it would be another 30 years before Congress would enact legislation designed to prevent the sort of disaster that occurred aboard the *Sultana* that night.

Steamboat travel always involved one major hazard, that of an overworked, exploding boiler. From the beginnings of steamboat travel very early in the 19th century until 1850, there had been 185 steamboat explosions resulting in the deaths of 1,400 people.

In just minutes on that one night, at least 1,500 people would meet their deaths in the spectacular explosion of the *Sultana*'s boilers, and the cause would be a compound of personal and political misjudgment.

In 1865, great numbers of Union prisoners were released from the Confederate prisoner of war camps at Cahaba and Andersonville. Vicksburg, Mississippi was the loading point for these emaciated survivors, who wanted nothing more than swift passage northward, to Cairo, Illinois, the debarkation point from which they could then go home.

Thousands of them boarded upriver steamers in the early spring of 1865, bound for safety and familiar sights. By April, however, there were ugly and probably founded rumors that the government was giving all of this lucrative business to one steamboat company, in return for a kickback of one dollar a passenger.

Anxious to scotch the rumors before they reached the public and official investigatory agencies, government officials at Vicksburg welcomed the arrival of the *Sultana*, which belonged to a rival company. Two years old, the *Sultana* was not a particularly impressive or big boat, weighing in at approximately 1,700 tons. It had a legal load limit of 376 passengers and crew members. Anything exceeding this would demand forced firing of its four tubular boilers, an extremely dangerous practice.

But neither the owners nor the government seemed to care about the regulations or the hazards that spring. By 2 A.M. on April 26, after it had ceased loading its war prisoners and cargo and repaired a faulty steam line leading from one of its boilers, the *Sultana* pulled away from Vicksburg with 2,300 to 2,500 veterans, 75 to 100 civilian passengers and a crew of 80. (The figures concerning both passengers and fatalities have remained approximate, since no accurate records were kept.)

Low in the water and lumbering against the current, the *Sultana* carried the greatest load any steamboat had ever carried on the Mississippi when she left Vicksburg. It would take an unprecedented 17 hours for it to reach Memphis, where she docked shortly after 7:00 P.M. on the 26th.

The coal bins had been almost emptied by the time the *Sultana* reached Memphis, and once she had unloaded 100 hogsheads of sugar, she was taken to the Arkansas side of the river to pick up another 1,000 bushels of coal. Once the ship had been loaded, stokers were ordered to 'pour on the coal, and keep this thing moving.' A plausible rumor ran along the river then and afterward that the chief engineer wired the safety valves in place so that every possible bit of steam was available to drive the side wheels of the *Sultana*.

Midnight came and went, and the boat beat against the current, heading steadily northward. At 2:00 A.M. on the 27th, while most of her passengers slept, the number three boiler exploded with a cataclysmic roar. Hot metal ripped through the ship like white-hot knives. Within minutes, two more boilers exploded, ripping half the steamer apart, collapsing the various decks and crushing those hapless passengers or crewmen who had not been either scalded to death or ripped apart by the metal pieces of boilers.

Some passengers were blown into the water and survived. Others who got through the initial explosion were trapped by the roaring fire that followed it. A small group huddled on the bow of the boat and were quickly pushed into the water by the advancing flames and the collapse of the *Sultana*'s two smokestacks.

Steamboats in the area, hearing the explosion, rushed to the rescue, as did the Union gunboat *Grosbeak*. They found a scene of unbelievable carnage. Having survived the hell of Andersonville, hundreds of homeward bound men were blown apart or burned by a disaster that, in retrospect, was nearly inevitable.

A later investigation failed to either fix the blame for the tragedy or accurately estimate the casualty figures. Trained observers guessed the number of dead to be

1,900, a total generally considered to be too high. A U.S. Army board of review released a figure of 1,238, a total obviously designed to minimize the tragedy. The estimate by customs service officials at Memphis of 1,547 has been the generally agreed on, if inconclusive, one, which makes the death toll of the explosion of the *Sultana* 30 more than that of the much more celebrated sinking of the *Titanic* (see p. 263).

UNITED STATES – TEXAS, NEW LONDON
March 18, 1937

The cataclysmic explosion of natural gas that destroyed the New London, Texas Consolidated School on March 18, 1937 was caused by 'wet' gas, used as an economy measure by the school system and ignited by a spark. Two hundred ninety-seven students and teachers were killed, 437 were injured.

UNITED STATES – TEXAS, TEXAS CITY
April 16–18, 1947

Human error caused the worst harbor explosion in American history, the explosion of the French ship Grandcamp *in Texas City Harbor, Texas on April 16, 1947. Seven hundred fifty-two were killed, 3,000 aboard neighboring ships and onshore were injured.*

UNITED STATES – UTAH, CASTLE GATE
March 8, 1924

No specific source was discovered for the ignition of accumulated gases that caused the explosion in the Utah Fuel Company's coal mine in Castle Gate, Utah on March 8, 1924. One hundred seventy-three miners were killed; 30 were injured.

UNITED STATES – UTAH, SCOFIELD
May 1, 1900

Human misjudgment was responsible for the storage of blasting powder underground in the Scofield, Utah coal works. The powder ignited on May 1, 1900, causing an explosion that killed 200 miners.

UNITED STATES – VIRGINIA, POCAHONTAS
March 13, 1884

A combination of overuse of blasting powder and faulty ventilation caused the explosion in the Laurel Mine of the Southwest Virginia Improvement Company in Pocahontas, Virginia on March 13, 1884. One hundred twelve miners were killed; two were injured.

UNITED STATES – WEST VIRGINIA, ECCLES
April 28, 1914

A dynamite blast that ignited gases caused the explosion in the New River Colliers Company mine in Eccles, West Virginia on April 28, 1914. One hundred seventy-nine were killed; 51 were injured.

UNITED STATES – WEST VIRGINIA, MONONGAH
December 6, 1907

A runaway rail car severed electrical cable that in turn ignited gases in the Monongah mine in Monongah, West Virginia on December 6, 1907. The resultant explosion killed 362 miners and injured four.

UNITED STATES – WYOMING, HANNA
June 30, 1903

Blasting powder ignited gas that caused the explosion in the Union Pacific Railroad's Hanna, Wyoming mine on

June 30, 1903. One hundred sixty-nine died; 27 were injured.

USSR – UFA
June 3, 1989

A leak in a liquefied petroleum gas pipeline was ignited by a spark from a passing passenger train near Ufa, USSR on June 3, 1989. The explosion killed 190 and injured 720. Another 270 were presumed dead.

Early in the morning of June 3, 1989, partway between the two Soviet cities of Asha and Ufa in the Ural Mountains of the USSR, a liquefied petroleum gas pipeline erupted. It was a Sunday morning, and the gas, which was being transferred from oil fields in Nizhnevartovsk to refineries in Ufa, was being monitored, presumably by a skeleton crew. Pressure gauges undoubtedly showed a drop in pressure, an indication of a leak. But for some unexplainable reason, instead of investigating the leak, the pipeline operators on duty simply turned up the pumps, thus feeding a mixture of propane, butane and benzene vapors into a ravine leading to a nearby railroad. By the time the vapors had settled into the valley surrounding the train tracks, they were composed mainly of methane, the highly volatile gas responsible for a multitude of mine explosions.

Shortly after this, two trains traveling in opposite directions between the Siberian city of Novosibirsk and the Black Sea town of Adler, passed each other in that ravine. The trains, loaded with vacationers, were not scheduled to pass at that particular point at that particular moment, but one was behind schedule, and as fate would have it, the two were parallel when they entered the valley. The heavy aroma of gas, hanging like a fog to the level of the train windows, became sickeningly apparent to the engineers of both trains as they sped through the pass.

Suddenly, a spark from one of the trains ignited the gas, which exploded with a deafening roar and bright orange flashes of flame. Its force – that of 10,000 tons of TNT – felled every tree within a three-mile radius and blew both locomotives and the 38 cars of the two trains completely off the tracks. Pieces of metal, smashed windows and fragments of bodies were blown in several directions.

A metal-melting fire followed instantly, incinerating the surviving passengers before they could extricate themselves from the mangled coaches.

Speaking later to Tass, the Soviet news agency, a Soviet army officer noted that he had been standing at an open window when he noticed the acrid, petroleum smell coming from the gas leak.

'I sensed that something must be wrong,' he said, 'but before I could do anything there was a glow and then a thunderous explosion.' The officer escaped from the burning car through a broken window.

Rescue squads immediately poured into the region from both Ufa and Asha, and surgeons, burn specialists and medical supplies were airlifted from Moscow throughout the day and night. The final casualty count was appalling: 190 were known dead, at least 270 were missing and presumed dead, and 720 were injured seriously enough to be hospitalized.

YUGOSLAVIA – KAKANJ
June 7, 1965

Gas ignited by a blasting fuse set off an explosion in a mine in Kakanj, Yugoslavia on June 7, 1965. One hundred twenty-eight were killed; 41 were injured.

Fires

The Worst Recorded Fires

Detailed in text

Austria
* * Vienna (1881) Ring Theatre

Belgium
* * Brussels (1967) L'Innovation department store

Brazil
* * Niteroi (1961) Gran Circo Norte-Americano
* Parana (1962) Coffee plantation fire
* * Sao Paulo (1974) Joelmo building

Canada
* * Montreal (1927) Laurier Palace Theater
* New Brunswick (1825) Forest fire
* North Ontario (1916) Forest fire

Carthage
* (146 B.C.) Sacking of Carthage

Chile
* Santiago
* (1863) Jesuit church fire
* (1945) Braden copper mine fire

China
* Antung (1937) Movie theater fire
* Canton (1845) Theater fire
* Chow-t'sun (1924) Fire outside city

* * Chungking (1949) Burning of the city
* Hankow (1947) Fire on the docks
* * Heilongjang Province (1987) Forest fire
* Tangshen (1993) Department store
* Tuliuchen (1936) Theater fire
* Wuchow (1930) Tea District fire

Colombia
* * Bogota (1958) El Almacen Vida department store

Egypt
* Cairo (1824) Burning of much of the city

France
* Paris
* * (1887) Opera Comique
* * Paris (1897) Charity bazaar
* * St. Laurent-du-Pont (1970) Cinq-Sept Club discotheque

Germany
* * Dresden (1945) Firebombing of city

Great Britain
* England
* * Bradford (1985) Valley Parade soccer stadium
* * Exeter (1887) Exeter Theatre
* London
* (1212) City burned

* (1666) Great Fire of London
* (1987) Underground

Guatemala
* Guatemala City (1960) Guatemala City Insane Asylum

Iran
* Abadan (1978) Movie theater

Jamaica
* Kingston (1980) Eventide nursing home

Japan
  Hakodate (1934) Much of the city burned
* Osaka (1972) Playtown Cabaret
  Yokohama (1955) Catholic Old Women's Home

Mesopotamia
  Babylon (538 B.C.) Burning of Babylon

Mexico
  Acapulco (1909) Flores Theater

Puerto Rico
* San Juan (1986) Dupont Plaza Hotel

Rome
* (A.D. 64) Burning of Rome by Nero

Russia
  Berditschoft (1883) Circus Ferroni
* Igolkino (1929) Factory fire
  Moscow (1570) Burning of city

Saudi Arabia
  Mina (1975) Tent city burned

South Korea
* Seoul (1971) Taeyunkak Hotel

Spain
* Madrid (1928) Novedades Theater

Syria
* Amude (1960) Movie theater

Thailand
* Nakhon Pathom (1993) Doll factory

Turkey
  Constantinople (1729) Burning of 12,000 houses
* Constantinople (1870) Fire originating in Armenian district
  Smyrna (1922) Burning of city

United States
  Connecticut
* Hartford (1944) Ringling Brothers, Barnum & Bailey Circus
  Georgia
* Atlanta (1946) Winecoff Hotel
  Illinois
  Chicago
* (1871) Great Chicago Fire
* (1903) Iroquois Theater
* (1958) Our Lady of the Angels School
  Massachusetts
* Boston (1942) Cocoanut Grove Night Club
  Minnesota
* (1918) Forest fire
* Hinckley (1894) Forest fire
  Mississippi
* Natchez (1940) Rhythm Night Club

New Jersey
* Coast (1934) See
    MARITIME DISASTERS,
    Morro Castle
* Hoboken (1900) Docks
New York
* The Bronx (1990)
    Happy Land Social
    Club
* Brooklyn (1876) Brooklyn
    Theatre
* New York (1899)
    Windsor Hotel
* New York (1904) See
    MARITIME DISASTERS,
    General Slocum

* New York (1911) Triangle
    Shirtwaist Factory
North Carolina
Hamlet (1991) Chicken
    processing plant
Ohio
* Collinwood (1908)
    Lakeview School
* Columbus (1930) Ohio
    State Penitentiary
Pennsylvania
Boyertown (1908)
    Rhoades Theater
Wisconsin
* Peshtigo (1871) Forest
    fire

Chronology

* Detailed in text

538 B.C.
   Babylon, Mesopotamia;
   Burning of Babylon
146 B.C.
   Carthage; Sacking of
   Carthage
A.D. 64
July 19
 * Rome; Burning of Rome
   by Nero
1212
   London, England;
   Burning of city
1570
   Moscow, Russia; Burning
   of city
1666
Sept. 2–6
 * London, England; Great
   Fire of London
1729
   Constantinople, Turkey;
   Burning of 12,000
   houses

1824
Mar. 22
   Cairo, Egypt; Burning of
   much of the city
1825
Nov. 7
   New Brunswick, Canada;
   Forest fire
1845
May
   Canton, China; Theater
   fire
1863
Jan. 17
   Santiago, Chile; Jesuit
   church fire
1870
June 5
 * Constantinople, Turkey;
   Fire originating in
   Armenian district
1871
Oct. 8
 * Chicago, Illinois; Great
   Chicago Fire

* Peshtigo, Wisconsin;
    Forest fire

1876
Dec. 5
   * Brooklyn, New York;
     Brooklyn Theatre

1881
Dec. 8
   * Vienna, Austria; Ring
     Theatre

1883
Jan. 13
     Berditschoft, Russia;
     Circus Ferroni

1887
May 25
   * Paris, France; Opera
     Comique

Sept. 4
   * Exeter, England; Exeter
     Theatre

1894
Sept. 1
   * Hinckley, Minnesota;
     Forest fire

1897
May 4
   * Paris, France; Charity
     bazaar

1899
Mar. 17
   * New York, New York;
     Windsor Hotel

1900
June 30
   * Hoboken, New Jersey;
     Docks

1903
Dec. 30
   * Chicago, Illinois; Iroquois
     Theatre

1904
June 15
   * New York, New York;
     See MARITIME
     DISASTERS, *General
     Slocum*

1908
Jan. 13
     Boyertown, Pennsylvania;
     Rhoades Theater

Mar. 4
   * Collinwood, Ohio; Lake
     View School

1909
Feb. 14
     Acapulco, Mexico; Flores
     Theater

1911
Mar. 25
   * New York, New York;
     Triangle Shirtwaist
     Factory

1916
July 30
     North Ontario, Canada;
     Forest fire

1918
Oct. 12
   * Minnesota; Forest fire

1922
Sept. 13
     Smyrna, Turkey; Burning
     of city

1924
Mar. 24
     Chow-t'sun, China; Fire
     outside city

1927
Jan. 9
   * Montreal, Canada;
     Laurier Palace Theater

1928
Sept. 22
   * Madrid, Spain;
     Novedades Theater

1929
Mar. 12
  * Igolkino, Russia; Factory
    fire
1930
April 21
  * Columbus, Ohio; Ohio
    State Penitentiary
Oct. 19
    Wuchow, China; Tea
    District fire
1934
Mar. 21
    Hakodate, Japan; Much
    of city burned
Sept. 8
  * New Jersey Coast; See
    MARITIME DISASTERS,
    Morro Castle
1936
Mar. 15
    Tuliuchen, China;
    Theater fire
1937
Feb. 13
    Antung, China; Movie
    theater fire
1940
April 23
  * Natchez, Mississippi;
    Rhythm Night Club
1942
Nov. 28
  * Boston, Massachusetts;
    Cocoanut Grove Night
    Club
1944
July 6
  * Hartford, Connecticut;
    Ringling Brothers,
    Barnum & Bailey Circus
1945
Feb. 13
  * Dresden, Germany; Fire
    bombing of city

June 19
    Santiago, Chile; Braden
    copper mine fire
1946
Dec. 7
  * Atlanta, Georgia;
    Winecoff Hotel
1947
Dec. 28
    Hankow, China; Fire on
    docks
1949
Sept. 2
  * Chungking China;
    Burning of city
1955
Feb. 17
    Yokohama, Japan;
    Catholic Old Women's
    Home
1958
Dec. 1
  * Chicago, Illinois; Our
    Lady of the Angels
    School
Dec. 16
  * Bogota, Colombia; El
    Almacen Vida
    department store
1960
July 14
  * Guatemala City,
    Guatemala; Guatemala
    City Insane Asylum
Nov. 13
  * Amude, Syria; Movie
    theater
1961
Dec. 17
  * Niteroi, Brazil; Gran
    Circo Norte-Americano
1962
Sept. 7
    Parana, Brazil; Coffee
    plantation fire

1967
May 22
  * Brussels, Belgium;
    L'Innovation
    department store
1970
Nov. 1
  * St. Laurent du Pont,
    France; Cinq-Sept Club
    discotheque
1971
Dec. 25
  * Seoul, South Korea;
    Taeyunkak Hotel
1972
May 13
  * Osaka, Japan; Playtown
    Cabaret
1974
Feb. 1
  * Sao Paulo, Brazil; Joelmo
    building fire
1975
Dec. 12
    Mina, Saudi Arabia; Tent
    city burned
1978
Aug. 20
  * Abadan, Iran; Movie
    Theater
1980
May 20
  * Kingston, Jamaica;
    Eventide nursing home

1985
May 11
  * Bradford, England;
    Valley Parade stadium
    fire
1986
Dec. 31
  * San Juan, Puerto Rico;
    Dupont Plaza Hotel
1987
May–June
  * Heilongjiang Province,
    China; Forest fire
Nov. 18
  * London, England; King's
    Cross underground
    station
1990
Mar. 25
  * Bronx, New York; Happy
    Land Social Club
1991
Sept. 3
    Hamlet, North Carolina,
    USA; Chicken
    processing plant
1993
Feb. 15
    Tangshen, China;
    Department store
May 10
  * Nakhon Pathom,
    Thailand; Doll factory

Fires

Even the staunch civil libertarian and guardian of the Bill of Rights, Justice Oliver Wendell Holmes, agreed that the protection of freedom of speech does not extend to a person yelling 'Fire!' in a crowded theater. That particular outcry has caused some of the worst catastrophes in history, as a quick glance through this section will amply prove. In fact, pandemonium during a fire is as responsible for its fatalities as the flames themselves or the smoke that causes asphyxiation.

And yet, how can anyone really be blamed for feeling terror at the very thought of a death by burning? Fire has always been a treacherous friend to humankind. It brings comfort, warmth, a romantic glow when the time and the season are right, and it stimulates a fertile imagination.

To the Greeks, fire, along with earth, air and water, was one of the four basic elements from which all things were composed, and the Greeks attached mythological powers to it. Religions have attributed the same fiery origins to either the entire religion or to aspects of it. Vesta, goddess of the hearth, and her virgins guarded the holy fire in ancient Rome. Fire is the earthly representation of the sun in Zoroastrianism. In Kashmir Shaivism, the fire of faith in the efficacy of spiritual practices burns away the karmas of the past and present.

Consider the wonder with which primitive people must have discovered fire – probably witnessing lightning igniting a forest. What a monumental discovery it must have been when these primitives first discovered the uses for fire; they made it the very center of their civilizations, and this continued for thousands and thousands of years.

Think of the Olympic flame. And think of the monumental moment in 1827 when an English druggist 1.amed John Walker invented the first match.

Fire has warded off the terrors of the dark and the life-robbing chill of the cold. When we love, we say the object of our love warms our heart, and we kindle the flame of love.

But as much as we love fire, we fear it. Rather than die by fire, human beings, over and over, have flung themselves from the tops of high buildings. Were they crazed at the moment? Perhaps. But possibly not. Those who have miraculously survived these falls have affirmed that they would rather have the swift death at the end of a fall than the horrible, prolonged pain of death by fire. Medieval zealots knew this; execution at the stake was one of the most inhuman and barbarous practices ever conceived by humankind.

And it is true; death by fire is an agonizing death, for fire consumes slowly and relentlessly. Some victims have had their lungs burst because the fires around them have superheated the air (3,000 degrees Fahrenheit is the usual temperature in the middle of a firestorm) or robbed it of its oxygen. Toxic gases unleashed by fire cause asphyxiation.

And fire, being as fickle as it is, can turn from benevolent provider to destroyer in an instant. A turned back, a momentary distraction, an error in judgment, and a small fire can become a conflagration. The friendliest campfire, or barbecue, the smallest match struck against the darkness can ignite infernos.

Knossos, in Crete – the greatest metropolis of the world in 1400 B.C. – was destroyed by a fire set by invaders. Carthage, Rome, Ninevah, Babylon, Moscow, London, Constantinople, Smyrna, Copenhagen, Munich, Stockholm, St. Petersburg, Cairo, Chicago, New York – every one of them has either been totally destroyed or severely crippled by fire. It is the most devastating destroyer we know.

The criteria for inclusion in this section are far more

complex than in any other category. First, the decision had to be made regarding the inclusion of fire disasters in the volume on natural disasters or in *Man-made Catastrophes*. Certainly, there are forest fires that are begun by lightning, or the smoldering fires brought on by long droughts. But these are small in number compared with those caused by human error, carelessness or design. Even the worst forest fire in U.S. history, that of the 1871 burn that destroyed the city of Peshtigo, Wisconsin and 23 other villages (see p. 244), did not begin from wholly natural causes. Though it is thought to have started spontaneously, its devastation is directly attributable to the mess left behind by loggers who continued to fell trees during a rainless summer, and to railroad workers who, at the same time, burned debris in the forest.

Even spontaneous combustion in a pile of oil-soaked rags is, ultimately, the responsibility of the human being who piled the rags there in the first place.

Thus, fires rightfully belong in this volume.

In some cases, fire is often the secondary disaster. Explosions cause fires; earthquakes cause fires. And so, whenever it seemed as though the fire damage was specifically caused by another primary source for which there was a category, it was not included in this section – hence, for instance, the omission of the San Francisco Earthquake fire, the 1934 fire aboard the *Morro Castle*, and the 1904 fire aboard the excursion steamboat *General Slocum*, in New York Harbor. The first can be found in the Earthquake section in the volume on natural disasters; the other two can be found in the Maritime Disasters section in this volume.

Although war disasters have been omitted from both volumes, one exception was included in this section: The firebombing of Dresden by Allied bombers in 1945. One hundred thirty-five thousand civilians lost their lives, not from bombs, but from the firestorm set by incendiaries. This was the worst fire catastrophe in the world during any age and, because of this, demanded to be included.

Finally, human suffering and casualty figures again dictated the inclusion or noninclusion of a particular fire. Generally speaking, a cutoff of around 75 deaths was utilized, with one notable exception: the London Fire of 1666. This fire, in which the bacteria that caused the bubonic plague were incinerated, and out of which modern fire-fighting equipment and materials and the concept of fire insurance evolved, only claimed eight lives. But its impact was enough to warrant – perhaps demand – its inclusion in any compendium of the world's fires.

AUSTRIA – VIENNA
December 8, 1881

Human error on the part of a stagehand caused the most tragic theater fire in history, at the Ring Theatre in Vienna, Austria on December 8, 1881. Eight hundred fifty died and hundreds were injured.

The most tragic theater fire in history took place the night after Offenbach's *Les Contes d'Hoffmann* premiered at Vienna's elegant, ornate Ring Theatre. It, like so many human catastrophes, was caused by human carelessness, compounded by human error and inaction.

The Ring Theatre, one of the jewels in the most elegant and artistically productive times in the history of this fabled city, had been built by the imperial government of Franz Joseph in 1873. Located off the famous Ringstrasse, which was already festooned with the Burgtheatre, the Opera House, the Kunstlerhause and the Musikverein, it immediately became a popular mecca for the city's lovers of popular entertainment.

Vienna under Franz Joseph was alive with the arts at the end of the 19th century. Brahms, the Strauss family and Mahler had all been drawn to it in the same way that Mozart and Beethoven had at the end of the 18th century and the beginning of the 19th. And while the Opera House was the home of grand opera, the masses flocked to the gilded splendor of the Ring Theatre, where the great Sarah Bernhardt and Signor Salvini's dramatic troupe appeared, and the lively and racy operettas of Jacques Offenbach were performed.

Royalty and the rich were also drawn to this theater by its glitter and its comfort, but they rarely arrived on time. Offenbach knew enough to write long overtures to fill in the time between the announced curtain time and their bejeweled entrances after 7:00 P.M.

Thus, on the night of December 8, 1881, the night after *Les Contes d'Hoffmann's* premier, only the two balconies were full at 6:45 P.M. Eager tradespeople, students, actors and actresses, attracted by critical praise and enthusiastic recommendations of the new Offenbach work, filled these two upper parts of the auditorium, while a few renegade knights and bank directors occupied the few boxes and stalls downstairs.

At that precise moment, a stagehand went about his usual task of lighting the upper row of gas jets above the stage. Possibly he was careless. Possibly the elaborate scenery required for the operetta was too abundantly or negligently hung. For whatever reason, his long-handled igniter set fire to the canvas trappings of several theatrical clouds. Within seconds, the flames swept to the stage curtains. The stage doors were open; the air blowing in through them fanned the flames and billowed the curtains outward, toward the audience. Huge tongues of flame leaped from canvas to canvas onstage and out into the auditorium.

At this point, the iron fire curtain that existed in every completely equipped theater of the time could and should have been lowered. It would have contained the fire onstage, curtailed the draft and snuffed out some of the flames. But, inexplicably, this was not done, nor was the fire brigade summoned, nor was the onstage water hose pressed into service.

Instead, panic spread as quickly as the fire. As the flames shot outward from the stage, crawling up drapes and running in fiery streams across the ceiling, the patrons stood up in their seats, screamed, 'Fire!' and began to shove at one another. To compound the hysteria, a stagehand shut off the gas, plunging the entire premises into darkness, save for the light of the rapidly accumulating fire.

The occupants of the stalls and boxes got out safely, walking rapidly to the lobby doors and out to the square, where gilded carriages containing royalty and the wealthy were just beginning to draw up.

In the balconies, the crush of humanity battered its way toward the exits, only to find them blocked by impenetrable walls of fire. Some patrons, pushed or panicked, leaped or fell from the front of the balconies. One woman landed on two other audience members, killing herself and both of them.

Summoned by spectators, the fire brigades arrived, but their ladders were too short to reach even the first balcony. By now, patrons were smashing the Gothic windows behind the balconies and leaping hysterically to their deaths in the square below. Firemen frantically ransacked the theater for drapes from which to fashion life nets, but most had been burned to charred threads. They finally found one huge stage drape, and, shouting to those in the balconies to jump into it, they stretched it taut beneath the balcony rails.

The patrons calmed. A commanding, aristocratic man ordered the children to jump first, then the women and finally the men. One hundred twelve children, women and some men thus survived before the walls began to cave in and the flames and smoke became so intense that the rescue attempt had to be abandoned. Those who remained were either incinerated or crushed under the falling walls and pieces of decor.

Members of the royal family – among them, Franz Joseph's grand nephews Charles, Albrecht, William,

Salvatore and Eugene – arrived at the scene, took one look at the inferno before them and, on the spot, began a collection of relief funds for the victims. Crown Prince Rudolf wept openly at the catastrophe, which claimed 850 victims – the highest number of fatalities that would ever be recorded in a European theater fire. Hundreds more were injured.

BELGIUM – BRUSSELS
May 22, 1967

Panic and the lack of a sprinkler system combined to cause the tragedy of the L'Innovation department store fire in Brussels, Belgium on May 22, 1967. Three hundred twenty-two died; scores were injured.

Panic kills as many people in mass fires as smoke or flames, and panic accounted for many of the deaths in the store fire with the greatest fatality count in history. Three hundred twenty-two people died in the noontime fire at L'Innovation, the five-story department store located in the heart of the old city in Brussels, Belgium.

Spring is a time of innovative sales, and L'Innovation, true to its name, featured a Salute to American Fashion in May 1967. On May 22, the 'million dollar showcase' attracted approximately 2,500 customers to the store. L'Innovation prided itself on its service, and another 1,200 clerks – one for every two customers – were in attendance at the height of the shopping day, when office workers on their lunch hour swelled the ranks of shoppers.

It was nearly noon when a fire broke out in three places on the fourth floor of the crowded store. There was some inconclusive evidence of an accelerant being used to begin the fire, though arson was never proved. Whatever its source, the fire spread rapidly and unchecked. The old building was without a sprinkler system. It did have 15 full-time firemen on duty at all times, to compensate for its lack of mechanical fire-fighting means, but for some reason, only two of the 15 responded to the alarm that day. Their sincere but ineffectual efforts to control the wildly spreading blaze with hand-held fire extinguishers did nothing to stop the gathering holocaust.

All 4,000 people in the store tried to reach the exits and elevators at the same time. Many were trampled to death in this insane rush; others had limbs broken and clothing stripped away. Those who could not reach stairways, elevators or doors fought their way to windows. Some smashed them out with their bare hands and leaped for the street, hoping to land on the forgiving hoods of parked cars. Some did and only suffered broken limbs. Others missed and died.

Firemen, hampered by the narrow, twisting streets of the Old Quarter, took an unconscionable amount of time to arrive on the scene. By the time they finally got there, hundreds of canisters of butane gas, destined for summer campers and stored on the store's roof, exploded, feeding the inferno still further. Desperate people still clinging to upper stories were turned into human torches as the flames consumed the entire building, destroying it totally, and burning to ashes many of the 322 people who perished in the fire.

BRAZIL – NITEROI
December 17, 1961

Either arson or sparks from a passing train were suspected of causing the worst circus fire ever recorded, in Niteroi, Brazil on December 17, 1961. Three hundred twenty-three died; 500 were injured.

This incredible circus fire killed 323 persons – most of them children – and cruelly burned 500 more. And it all happened in a little more than three minutes.

As part of its annual Christmas week celebration in

1961, Brazil featured the Gran Circo Norte-Americano, a Brazilian version of Ringling Brothers. In the town of Niteroi, which is located across the bay from Rio de Janeiro, the circus played out its thrills and fantasies in a blue and white nylon tent large enough to accommodate high-wire acts, animal acts, clowns and 2,500 spectators.

On the afternoon of December 17, 1961, the tent was packed to capacity. Most of the audience was composed of children, on holiday from school. They were transfixed by the death-defying high-wire acrobatics of the featured trapeze artist, Antonietta Estavanovich. And it was Ms. Estavanovich who first saw the flames. What must have gone through her mind as she soared through the air toward her partner and saw flames beneath her, in the upper wall of the tent, she never said. But by the time she and her partner had spun into the safety net and had headed for the exits, the fire had made its way to the center of the tent and was edging downward along the tent poles.

Within three minutes, the entire tent had become one huge flame, and the screaming children were stampeding. Three hundred of them ran toward the center ring. The tent collapsed around them, suffocating them. Some others fell as the mob surged in several directions, and they were trampled underfoot.

Sergio Pfiel Manhaes, a heroic young Boy Scout, pulled out his knife, cut a hole in the side of the tent, hauled his family through it and then went back into the conflagration and led an adult, blinded by smoke, to safety.

Joao Goulart, the president of Brazil, broke down in tears when he went into the children's ward in Niteroi's Antonio Pedro Hospital to visit the 500 injured. The investigation he ordered turned up no conclusive reason for the fire. Opinion on the cause of the disaster was divided between arson and sparks from a passing train.

BRAZIL – SAO PAULO
February 1, 1974

*An overheated air-conditioning vent ignited plastic con-
struction material piled near it in the Joelmo building,
which housed the Crefisul Bank, in Sao Paulo, Brazil
on February 1, 1974. Thrill seekers hampered firemen,
and 220 died. Hundreds more were injured.*

Sao Paulo is one of the wealthiest cities in Brazil,
boasting a population of six million and some of the
country's most modern office buildings.

But Sao Paulo is lacking in elementary safety protection for its populace. Safety codes in most major cities
of the world decree that nonflammable materials be
used in major office buildings. The interior of the
Joelmo building, a skyscraper in downtown Sao Paulo
that housed the offices of the Crefisul Bank, was
composed almost entirely of highly flammable materials. And these two factors accounted for the deaths of
220 people on February 1, 1974.

It was one of the worst office building disasters in
history, and it will be forever memorable for the
extremes of human behavior that it revealed. At one
end of the spectrum were the acts of touching and
staggering heroism on the part of firemen, swinging on
ropes high over the streets to rescue panicked victims.
At the other, was the crush of spectators straining to
watch flaming people fling themselves to their deaths
from upper stories. Over 300,000 cars, abandoned by
these morbid, sensation-hungry spectators, clogged
streets and prevented rescue equipment from getting
through.

The fire began in an overheated air-conditioning
vent on the 12th floor of the 25-story building. Plastic
material piled near the vent quickly ignited and spread
to other plastic constructions built into the building.
The first six floors of the structure were occupied by a
car park; thus, most of the employees trapped by the

flames were in upper stories beyond the reach of firemen's ladders, which only extended to the seventh floor.

Some managed to battle their way to exits and ran from the building. Others rushed to save themselves, trampling some of their fellow employees to death. Thirty-four people locked themselves in a washroom and turned on the watertaps, in hope of keeping the flames away. They were discovered the next day, every one of them suffocated to death.

People at some of the windows and on some of the ledges of the building, seeing that the ladders could not reach them, jumped, preferring a quick death to a slow one. One man hit two firemen on a ladder, carrying them with him to their deaths. One woman jumped with a baby in her arms. She died; the baby survived. Twenty-five people tried to leap to the roof of a nearby building. All twenty-five died.

Others heeded the large signs that firemen held up to them reading, 'Courage. We are with you. Don't jump.'

One heroic fireman, Sergeant Jose Rufino, swung on a rope secured to a nearby building, grabbing 18 survivors and swinging with them on his back to safety. During one attempt, a man leaping from the 16th floor collided with Rufino, peeling the man from the fireman's back and sending him to his death. Rufino managed to hang on to the rope and thus saved himself, but his hands were torn and bleeding when he finally rejoined his fellow firemen.

Helicopters sent to rescue survivors from the roof could not land because of the intensity of the heat and the density of the smoke. At one point, the paint began to scale off the doors of one helicopter. Firemen finally dropped cartons of milk to survivors who had made their way to the building's roof. The detoxifying properties of the milk were credited with keeping these near-victims alive until an army helicopter was brought to the roof of the building. The helicopter landed on the slowly buckling roof and lifted off, in a series of staccato landings and takeoffs, 85 people. As the last 10 people were rescued, the roof collapsed.

It would be four hours before firemen could bring the blaze under any sort of control. Almost all of the interior of the building from the 12th floor upward was reduced to charred and sodden rubble.

There was some talk of sabotage, some reports that a telephone operator at the Crefisul Bank had received an anonymous call the day before saying that a bomb would explode on Friday morning. But the report was never considered in the inquiry that followed the fire. The cause was multiple; 220 people were dead; hundreds had been injured; and the municipality had much to do to prevent a recurrence.

CANADA – MONTREAL
January 9, 1927

Employee negligence and political payoffs that allowed fire code violations to exist were the causes of the fire in the Laurier Palace Theater in Montreal, Canada on January 9, 1927. Seventy-eight children died; 30 were severely injured.

CHINA – CHUNGKING
September 2, 1949

Arson was suspected in the fire that began in the slum district of Chungking, China on September 2, 1949 and destroyed 10,000 homes and left 100,000 homeless. One thousand seven hundred died in the fire; thousands were injured.

The year was one of extreme turmoil in China, the turning point between Nationalist and Communist control of the country. Until 1947, Chiang Kai Shek's Nationalists, supported by U.S. supplies and money, had tenaciously held on to the control of the country.

But by November 1948, when the Chinese Communists, under Mao Tse Tung, captured Mukden and thus the industrial heartland of the country, the standoff between the two factions had all but been won by the Communists. Sweeping inflation, increased police repression and a grinding, endless famine had so eroded public confidence in the Nationalists that a state of civil strife, trembling on the brink of civil war, existed.

In January 1949, Peking fell to the Communists. From April to November, other major cities also fell, most without a fight. Nanking, Han-kou, Shanghai, Canton and · eventually Chungking, the Nationalist capital, all surrendered.

In September, the tensions in the city were at their highest point. And on September 2, 1949 at 4:00 P.M., a fire of mysterious origin began in Chungking's slum district. Whether the arsonist was a Communist or whether it was someone directed by the Nationalist government to set the blaze in the hope of turning public opinion against the Communists will probably never be known. In the holocaust's aftermath, the Nationalists rounded up suspected Communists and, a week later, executed for arson a man known to be part of the Communist underground.

The human toll was staggering. The fire, once begun, spread unchecked in several directions. It ate into the residential district, consuming nearly 10,000 homes and leaving more than 100,000 people homeless. It devastated the business district and then, fanned by winds, roared toward the waterfronts of the Yangtze and Chialung rivers. Refugees, running ahead of the advancing wall of fire, had come to this part of the city in the hope of escaping in one of the hundreds of boats docked there. Hundreds of people were burned to death both on the docks and in the moored boats, as the roaring inferno outraced and enveloped them.

Chungking would burn for 18 hours that afternoon and night, and when it was over, more than 1,700 residents of that embattled city would be dead.

CHINA – HEILONGJANG PROVINCE
May–June, 1987

It took tens of thousands of firefighters over a month to extinguish the worst forest fire in China's history. Started for unknown reasons on May 6, 1987, it killed over 200 people, burned 1.48 million acres of forest and left over 50,000 homeless.

COLOMBIA – BOGOTA
December 16, 1958

A light bulb ignited a creche in El Almacen Vida, one of Bogota, Colombia's largest department stores, on December 16, 1958. Eighty-four died in the resultant fire; scores were injured.

FRANCE – PARIS
May 25, 1887

A gaslight igniting scenery followed by human error – the failure to lower a fire curtain – caused the fire in Paris's Opera-Comique on May 25, 1887. Two hundred died.

FRANCE – PARIS
May 4, 1897

A lamp used to illuminate a kinematograph ignited the structure erected at Paris's annual Grand Bazar de Charite on May 4, 1897. One hundred fifty people died in the fire; hundreds were injured.

FRANCE – ST.-LAURENT-DU-PONT
November 1, 1970

A dropped, lighted cigarette combined with multiple

violations of fire codes caused the fire in the Cinq-Sept Club, a disco in St.-Laurent-du-Pont, France, on November 1, 1970. One hundred forty-six patrons died; hundreds were injured.

The Cinq-Sept Club, in the small French village of St.-Laurent-du-Pont, 20 miles south of Grenoble, was a disaster aching to occur. A multiple array of safety violations and a disregard of common sense rendered this huge disco, a gathering place for young people from Grenoble, Aix-les-Bains and Chambery, a dangerous fire trap.

In clear violation of French fire regulations, one of the two required access doors as well as the main entrance was sealed, and the other locked. The two regulation fire exits were unlit; one was hidden by a screen behind the bandstand, and the other was blocked by stacks of chairs. The main entrance itself was an eight-foot-high, spiked turnstile.

The psychedelic decor in this hangar-like club consisted of an arched grotto sculpted from highly flammable polystyrene, another violation of fire regulations. Above the dance floor were tiny alcoves, reachable by one spiral staircase. There were no fire extinguishers on the premises.

And finally, and most astonishing of all, the club possessed no telephone.

On the night of November 1, 1970, the Cinq-Sept was packed with youngsters in their late teens and early twenties gyrating to the sounds of 'Storm,' a new group from Paris. Around 1:40 A.M., the group had just begun its last set with the Stones' 'Satisfaction.'

Upstairs, in one of the alcoves, someone dropped a lighted cigarette on a cushion. It immediately caught fire, and several patrons tried to beat it out with their hands and jackets. But the fire was stubborn, and in moments it had spread to the plastic arches that separated the alcoves. A vast tongue of flame shot the length of the dance floor as the plastic arches began to melt, dropping molten lumps of plastic on those near them.

At first, there was an orderliness about the exodus of the crowd. Some in the alcoves descended the staircase and exited through the one obvious and available, if obstructed, exit. Thirty left this way. But moments later, panic took over. The flames and the heat intensified enormously, and heavy, suffocating fumes filled the club, asphyxiating some couples, who were later discovered still locked in each other's arms on the dance floor and near the bar.

One barman hurled himself against one of the emergency exits near him, and he and a handful of patrons escaped through it. Simultaneously, one of the owners, 25-year-old Gilbert Bas, saw an emergency light come on in his office. Walking toward the door, he heard the anguished cries of 'Fire!' but did not open the door to the club. With no telephone, he was unable to call the fire department. He exited through his office door and drove almost two kilometers to the fire station to report the fire in person.

Meanwhile, people in the club were dying. The pandemonium induced by panic had pressed the crowd against the turnstile at the main entrance, jamming it. Later rescuers would discover the body of one young man impaled upon one of the spikes of the turnstile.

The club had become an inferno. The corrugated iron roof turned red hot and collapsed on those inside. One hundred forty-four young people would perish horribly in the flames. Two more would die later of their burns, bringing the mortality total to 146.

The next day, morbid curiosity would attract thousands to the tiny village to view the grisly sight. It would take a combined force of 200 policemen and law enforcement officials to move the crowd away from the ruins of the club.

The sheer magnitude of the disaster forced an intense investigation, and the village's mayor, Pierre Perrin, and secretary-general of the prefecture de l'Isere Albert Ulrich were immediately suspended from their jobs. As the investigation progressed, a tangled web of bureaucratic fumbling, backturning and compromise was revealed. There was scarcely a municipal agency that was not involved in some way. The rules were in place. But they had never been enforced.

In June 1971, the mayor and two building contractors were charged with causing injury through negligence. Gilbert Bas, the sole surviving owner (his two partners had died in the blaze), was charged with manslaughter. In November 1971, all were found guilty but received suspended sentences – Bas for two years, Mayor Perrin for 10 months, the three building contractors for 15, 13 and 10 months each.

The fire would go down in record books as the worst in the history of France.

GERMANY – DRESDEN
February 13, 1945

The Allied firebombing of Dresden on February 13, 1945 caused a fire storm that destroyed the city, killed 135,000 residents and injured hundreds of thousands more.

GREAT BRITAIN – ENGLAND, BRADFORD
May 11, 1985

Fifty-six people – most of them children and the elderly – died and 210 were injured when a fire erupted in the main stand of Bradford City's Valley Parade ground shortly before half-time in a game between Bradford City and Lincoln City on May 11, 1985. The 77-year-old wooden stand was consumed by flames in minutes. Padlocked gates accounted for some of the fatalities.

GREAT BRITAIN – ENGLAND, EXETER
September 4, 1887

A gaslight ignited scenery onstage, causing the fire in the Exeter Theatre in Exeter, on September 4, 1887. Two hundred were killed; hundreds were injured.

'The bodies were lying so thick [at the bottom of the gallery stairs] that they quite occupied the entire width of the staircase,' said Harry Foot to the *Illustrated London News* on September 5, 1887; 'in some cases they were four and five rows deep. At the bottom of the stairs they lay thicker than at the top, almost as if shot down a shoot. In the majority of cases the arms were outstretched beyond the head, as if they had struggled to the last to drag themselves forward; but their legs were rendered immovable by the bodies of those who had followed and partly fallen on them.'

Foot and nearly 1,400 other playgoers had attended a performance at the stately Exeter Theatre, one of the prides of the city of Exeter on the night of September 4, 1887. The performance had hardly begun when the nemesis of safety in 19th century theaters, an onstage gaslight, ignited some canvas scenery. As in the Ring Theatre disaster in Vienna six years before (see p. 194), the initial ignition occurred in the flies above the stage and slightly behind the top of the proscenium. Overhead gas lamps set fire to the uppermost reaches of a tall piece of scenery, just behind the act drop, and spread rapidly to the act curtain, then to the drapes in front of the proscenium. From there, the flames shot out in lethal sheets into the audience.

The actors onstage and the wealthy in the stalls and boxes were able to file out without injury. Some 900 of them emerged unscathed.

It was, as usual, a different scene entirely in the gallery. There, pandemonium and hysteria took an early toll. Men, women and children fled toward the one stairwell that might allow them to escape the huge, billowing clouds of smoke that were now blotting out whatever light had been left in the theater.

By the time many of them reached the stairwell, it had become a fatal flue, collecting the smoke from other parts of the structure, containing it and shooting it upward. Some gallery patrons were trampled underfoot; others who managed to reach the stairwell suffocated from the smoke, fell in place and blockaded the exit, trapping others behind.

George Cooper, a soldier, William Hunt, a sailor, and the aforementioned patron Harry Foot were among the heroes of the day. Ignoring their own safety, they dashed into the theater, plucking survivors from the steadily accumulating piles of the dead and dying and dragging or carrying them from the flaming theater.

Eventually, the flames reached the lead roof and heated it to the melting point. Flames descended the stairwells, followed by drops of molten lead. It was only at this point that the rescuers abandoned their efforts. 'It would have been suicidal to have continued our work,' Foot confessed to reporters later.

Two hundred patrons died in this fire, most of them in one stairway.

GREAT BRITAIN – ENGLAND, LONDON
September 2–6, 1666

A fire in the chimney of a bake shop, coupled with a long drought, caused the Great Fire of London on September 2, 1666. Thirteen thousand houses and 87 churches were destroyed; only eight people died.

The Great Fire of London was monumental in many respects. It destroyed 13,000 houses and 87 churches – including Saint Paul's – on 400 streets, laid waste to the Royal Exchange and Guild Hall and reduced a score of other public buildings to charred ashes. It burned for five days and was only stopped by a change in the direction and velocity of the wind. It reduced to rubble a large portion of the largest city in the world at that time and exposed to the public the woeful inadequacy of the fire-fighting apparatus and techniques of the age.

Yet there were positive aspects to this holocaust. If records are at all accurate, it only claimed eight lives. The bubonic plague, which had raged through Europe for decades, disappeared in England, apparently burned out of existence by the Great London Fire of 1666. Scientists theorize that the intense heat incinerated the plague bacillus, thus freeing the British Isles from what would continue to roam the continent of Europe for another 150 years.

The methods of forcing water through hoses by compressed air had been known and feasible since the invention, in 1590 by Cyprian Lucar, of the 'portable squirt' – a brass tank powered by three men and used to some effect in fighting the 1666 fire. Decaus's 'rare and necessary engine,' developed in 1615 and outfitted with a swivel joint, and Hans Hautch's engine at Nuremberg, built in 1655, which was designed to force, by air, a steady stream of water at a fire, were also in limited use. But only the least effective of these, the portable squirt was brought into play during the Great Fire, and even then on a very limited basis. Firemen simply pulled down flaming houses by grappling their walls with iron hooks on poles.

Afterward, however, modern methods of climbing ladders, extinguishing flames and carrying people to safety were begun. After the fire, when a new engine designed to fight fires was invented or introduced, it was not ignored, as it had been before 1666, but tested and, if found effective, was adopted.

Furthermore, as a result of the extent of this calamity, the concept of fire insurance was developed, and less than a year later, the world's first fire insurance policy was written by Dr. Nicholas Barton, who had built houses in the burned-out districts of London following the fire. His policies guaranteed to replace a house if it was destroyed by fire, and he did an immediate, brisk business, which eventually developed into Phoenix Fire Insurance, a firm that is still functioning today.

A long, pervasive drought preceded the London fire, very much like the long dry spell that occurred before the famous Chicago fire of 1871 (see p. 230). That fire began early in the evening. The London conflagration started at 2 in the morning in the chimney of the King's Baker's Shop on Pudding Lane, near London Bridge. From there, borne on a brisk wind, it ignited house after house and worked its way to the Thames wharves, where piles of flammable goods were stored.

The two most important men in the fighting of the Great Fire were Samuel Pepys and William Penn. Pepys, the son of a London tailor, was then secretary of the admiralty, an accomplished musician, a critic of painting, architecture and drama, a charming host and a connoisseur of beautiful women. He also kept a meticulous diary, and it is in the pages of this diary that the most vivid and precise record of the fire was set down:

> September 2, 1666. Some of the maids sitting up late last night to get things ready against our feast today . . . called us up about three in the morning to tell us of a great fire they saw in the City. So I rose, and slipped on my nightgown, and went to [the] window; and thought it to be on the back side of Mark Lane at the farthest, and so went to bed again and to sleep.

The next morning, Pepys's wife Jane informed him that 300 houses had been burned down and that all of Fish Street by London Bridge had been consumed. Pepys went to the Thames:

> I . . . got a boat, and through the bridge, and there saw a lamentable fire, everybody endeavoring to

remove their goods, and flinging into the river, or bringing them into lighters that lay off; poor people staying in their houses till the very fire touched them, and then running into boats or clambering from one pair of stairs by the water – one side to another . . . Having stayed and in an hour's time seen the fire rage every way, and nobody, to my sight, endeavoring to quench it, but to remove their goods and leave all to the fire . . . and the wind mighty high and driving into the city; and everything, after so long a drought, proving combustible, even the very stones of churches, I to White Hall.

At White Hall, Pepys informed the king and the Duke of York of the horrendous state of London and got from them an order to pull down every house that might carry the fire forward.

'At last,' he goes on, 'met my Lord Mayor in Canning Street, like a man spent, with a handkercher about his neck, to the King's message, he cried, like a fainting woman:

'Lord! What can I do? I am spent. People will not obey me. I have been pulling down houses; but the fire overtakes us faster than we can do it . . .' The houses so very thick thereabouts, and full of matter for burning, as pitch and tar in Thames Street, and warehouses of oil and wines and brandy and other things.

As the days and nights ached forward, the fire seemed to increase. Pepys went back and forth between the lord mayor, the king, and the Duke of York, bearing one repeated order: 'Pull down the houses.' He laments:

and to the fire up and down, it still increasing, and the wind great. So near the fire as we could for smoke; and all over the Thames, with one's faces in the wind you were almost burned with a shower of firedrops . . . and, as it grew darker, appeared more and more; and in corners and upon steeples, and between churches and houses, as far as we could see up the hill of the City, in a most horrid, malicious, bloody flame, not like the fine flame of an ordinary fire . . . We saw the fire as only one entire arch of fire from this to the other side of the bridge, and in a bow up the hill for an arch of above a mile long. It made me weep to see it. The churches, houses, and all on fire and flaming at once; and a horrid noise the flames made, and the cracking of houses at their ruin.

By the morning of the fifth, William Penn, an important enough personage to command attention both in court and in the city, had taken a hand, and instead of simply pulling down houses, fire brigadiers were now, under his direction, blowing them up.

Pepys looked on:

I up to the top of Barking steeple, and there saw the saddest sight of desolation that I ever saw; everywhere great fires, oil cellars and brimstone and other things burning . . .

I walked into the town, and find Fenchurch Street, Gracious Street, and Lombard Street all in dust. The exchange a sad sight, nothing standing there of all the statues or pillars but Sir Thomas Gresham's picture in the corner. Into Moorfield's our feet ready to burn walking through the town among hot coals and flint that full of people and poor wretches carrying their goods there . . . Thence homeward, having passed through Cheapside and Newgate market, all burned . . . and took up, which I keep by me, a piece of glass of the Mercers' Chapel in the street, where much more was, so melted and buckled with the heat of the fire like parchment.

The wind changed; the fire abated. Less than a third of

the walled city remained after this cataclysmic fire, which consumed most of London.

GREAT BRITAIN – ENGLAND, LONDON
November 18, 1987

Thirty-one people died and 80 were injured in the worst fire in the history of the London Underground at King's Cross station on November 18, 1987. A lighted match dropped on grease and debris under a wooden escalator started the blaze, which trapped its victims in a wall of flame.

King's Cross underground station is one of London's busiest, a place where no fewer than five lines converge, and British Rail maintains two terminals, King's Cross and St Pancras. The Piccadilly, Northern, Metropolitan, Victoria and Circle underground lines all disgorge thousands of commuters on weekday afternoons and before holidays, and this was the situation on the late afternoon of Wednesday, November 18, 1987.

The Piccadilly line is connected to the main ticket hall by a long, wooden escalator. Sometime during that afternoon, near the bottom of the staircase, someone dropped a lighted match into a gap beside the moving treads of the Piccadilly Line escalator. It was a thoughtless move, or perhaps a prank; no one knows precisely which, but its effect was gradual and lethal.

As the afternoon turned to early evening, and more and more commuters poured into the station and rode the escalator upward to the ticket hall, the match ignited grease and debris that had accumulated beneath the escalator. The flames built steadily, and at 7:50 p.m., just as the last wave of commuters was emptying onto the upper level of the station, clouds of smoke began to emerge from the escalator.

Suddenly, an immense fireball erupted out of the regions below the moving stairs, shot up the railing in a white-hot wall of flame, and exploded into the turnstile area.

Horrified people began to panic, as smoke obscured the station, and flames enveloped some who were in the path of the fireball. Underground staff directed passengers from the Piccadilly to the Victoria line escalator, but it, too, emptied into the turnstile area, which was now a roaring inferno. 'We followed their instructions and got on to the other escalator,' survivor Andrew Lea told reporters. 'About halfway up, a sheet of flame shot across the top of that escalator and very soon the ceiling was on fire and debris started falling down . . .'

Chaos consumed the station. Staff used no fire extinguishers, and no one seemed to know where to direct the panicked passengers. Finally, 150 members of the London Fire Brigade arrived and began to gather the dead and dying, lead the choking survivors from the station, and extinguish the blaze.

Thirty-one people died; 80 were injured, 21 of them seriously enough to require hospitalization. It was the worst fire in the history of the London Underground, surpassing the one in 1985 in which one person died and 47 were injured.

A year-long inquiry resulted in charges of negligence and incompetence on the part of staff and safety and maintenance personnel in the London Underground. Sir Keith Bright, chairman of London Regional Transport, and Dr. Tony M. Ridley, chairman and chief executive of the London Underground, resigned. The next week, the installation of new metal escalators and millions of pounds in safety improvements were announced in Parliament.

GUATEMALA – GUATEMALA CITY
July 14, 1960

Either faulty electrical wiring or a candle collapsing onto flammable material in front of a religious statue ignited the fire in the Guatemala City Insane Asylum on July 14, 1960. Two hundred twenty-five died; 300 were injured.

The Guatemala City Insane Asylum was madness personified. A structure built in 1890, its facilities, its design and its safety had all outlived their capacity by the summer of 1960. Sometime during the early hours of July 14 of that year, a fire began in the asylum, started either by faulty electrical wiring or a candle collapsing onto flammable material in front of a religious statue. Within minutes, the ancient structure was ablaze, and 600 of its 1,500 inmates and attendants were trapped behind nonfunctioning doors.

The children who were housed in the asylum were the first to be evacuated, and every one of them survived. But there were still hundreds of adults who were incapable of saving themselves, and they were driven to wild hysteria by a fire that resisted every effort of the Guatemala City fire department to extinguish it.

Finally, realizing that most of the exits were blocked, and that those that were open were not being used by the patients to free themselves, the fire department, led by Guatemalan president Miguel Ydigoras Fuentes, brought a bulldozer onto the premises and knocked down a wall. Hundreds fled the building to safety through the hole in the wall, but others still had to be led, fighting and screaming, from the flames by rescuers. Thirty-one maximum-security patients, each considered dangerous, were never freed from their cells and burned to death in them.

The fire was brought under control by early morning of the 14th, and by that evening, 27,000 pounds of relief supplies had arrived from the United States. Two hundred twenty-five patients, most of them women, perished in the fire, and 300 were severely injured.

In the grim aftermath, murder and arson in the city increased after the fire. They were attributed to 48

criminally insane inmates who escaped from the burning asylum that night and were never recaptured.

IRAN – ABADAN
August 20, 1978

Arson caused a fire in a movie theater in Abadan, Iran
on August 20, 1978. Four hundred twenty-two died in
the conflagration.

In 1978, Shah Mohammad Reza Pahlavi was trying to
Westernize Iran. He ran head on into Muslim extremists, who announced that, in his efforts to emancipate
women and redistribute church lands, the shah was
violating the teachings of the Koran. Further, the
general atmosphere engendered by his 'Westernizing'
process had resulted in a general laxity on the part of
segments of the public in observing the strict dictates of
the Muslim holy month of Ramadan. One of the
consequences of this that angered the extremists was
the showing of movies during Ramadan.

Saturday night, August 20, 1978 was a hot and
muggy night in the oil-refining city of Abadan, at the
northern tip of the Persian Gulf. A crowd had gathered
at the Rex Theatre to see the Persian-language film *The
Deer* and escape the heat.

Partway through the evening, a group of Muslim
terrorists, aided by two employees of the Rex who were
sympathetic to their cause, approached the theater
from the outside. They carried several cans of gasoline,
which they proceeded to splash on every outside wall.
Then, as several of them ignited the gasoline, others,
aided by the employees, opened the only exit door and
doused the interior section of the theater near it with
flaming gasoline. They then slammed the door and
locked it.

Inside, the terrified audience went berserk. Flames
roared through the building, consuming its interior and
the people within. An enormous hill of grappling

human beings piled up at the barricaded exit. Those who arrived there first were crushed under the pile; others were overcome by smoke; those at the top were incinerated.

The heat rose to inhuman levels. The entire building was consumed by flames. Some managed to smash windows; still others discovered a roof exit that had been overlooked by the arsonists and escaped. But they were the lucky few. By the time firemen arrived on the scene, smashed windows and broke in the barricaded door, the screaming from within the inferno that was once a theater had stopped.

Four hundred twenty-two people were burned to death, died of suffocation or were trampled to death. Entire families from the working-class neighborhood in which the theater was located were wiped out.

Ten arrests were made the following Monday, and the theater's manager was arrested and charged with negligence for ignoring police orders to hire more employees and guards. It would be one of the last futile gestures of opposition to the Muslim extremists, who would soon command the country.

JAMAICA – KINGSTON
May 20, 1980

Overcrowding, combined with a short circuit in the wall of Eventide Home, a nursing home in Kingston, Jamaica, caused a fire on May 20, 1980. One hundred fifty-seven perished in the blaze.

On the night of May 20, 1980, there were 204 elderly, indigent women asleep in a 110-year-old, two-story building in a three-building complex called Eventide Home, located in Kingston, Jamaica. The other two buildings housed elderly men and handicapped children, and the entire complex was city owned and city run.

The structure sheltering the women was particularly

decrepit and dangerous. Built of highly inflammable pitch pine wood, it had been branded a 'tinder box' by Kingston fire chief Allen Ridgeway several times, but the city had ignored his warnings and had packed the building, which had a legal capacity of 180, with 204 elderly women.

'It was a place of indigent people,' the fire chief explained to reporters after the fire that destroyed it. 'The ratio of indigent rose and the capacity of the complex couldn't be expanded. The normal statutes just couldn't be kept.'

And this breaking of its own statutes by the city only intensified the tragedy when the inevitable finally happened. At 1 A.M. on Wednesday, May 20, 1980, a short circuit in the building's electrical system started a fire in one of the walls. By the time anyone had even smelled the smoke, the flames had begun to consume the building. Screaming women, some unable to leave their beds, remained helpless before the onslaught of the flames, which raced with lightning speed through the entire building, collapsing walls and floors and igniting everything burnable within moments.

Some women managed to reach windows, but the fire spread so rapidly that it had become a hopeless situation long before the fire department even arrived. There were neither ladders nor safety nets for them, and the women who jumped from the upper level of the two stories injured themselves seriously.

The fire department arrived on the scene within five minutes. Four minutes later, the entire building collapsed upon itself with a sickening roar that mixed with the piercing screams of the women still trapped within it. A huge funeral pyre, it instantly silenced the last frantic efforts of any remaining survivors. Of the 204 women who had just 20 minutes before been sleeping peacefully within the shelter, only 47 would escape. One hundred fifty-seven died in the flames, most of them burned alive. It would be almost impossible to identify most of them the next day.

The best the fire department could do was to evacuate the children from their nearby shelter. The men, at a far corner of the complex, were not disturbed, and many slept through the entire holocaust.

A political campaign was warming up in Jamaica, and both sides in the contest irresponsibly accused the other of sending arsonists to start the fire. Prime Minister Michael N. Manley informed local radio stations that night that arsonists began the blaze, and a Kingston police spokesman perpetuated the rumor that telephone wires to the complex had been cut shortly before the blaze started. But Fire Chief Ridgeway steadfastly refused to blame arsonists, and his investigation proved that the immediate cause of the fire had been an electrical short circuit. The resultant tragedy was caused by housing helpless people in an overcrowded fire trap.

JAPAN – OSAKA
May 13, 1972

A short circuit in a room containing oil-soaked rags, plus obscured fire exits, combined to turn the fire in the Playtown Cabaret in Osaka, Japan on May 13, 1972 into a fatal inferno. One hundred eighteen died; 38 were injured.

PUERTO RICO – SAN JUAN
December 31, 1986

Labor troubles led to arson that caused the catastrophic fire on New Year's Eve, December 31, 1986 in the Dupont Plaza Hotel in San Juan, Puerto Rico. Ninety-six died; hundreds were injured.

ROME
July 19, A.D. 64

Imperial arson, ordered by Nero, caused the fire that

consumed three of Rome's 14 districts and damaged seven more on July 19, A.D. 64. No fatality or injury figures survive.

One of the more despicable pictures of ancient times is that of Nero fiddling while Rome burns. But the picture is not entirely accurate. Actually, the mad emperor fingered the lyre while he sang verses from *The Fall of Troy* and watched the conflagration from a safe hilltop.

There is unanimous consent among contemporary historians that Nero ordered this terrible fire set – possibly so that he could expand his already grandiose palace, which occupied two of Rome's seven hills, possibly because he had tired of the drabness of Rome's ancient buildings, possibly because he liked fires.

In any case, Nero departed on a short trip to Actium on July 17, A.D. 64, and on July 19 a mysterious blaze began in the vicinity of the Circus Maximus, at the bottom of the Palatine Hill. From the Circus Maximus, it spread swiftly, helped by a strong wind and the narrow streets of the quarter. It moved on without mercy, consuming buildings that had stood since the time of Romulus, the founder of the city 800 years before. Romulus's temple dedicated to the god Jupiter was one of the many venerable and irreplaceable buildings that burned during the six days and seven nights of the conflagration.

Tacitus, the historian of Rome, described the sorry scene:

Terrified, shrieking women, helpless old and young . . . fugitives and lingerers alike – all heightened the confusion. When people looked back, menacing flames sprang up before them or outflanked them. When they escaped to a neighboring quarter, the fire followed – even districts believed remote proved to be involved. Finally, with no idea where or what to flee, they crowded onto the country roads, or lay in the fields. Some who had lost everything – even their food for the day – could have escaped but preferred to die. So did others, who had failed to rescue their loved ones.

That the fire was officially set was supported by Tacitus, too. 'Nobody dared fight the flames,' he wrote. 'Attempts to do so were prevented by menacing gangs. Torches, too, were openly thrown in, by men crying that they acted under orders.'

Finally, before the entire city was destroyed, fire brigades demolished buildings in the fire's path, and it ended, but not before consuming three of the city's 14 districts entirely and severely damaging seven more. Nero forbade homeowners from returning to salvage what they could from the ruins of their homes. The reason? Tacitus answers: 'to collect as much loot as possible for himself.'

Rumor, based on fact, spread through the city as fast as the fire; Nero had ordered it. To stop the rumor, Nero publicly speculated that the Christians in Rome, among them Saint Peter, were behind the arson that had wreaked such havoc. He ordered mass arrests and public crucifixions. Christians were set afire in Nero's gardens, and others were forced to enter the Circus dressed as animals, where killer dogs tore them to pieces.

According to the historians, even this failed to hide Nero's guilt. He rebuilt the city, after reconstructing his own palace on a hitherto unprecedented scale of opulence. There was a 120-foot-high statue of himself in the entrance hall, a pillared arcade a mile long and gardens containing lakes and complete forests. In the city, rebuilt public buildings were restricted in height, built of non-flammable stone, and porches were dictated as part of their approved design, so that fire fighters could have easy access in case of future fires.

RUSSIA – IGOLKINO
March 12, 1929

Drunken negligence on the part of a projectionist, compounded by the overcrowding of a room with inadequate exits above a factory in Igolkino, Russia, caused the March 12, 1929 fire in that city. One hundred twenty died in the blaze.

March 12, 1929 was the 12th anniversary of the abdication of Czar Nicholas II. In the tiny Russian village of Igolkino, 250 miles northeast of Moscow, a group of drunken workers and their families decided to celebrate by viewing Victor Seastrom's classic film *The Wind.* Igolkino possessed no movie theater, but this did not dissuade the celebrants. They commandeered a 24-by-24-foot room above a factory. The factory manager had protested vehemently against the use of the room. First, according to *New York Times* reporter Walter Duranty, '[he] feared the peasants would steal tools stored in the room.' But more importantly, and perhaps a bit more believably, he knew that 30 gallons of gasoline had been accidentally spilled on the floor of the room the day before, that there was only one exit from the room and that the windows were too small to accommodate people trying to flee from a fire.

His protestations fell on deaf ears. The village Soviet warned him that he would be arrested if he tried to prevent the workers from using the room. The factory manager acquiesced, and workers, led by Bazarnof, a drunken projectionist who carried the projector and film in one hand and a bottle of vodka in the other, crammed themselves into the fetid room.

Most of the revelers could not have cared less about the motion picture. They in fact shouted for music. Bazarnof complied, turning the running of the film over to an unskilled and equally drunk friend. Lighting up a cigarette and strapping on an accordion, Bazarnof squatted in the doorway of the only exit and began to play Russian folk songs. The substitute projectionist allowed the film to run off the take-up reel and accumulate in a pile on the floor.

Unconcerned, Bazarnof continued to play the accordion. When his cigarette had burned down to a butt, he flipped it. The still-glowing cigarette landed in the middle of the nitrate-treated film and instantly ignited it. The flames rushed to the gasoline-soaked floor, and within seconds the entire room and its occupants were ablaze. Bazarnof leaped up and ran. He did not stop until he reached a nearby village, where, a day later, he was arrested.

Meanwhile, people choked and suffocated on the thick black smoke generated by the ball of fire that had now consumed the room. Some were trampled to death underfoot; others were burned alive.

In the midst of this, someone discovered a trapdoor that opened onto the factory below. One hundred thirty people managed to squeeze through either the trapdoor or the one exit, but 120 died in that 24-by-24-foot cauldron.

One more victim would be claimed in a ghoulish and grisly charade. Furious and distraught over the mayhem and death, the village's peasants vented their rage not on the absent projectionist who had caused the fire, but on the factory manager who had tried to warn their dead comrades away from the firetrap. A mob of workers cornered him, stoned him, beat him unconscious and flung him into the still-raging fire, where he burned to death.

SOUTH KOREA – SEOUL
December 25, 1971

Human negligence in failing to contain a small fire caused by a propane tank explosion in a coffee shop led to the huge fire in the Taeyunkak Hotel in Seoul, South Korea on Christmas Day, December 25, 1971. One hundred sixty-three died in the fire; 50 were injured.

Holiday times seem to be particularly vulnerable to tragedies resulting from human carelessness.

Eight workers and executives of the luxurious 21-story Taeyunkak Hotel in the center of Seoul, Korea were arrested and charged with negligence after the December 25, 1971 fire that raked the hotel with roaring flames and caused the death of 163 persons.

The fire began at 10:00 A.M. when a propane tank used for cooking in a second-floor coffee shop exploded and burst into flames. Under ordinary circumstances, this manageable fire should have been extinguished, or at least contained within the confines of the coffee shop. But it was not, and the flames soared up through conduits and elevator shafts, climbing 20 stories to the hotel's roof within minutes.

Fortunately, because of the Christmas holiday, the offices in the building were unoccupied. Still, 317 people – 187 guests and 130 hotel employees – were in the building when the fire began. Again, as in so many fires in public buildings, there were too few fire escapes, and those that existed were blocked by fire, smoke or debris.

Firemen arrived quickly, but an incredible situation developed as soon as they came upon the scene. Amazingly, in a city of skyscrapers, they had ladders that only reached to the fourth floor. Their hoses only drove water as high as the ninth floor, and the flames were shooting out of the building all the way to the 22nd story and beyond.

Panicked, hysterical people began to fling themselves from windows. Even when 13 helicopters arrived, the mayhem and dying scarcely ceased. The roof was consumed in flames; there was no landing space for the helicopters, and so their pilots and crews attempted to rescue survivors by ladder from window ledges. It was a risky exercise for professionals under ideal circumstances. It proved disastrous in this situation. Only a small number of people managed to clamber up the swinging ladders to safety, and two who were rescued from the flames lost their grip and fell to their deaths.

Everything was tried, even the pieced-together poles of circus acrobats, but little could be done for those trapped on the upper floors of this flaming modern hotel, and it was considered fortunate that only 163 people died and approximately 50 were injured.

SPAIN – MADRID
September 22, 1928

A short circuit set fire to scenery in the Novedades Theater in Madrid on September 22, 1928. The resultant fire killed 110 people; 350 were injured, many seriously.

SYRIA – AMUDE
November 13, 1960

An unexplained explosion in the projection booth of a movie theater in Amude, Syria on November 13, 1960 caused a fire that gutted the building. One hundred fifty-two children attending a special program were killed; 23 were injured.

THAILAND – NAKHON PATHOM
May 10, 1993

Two hundred six workers were killed and 500 were injured in the worst factory fire in history, at a doll factory in Nakhon Pathom, Thailand on May 10, 1993. As in the Triangle Shirtwaist fire (see p. 238), substandard working conditions, blocked exits and a lack of safety precautions caused the appalling loss of life.

The parallels were eerie and disturbing.

The Triangle Shirtwaist Factory in 1911 (New York City) employed young, immigrant girls and paid them starvation wages of $18 a week; the Kader Industrial Company doll factory in 1993 (Nakhom Pathom, Thailand) employed immigrant girls and paid them starvation wages of between $120 and $160 a month.

Working conditions at the Triangle Shirtwaist Factory were crowded and abominable, and the doors were bolted shut in order to prevent the girls from stealing the stock; Working conditions at the Kader Industrial Company were substandard, and the doors were bolted shut to prevent the girls from stealing the dolls and novelty items they assembled.

Fire escapes and safety precautions at the Triangle Shirtwaist Factory were either inoperative, decaying, or nonexistent, and when, on March 25, 1911, a fire began in a rag bin and rapidly consumed the factory, hundreds died needlessly, piled up against the blocked doors or in headlong leaps from upper stories when the fire escapes failed; fire escapes and safety precautions at the Kader Industrial Company were nonexistent, and when, on May 10, 1993, a fire began in the cloth-cutting area and rapidly consumed the factory, hundreds of helpless girls died needlessly, piled up against the locked doors or in headlong leaps from the factory's roof when they found no fire escapes.

One hundred forty-five girls were burned to death and scores more were injured at the Triangle Shirtwaist Factory; 206 girls were burned to death and 500 were injured at the Kader Industrial Company, making this the worst factory fire in the history of the world.

There were four buildings in the complex of the Kader Industrial Company, Ltd., a Thailand, Hong Kong and Taiwan-owned manufacturer of dolls and novelty items for export. Eight hundred employees were working in the four-building complex on May 10, 1993, when a short circuit apparently caused a fire in the ground-floor cloth-cutting room of one of the buildings.

Within minutes, the flames spread to the top floors of this building, then leaped to two other structures. Workers clawed their way to staircases leading to the exits. But the doors were bolted shut, and, as fireballs of flame pursued them, more and more frantic workers piled onto the staircases, which collapsed under their weight. Scores were incinerated as they flung themselves in clusters against the doors, or were crushed by the collapsing stairs.

Meanwhile, those who escaped this fate dashed to windows, from which fire escapes should have taken them to the ground. But there were no fire escapes, and so they did what they had to do, and leaped six stories to the earth below. Most suffered broken bones or concussions.

'It's not our fault,' one guard, in charge of a locked door, told reporters. 'The company told us to lock the doors so people would not sneak out or steal.'

'It's not our fault,' echoed company executives to television reporters. 'We simply complied with government regulations.'

The next day, as Thai soldiers began the grim task of searching through the smoking rubble of the factory, the government launched an investigation into the numerous safety violations in the factory. Not a single fire alarm was discovered, and charges of gross negligence were filed against the company's executives.

TURKEY – CONSTANTINOPLE
June 5, 1870

Hot charcoals spilled from a brazier onto the wooden steps of a home in the Armenian section of Constantinople, Turkey on June 5, 1870 and fanned by high winds led to a conflagration that destroyed 3,000 homes and set fire to the entire city. Nine hundred residents died.

There seems to be some dispute about some of the details of the great fire that swept through Constantinople, Turkey on Sunday, June 5, 1870. Several versions indicate that it was a balmy spring day, and a large portion of the population was out of the city, enjoying picnics and the country. But these same reports also indicate that a gale-force wind was blowing, and this wind was responsible for the wildfire nature of the disaster. Considering the enormous number of casualties – 900 persons burned to death, more than 3,000 buildings destroyed – it would seem that the population was at home, not out battling the winds on open picnic grounds.

One detail runs consistently through the chronicles of that terrible day, however: the origins of the fire. An Armenian family in the Valide Tchesme district was definitely at home at dinnertime, and the mother of the household instructed her young daughter to go upstairs, fill an iron pan with burning charcoal and bring it downstairs to the cooking quarters. The daughter obeyed, but on the way back she dropped some of the glowing charcoal on the steps. The gale, blowing through an open window on the staircase, scattered the sparks onto the roof of an adjoining home, and the blaze was under way.

Flames leaped from home to home, leveling both the Armenian and Christian quarters in a matter of hours, and then roared to the docks on the Bosporus and up Feridje, the grand street that contained churches, shops, hospitals, legations and consulates.

The churches, hospitals and diplomatic missions were surrounded by stone walls and sustained little damage. Sir Henry Elliott, the British consul, only suffered a singed silk dressing gown, which he wore while directing fire prevention within his compound. But the damage to the remainder of the city was devastating: 900 dead, 3,000 buildings in ruins, and more than a square mile of Constantinople reduced to rubble.

UNITED STATES – CONNECTICUT, HARTFORD
July 6, 1944

The most tragic circus fire in history, the Ringling Brothers, Barnum & Bailey fire in Hartford, Connecticut on July 6, 1944, was caused by a combination of arson and a shortage of fireproof materials because of World War II. One hundred sixty-eight died; more than 480 were injured.

UNITED STATES – GEORGIA, ATLANTA
December 7, 1946

The worst hotel fire in U.S. history took place in the 'fireproof' Winecoff Hotel in Atlanta, Georgia on December 7, 1946. Caused by a smoldering mattress that burst into flames in a momentarily unattended corridor, it killed 119 and injured 100.

UNITED STATES – ILLINOIS, CHICAGO
October 8, 1871

A combination of a long drought, wooden construction and the overturning of a kerosene lantern in the O'Leary barn on DeKoven Street led to the Great Chicago Fire of October 8, 1871. Some 250 to 300 died, 90,000 were made homeless. There was $196 million in property damage.

UNITED STATES – ILLINOIS, CHICAGO
December 30, 1903

The worst theater fire in U.S. history, that of the Iroquois Theatre in Chicago on December 30, 1903, was caused by a combination of negligence in design, blocked fire exits, a snagged fire curtain, an absent stage manager and a calcium light igniting scenery. Five hundred ninety-one died and scores were injured in the resulting inferno.

UNITED STATES – ILLINOIS, CHICAGO
December 1, 1958

A lack of fire drill regulations led to tragedy in the fire, begun in a pile of trash in the basement, in Our Lady of the Angels grade school in Chicago on December 1, 1958. Ninety-three perished in the blaze.

UNITED STATES – MASSACHUSETTS, BOSTON
November 28, 1942

A smoldering match carelessly tossed onto an artificial palm caused the tragic fire in Boston's Cocoanut Grove Night Club on November 28, 1942. Four hundred ninety-one died, and hundreds were injured.

UNITED STATES – MINNESOTA
October 12, 1918

Ordinary spring and summer smolderings were fanned into Minnesota's worst forest fire by 60-mile-per-hour winds on October 12, 1918. Eight hundred people died.

UNITED STATES – MINNESOTA, HINCKLEY
September 1, 1894

Smoldering ashes on a forest floor were fanned into flames by a sudden burst of wind on September 1, 1894 near Hinckley, Minnesota. The resultant forest fire killed 413 people – one-third of the population of the town – and destroyed every building.

UNITED STATES – MISSISSIPPI, NATCHEZ
April 23, 1940

The ignoring of fire regulations by both owners and officials and a carelessly thrown match were the causes of the fire that devastated the Rhythm Night Club in Natchez, Mississippi on April 23, 1940. One hundred ninety-eight died; 40 were injured.

UNITED STATES – NEW JERSEY COAST
September 8, 1934

See MARITIME DISASTERS, *Morro Castle* (p. 263).

UNITED STATES – NEW JERSEY, HOBOKEN
June 30, 1900

A smoldering fire of unknown origin in cotton bales piled on the docks in Hoboken, New Jersey on June 30, 1900 suddenly burst into flames, igniting the entire docks and four German Lloyd ships loaded with Sunday sightseers. Three hundred twenty-six died in the blaze; 250 were injured.

UNITED STATES – NEW YORK, BRONX
March 25, 1990

In the worst mass murder in U.S. history, and the worst fire in New York City since the Triangle Shirtwaist tragedy of 1911, Julio Gonzalez set fire to the Happy Land Social Club in the East Tremont section of the Bronx, New York on March 25, 1990. Eighty-seven people perished in the blaze.

Exactly 79 years to the day after the Triangle Shirtwaist fire, which killed 149 young girls in New York City (see p. 238), the Happy Land Club, an illegal social club crowded with Honduran immigrants, was the scene of an infernal catastrophe that took the lives of 87 people at 3:30 A.M. on Sunday, March 25, 1990.

In March 1990, there were 177 illegal social clubs dotted throughout the five boroughs of New York City. Usually open only on weekends, and catering to groups of people united by ethnicity, nationality, geography or shared interests, they sold liquor illegally, allowed dancing without benefit of cabaret licenses and generally provided congenial, if illegitimate, neighborhood nights out.

The Happy Land Social Club was one of these illegal oases. Located on the west side of Southern Boulevard in the East Tremont section of the Bronx, in the heart of a Honduran community, it sported a stone face, painted red and adorned by a large sign that read:

HAPPY LAND SOCIAL CLUB INC.
LITTLE LEAGUE – PONY
FOR HIRE HALL
ALL SOCIAL EVENTS

A smiling face beamed down from the space between 'Happy' and 'Land.'

The club was 22 feet wide by 58 feet deep and was on two stories. On the left side was the entrance door, which led to a coat-check and admission area, where patrons paid a $5 cover charge. There was a bar at the rear of the downstairs room, and one in the same position upstairs, whose windowless upstairs room most people favored, since it contained a disc jockey and a dance floor. Celebrants paid $3 a drink to talk, sing and dance in the small, low-ceilinged room. A narrow, steep front staircase and a back set of stairs connected the two parts of the club.

'It was like a headquarters for Hondurans,' said Steven McGregor, who lived near the club and was interviewed by the *New York Times* after the fire. 'They threw parties every weekend.'

The club had been pronounced a firetrap by the city fire department, and its landlord had issued an eviction notice 10 months before for nonpayment of rent. On November 21, 1988, the city had ordered the building vacated because it lacked a second exit, a fire alarm and a sprinkler system. In the meantime there had been two arrests made for selling liquor without a license. On November 1, 1989, the police visited the club but found it padlocked. It always was during the week, neighbors said, and it was on a weekday that the police made their visit.

But March 24, 1990 was a Saturday, and the place was packed with noisy, friendly partygoers, except for one disgruntled customer. Early in the morning of Sunday the 25th, 36-year-old Julio Gonzalez came to the club, had two beers and had an argument with his former girlfriend, Lydia Feliciano, who worked there as a coat-check attendant.

Gonzalez was well known at the club and in the neighborhood. In 1980, he had deserted the Cuban Army and had fabricated a record of drug trafficking in Cuba in order to win expulsion to the United States in the 1980 Mariel boatlift. In the intervening 10 years between his arrival in New York City and the fateful night of March 25, 1990, he had worked at and been fired from various jobs. His latest job as a warehouse worker at a lamp company in Long Island City had terminated just six weeks earlier.

Most of the time, he lived as a street person who hustled money washing cars or peddling. He and Ms. Feliciano had lived together for eight years and had recently broken up, and for the past few days he had tried to convince her to come back to him. That night, in his entreaties and demands, he became loud, boisterous and profane. A bouncer, noting the escalating argument, kicked him out.

Gonzalez became furious and shouted a vow that he would shut down the club. He picked up a plastic jug that was sitting near its entrance, walked to a nearby Amoco station and bought $1 worth of gasoline. Returning to the Happy Land, he entered its one street door and encountered a lone man, who was exiting. He pretended to make a phone call on the pay phone in the hallway, until the other man was out of sight, and then poured a trail of gasoline from the street, through the entrance and into the inside hall. He drew out a match, tossed it into the gasoline and watched it ignite. Satisfied that it was burning, he turned and walked home.

Upstairs, the disc jockey, Ruben Valladares, began

his favorite Jamaican reggae song, 'Young Lover,' by Coco Tea.

'The floor got so full that a lot of people couldn't dance,' Felipe Figuero, one of the only three people on the second story of the club who would survive, later told a *Times* reporter. 'Then you heard it coming up the stairs.'

What he heard were shouts, from one of the club's two doormen. (The other was on the dance floor with his girlfriend.) He was yelling 'Fire! Fire!' and shoving his way through the mass of humanity.

'Right away, people went crazy,' said Figuero. 'Some ran this way and that way. Some people didn't make a big deal out of it. I could see a little smoke coming upstairs.'

The doorman shoved through the crowd, looking for his girlfriend, and Figuero took up the cry, in Spanish. 'Fuego!' he yelled, while his friend, disc jockey Ruben Valladares, turned up the lights and shouted 'Fuego!' into a microphone.

'People were already desperate,' continued Figuero. 'Everybody was running around.'

Figuero headed for the stairs. 'Everyone saw me go for it,' he said. 'I yelled "Down, let's go!" There were a lot of people around those stairs, but nobody followed me. I could hear all the cries, lots of people saying "Mama!" I heard something explode, like a light.'

It was the fire, roaring up and onto the second story. Figuero plunged down the stairs, into the smoke, threw himself against the crash bar of the back entrance to the club and found himself on the sidewalk with Ms. Feliciano and several patrons from the downstairs room.

A minute later, Ruben Valladares exploded through the door, his clothes in bright flames. 'He let out some screams that I remember too much,' Figuero said. 'I didn't even know who he was – he was so burned.' Valladares would survive, with burns over 50% of his body.

The fire had been set at 3:30 A.M. The alarm was turned in at 3:41 A.M. According to Albert Scardino, New York City Mayor David Dinkins' press secretary, fire equipment was there within three minutes. But it was already too late for 87 people.

Nineteen died from burns or smoke inhalation on the stairs or in the ground-floor room. But the greater number perished in a mountain of humanity that resembled the mass murders in the gas chambers of Auschwitz. The upstairs room, so low-ceilinged that the 5-foot, 6-inch tall Felipe Figuero could stand flat-footed and touch the mirrored, revolving globe suspended above its dance floor, contained precious little air under ordinary circumstances. When the flames reached it, they abruptly sucked all of the oxygen out of the room, and all of the second-floor victims died in seconds of suffocation and smoke inhalation.

'It was shocking,' First Deputy Mayor Norman Steisel told reporters afterward. 'None of the bodies I saw showed signs of burns. They looked waxen.' 'Some looked like they were crying,' one of the fire fighters from Ladder Company 58 told reporters. 'Some were horrified. Some looked like they were in shock. There were some people holding hands. There were some people who looked like they were trying to commiserate and hug each other. Some people had torn their clothing in their panic to get out.'

Later, emergency crews would break a hole through the wall of the upstairs room and into a construction office next door. They would drag the bodies through it and then take them to nearby Public School 67, which was turned into a temporary morgue. All day Sunday, its corridors were choked with grieving relatives and friends, who identified their loved ones through Polaroid pictures supplied by police officials.

Detectives, acting on information supplied by eye-witnesses, arrested Julio Gonzalez at his home that day. He offered no resistance and was brought before Bronx Criminal Court Judge Alexander W. Hunter Jr.

at 2 A.M. on March 26. There, Bronx District Attorney Robert T. Johnson charged Gonzalez with 87 counts of arson felony-murder and 87 counts of murder by depraved indifference to human life.

He went to trial in July 1991, pleading not guilty by reason of insanity. Justice Burton B. Roberts of the state supreme court denied a motion by the defense to suppress Gonzalez's admissions to detectives that he had set the fire, as well as physical evidence that included his sneakers containing residue from the gasoline that had been used to fuel the fatal blaze.

On August 19, 1991, the jury found Julio Gonzalez guilty on all charges, and he was sentenced to 25 years to life in prison, the maximum penalty under the law.

UNITED STATES – NEW YORK, BROOKLYN
December 5, 1876

A gaslight ignited scenery in the fly space of the Brooklyn Theatre in Brooklyn, New York on December 5, 1876. Two hundred ninety-five died; hundreds were injured.

UNITED STATES – NEW YORK, NEW YORK
March 17, 1899

New York's Windsor Hotel was totally destroyed by a fire on March 17, 1899 caused by a combination of a carelessly thrown match igniting dining room curtains, a stubborn policeman and St. Patrick's Day crowds. Ninety-two died; there is no record of the number of injuries.

UNITED STATES – NEW YORK, NEW YORK
June 15, 1904

See MARITIME DISASTERS, *General Slocum.*

UNITED STATES – NEW YORK, NEW YORK
March 25, 1911

One of the most tragic fires of all time, the Triangle Shirtwaist Factory fire in New York City on March 25, 1911, began unexplainably in a rag bin but was compounded by overcrowding, inadequate, decaying or bolted fire exits and fire escapes and a wholesale ignoring of safety regulations. One hundred forty-five died; scores were injured.

One of the grisliest and saddest fires ever to take place lasted a mere 18 minutes. If it had begun only 30 minutes later, it might have only consumed three floors of the 10-story Asch Building, located on the northwest corner of Greene Street and Washington Place in New York City. Instead, it took the lives of 145 young and trusting immigrant employees of the Triangle Shirtwaist Factory.

The factory, a sweatshop in the worst sense of the word, was located on the top three floors of the Asch Building and was owned and operated by Max Blanck and Isaac Harris. There were almost 800 such factories in New York in 1911. Because of a shortage of appropriate factory space, the top floors of existing buildings were commandeered as loft factories.

Working conditions were unbearable by today's standards – standards that began to be established as a result of the Triangle Shirtwaist Factory fire. On the eighth and ninth floors of the Triangle Shirtwaist loft, young women worked elbow to elbow at sewing machines that were arranged in long lines. The backs of the chairs on one line touched the backs of those on the next, making it difficult to move about. A few men, called cutters, worked at long tables nearby.

Most of the young workers were between 13 and 20 years old, and practically all were Italian, Russian, Hungarian and German immigrants who could speak little or no English. Most had worked up from messenger status, for which they had been paid $4.50 a week. They moved up to sewing on buttons for $6 a week and from there to the position of machine operator at $12. By working overtime – 13 hours a day, seven days a week – a few facile girls could and did earn as much as $18 a week.

There were exits from the building, but they were criminally inadequate. There were four elevators, but only one operated efficiently. Access to the elevator was down a long, narrow corridor that was made narrower by piled remnants, so that the girls would have to pass, single file, by inspectors, who examined their purses to make sure they did not steal anything.

There were two stairways leading to ground level, but the Washington Place doors were bolted shut and could not be opened from the inside – again, another device to keep the employees from stealing. The other door opened inward.

The only other exit was a decrepit fire escape, a foot and a half wide and rotting. After the blaze, it was estimated that it would have taken three hours for those working on the top three floors to descend it.

The Triangle Shirtwaist Factory had several fire buckets full of water lined up at its walls; there was a fire hose, but it had rotted to pieces long ago; there was a No Smoking sign, but it was regularly ignored and unenforced.

For years, safety regulators were aware of the dangerous conditions that existed in the brick buildings from Canal Street north to Eighth Street. A fire in one such building had taken the life of Assistant Fire Chief Charles W. Krueger. But the efforts of Fire Chief Edward Croker were frustrated by Wall Street interests, factory owners and the apathy of the city government.

The Triangle Shirtwaist owners were particularly arrogant in their defiance. They, after all, had been responsible for destroying the shirtwaist strike in 1910. It had started there and spread until 40,000 workers were out in the industry. Triangle refused to sign a contract and was credited with finally breaking the strike.

At 4:40 on Saturday afternoon, March 25, 1911, roughly 600 workers were working an overtime shift to make up for a backlog in orders. The narrow aisles were stacked with baskets of cut goods of lace and silk. On the cutting tables, layers of linen and cotton fabric were piled high. Huge bins were filled with scrap and waste material; the floor was littered with remnants. On overhead lines, finished shirtwaists were hung.

The shift was almost over; some employees had already begun to draw on their coats. And then, for a reason that has never been established, the fire started, in a rag bin on the Greene Street side of the eighth floor. It was tiny, and nobody noticed it until it had gotten an impressive, fatal start.

One of the women workers spotted it then and screamed 'Fire!' Factory manager Samuel Bernstein and foreman-tailor Max Rother, who were on the Washington Place side of the eighth floor, heard the cry and, grabbing fire buckets, raced to the fire. But it had gained too much headway to be snuffed out by two buckets of water. Other men rolled out the hose, which rotted away in their hands. The valve was rusted shut.

Now the flames leaped upward, igniting the shirtwaists that were hung overhead. Women shoved at one another, knocking over chairs as they tried to squeeze toward the exit from the room. The fire vaulted to a cutting table, setting a blaze there. The narrow hallway to the elevators became jammed with crying, terrorized women. The elevator held only 12 people, and its operator, Giuseppe Zito, could only make four or five round-trips before his car was rendered immovable by burned cables and the weight of the bodies of those who had flung themselves down the elevator shaft.

Those who got down the narrow staircase to the Greene Street exit ran into the inward-opening door. Scores of bodies piled up against it before some men bodily wrested the door open and shepherded a few frantic workers through.

On the Washington Place side of the building, workers piled up against the unyielding, bolted door. Tearing at one another's clothing, most of them died there as flames roared down the stairwell, burning them alive.

The fire had spread to the ninth floor now, where 300 more workers stampeded to escape the flames. On the 10th floor, in the executive offices, Blanck and Harris, along with Blanck's children and governess, who had come to visit him in his office, got to the roof and made their way to an adjacent building via a fire ladder.

Meanwhile, the eighth floor had become a raging inferno. Those who were trapped at the Washington Place exit were already blackened corpses. Some workers frantically tried to leave via the eighth-floor fire escape. Too flimsy to stand either heat or the weight thrown upon it, the iron ladder warped and then gave way. Those on it fell to the ground.

The fire roared on to the ninth floor. The heat was intense enough to curl sheet-iron shutters on a building 20 feet away.

The fire alarm had been turned in, and in moments, Engine Company Number 18, led by Foreman Howard Ruch, Company Number 72 and Hook and Ladder Company Number 20 were all there. But even though they arrived no more than eight minutes after the blaze began, they were too late. The most horrible phase of the drama had begun before they could get there.

Foreman Bernstein later told a UPI reporter that a shopgirl named Clotilda Terdanova was the first to jump from the building to her death. 'She tore her hair and ran from window to window,' he said, 'until finally, before anyone could stop her, she jumped out. She was young and very pretty. She was to leave us next Saturday to be married three weeks later.'

More and more women, some of them clinging together, jumped. It was literally raining bodies. The firemen could not unravel their hoses because of the smashed corpses piling on the sidewalks. Some finally did, and Battalion Chief Edward Worth used his first two lines to cool the building over the heads of the hysterical girls clinging to ledges and standing in windows. Then, a gust of wind sucked flames out of windows and onto the clothes of the trapped girls.

A cry of 'Raise your ladders! Raise your ladders!' came from the spectators who had begun to accumulate. A girl on a ninth-floor ledge waved a handkerchief, directing one of the ladders, which ascended toward her. But Chief Croker had warned long ago that their ladders would only reach to the seventh floor of any blazing building, and that is where the ladders stopped that afternoon. The girl, her skirt ablaze, leaped for the ladder 30 feet below her and missed. Her flaming body hit the sidewalk.

All of the fire hoses were now crushed by falling bodies, and no water was reaching the blaze. Company Number 18 spread the first life net, a new one 14 feet long. Three girls dove simultaneously from the ninth floor. When they landed, they ripped the net to shreds and pulled a dozen firemen inward on top of their bodies.

Company Number 20 set up a 20-foot Browder net. Bodies rained on it so rapidly that the tube steel frame buckled and gave way.

Two policemen improvised a blanket and caught one girl dead center. The blanket held for a minute and then gave way, and she crashed against the grating of a sky-light.

Another net received a girl who landed safely. Battalion Chief Worth pulled her upright. 'She blinked and said nothing,' Chief Worth later told reporters; 'I told her to "go right across the street." She walked ten feet – and dropped. She died in one minute.

'Life nets?' continued Worth. 'What good were they? The little ones went through life nets, pavement, and all. I thought they would come down one at a time.

I didn't know they would come with arms entwined – three and even four together.'

Bill Shepherd, the UPI reporter, wrote of the floods of water from the firemen's hoses that ran into the gutter. '[They] were actually red with blood. I looked upon the heap of dead bodies, and I remembered these girls were shirtwaist makers. I remembered their great strike of last year, in which these same girls had demanded more sanitary conditions and more safety precautions in the shops. These dead bodies were the answer.'

In 18 minutes, it was over. The doors on the ninth floor were chopped down, and the firemen quickly extinguished the flames. All of the damage had been done in the first 10 minutes. Firemen found 49 burned or suffocated bodies on the ninth floor. Thirty-six more were found at the bottom of the elevator shaft. Fifty-eight lay on the sidewalk. Two more would die of their injuries. All in all, 145 innocent, exploited young immigrants would perish in those terrible 10 minutes.

The reaction to the tragedy was immediate and immense. The Waistmakers Union organized a mass funeral for the victims, and 10,000 mourners attended. New York's East Side, from which most of the dead had come, seethed with anger. On April 5, more than 80,000 people marched up Fifth Avenue, following an empty hearse pulled by six horses draped in black.

The testimony at the trial of Harris and Blanck brought forth horrifying admissions. Safety expert H. F. Porter, who had pleaded with the Triangle owners to institute fire drills, told the *New York Times*, 'One man whom I advised to install a fire drill replied to me: "Let 'em burn. They're a lot of cattle, anyway." '

In December, a grand jury exonerated the Triangle owners of manslaughter charges, claiming that the bolted door might have been locked by an employee. The *New York Times* erupted in an editorial. 'The monstrous conclusion of the law is that the slaughter was no one's fault,' it thundered, 'that it couldn't be helped, or perhaps even that, in the fine legal phrase which is big enough to cover a multitude of defects of justice, it was "an act of God!" This conclusion is revolting to the moral sense of the community.'

But the country was shocked, and labor gained much. The International Ladies Garment Workers Union was formed as a direct result of the tragedy. The day of the sweatshop was nearing an end. Uniform fire and factory codes, led by New York's Sullivan-Hoey Fire Prevention Law of October 1911, were instituted all over the country. Fire Chief Edward Croker turned in his badge in order to lead a crusade for safety. Nothing would be quite the same in either fire prevention or factory working conditions ever again, and it had taken a tragedy of incredible proportions to bring this about.

UNITED STATES – OHIO, COLLINWOOD
March 4, 1908

The fire that began unexplainably in the boiler room of the Lake View School in Collinwood, Ohio on March 4, 1908 turned tragic because of blocked and faulty exits. One hundred seventy-six died; scores were injured.

UNITED STATES – OHIO, COLUMBUS
April 21, 1930

Arson and overcrowding conspired to intensify the fire in the Ohio State Penitentiary on April 21, 1930. Three hundred twenty-one died; 130 were injured in the resultant blaze.

UNITED STATES – WISCONSIN, PESHTIGO
October 8, 1871

The worst forest fire in U.S. history destroyed the entire town of Peshtigo, Wisconsin on October 8, 1871. No specific cause was recorded, but it was probably a combination of smoldering fires, a drought, indiscriminate logging and the burning of debris by railroads. Two thousand six hundred eighty-two people died in Peshtigo and the rest of Wisconsin, and hundreds were injured.

On October 8, 1871, the very day that the Great Chicago Fire began in Mrs. O'Leary's barn, the worst forest fire in the history of the United States started, 250 miles to the north of Chicago. It would claim 2,682 lives and level an area of 400 square miles of forest.

Peshtigo, built in the midst of an enormous forest a few miles from Green Bay, was a hugely successful logging town in 1871. It boasted 350 houses, three hotels, two churches, four saloons, a dozen stores, a sawmill and a woodenware factory. The Peshtigo River ran through the heart of town, and a large wooden bridge allowed those on one side of the settlement to get to the other. Most of Peshtigo's population of 2,000 was in the logging business, and they looked forward to the not too distant day when the Chicago and North-western Railroad would link their town with Milwaukee and Chicago.

All of the spring and summer preceding the fire was relentlessly dry. Early in July, a day of rain held out false hope. From then until September, no more rain fell. Springs began to dry up; rivers fell. During the summer, a number of small, fussy fires smoldered in dry peat bogs and in the webwork of roots that dried-up swamps revealed.

In August, citizens of Peshtigo carved a fireline out of the forest ringing the city. Accomplishing this, they felt safer, and when, on September 5, rain finally fell, they felt even more secure. But the rain was shortlived and inadequate, turning the forest into a steaming jungle. It was ripe for a forest fire, and the forest dwellers and logging interests only increased the danger by two foolish activities.

First, figuring that the rivers would soon be filled with water from expected rains, the logging interests continued to harvest trees. Limbs and slashings carpeted the forest floor.

Second, railroads cutting through the forest south of the city ignored the dryness of the brush around them and burned their debris.

Whether the final fire began from the spontaneous combustion of marsh gases, or the small smoldering fires finally burst into full-blown flames, or the railroaders kindled it with their fires, or a careless forest person began it, no one would ever determine. In fact, the fire itself received little notice in the press, except in the pages of Luther B. Noyes's three-month-old *Marinette and Peshtigo Eagle*, which published a Fire Extra on October 14 and has supplied practically all of the information on this fire for historians. The national Fourth Estate was too busy at the time with the Chicago Fire.

But to the people of Peshtigo, on the chilly Sunday of October 8, 1871, the approaching fire was very real. A pall of brownish smoke hung over them as they went to church to hear sermons warning of Judgment Day.

By seven o'clock that night, the wind had picked up, and ashes were beginning to fall on the city in a steady rain, much as if a volcano were erupting nearby. When the townspeople left services an hour later, a steady, full-throated roar could be heard nearby in the forest. Frightened, many of them went home, closed their doors and windows against the smoke and waited.

Meanwhile, farmers in the forest were in dire trouble. The flames of the fire were undeniably visible to them. By seven o'clock, huge tongues of flames licked at a score of farms and then rushed forward, consuming them. The network of paths through the woods became impassable, and forest animals began to mix with farm animals as they tried to escape the advancing fire.

One farmer gathered his wife and five children together into a wagon and tried to outrace the flames. They overtook them, killing everyone but the farmer.

By 9:00 P.M. church bells began to toll in Peshtigo, warning of the approaching inferno, which was now brutally apparent. The night was rimmed in the crimson glow of the fire advancing from the south. Cinders began to fall more rapidly on the city, setting small fires. The fire department shuttled between them, putting some out, being beaten back by others.

Now women began to gather up their children and, wrapping them in covers, fled to the streets with them. Sparks ignited trees within the city. Some townspeople began to turn toward the Peshtigo River.

Suddenly, a tornado-like gale whipped around the city, scattering a rain of fire. Sheets of flame and huge fire-brands began to fly through it. Balls of burning grass uprooted from the swamps and explosions of methane gas from the marshes rocked the night air.

The fleeing townspeople turned into a mob. Men joined the women and children. Those on one side of the river tried to reach the other side, and those on that side tried to cross the bridge at the identical moment. Two frantic, terrified mobs met each other at midspan, milling, fighting, tearing at each other. The bridge groaned and collapsed, flinging the mob into the river, where many drowned.

In the midst of this, the telegraph operator at the railroad station received some news that caused him to dash out into the street and inform nearby fire fighters: 'This fire is bigger than we thought. We just got a message on the telegraph from Green Bay. Chicago is burning!'

The fire fighters figured that it was indeed Judgment Day.

The firestorm erupted in another destroying wind. Flames roared through the city. Houses were bowled over. Roofs exploded from the tops of houses and flew through the superheated air. Burning trees became flaming battering rams. And the wall of fire roared on.

The air was so hot now that a person could burst into flames without being touched by fire at all. People simply became human torches, incinerated on the spot. Vacuum pockets developed in the air, and those who ran into them lost their breath, collapsed and died within a few steps.

Bizarre incidents flared up as easily as the fires set by the fire storm. One husky husband running through the streets toward the river with his wife in his arms collided with someone in the semidarkness brought on by the smoke. They all crashed to the ground. Frantically, he picked up his wife and continued toward the river. Reaching it, he plunged in up to his shoulders and set her down on her feet.

But it was not his wife. She was a total stranger. In the confusion after his fall, he had picked up the wrong woman. His wife was now a blackened corpse by the side of a road.

Another man dragged a heavy bed with his wife, who was suffering from a fever, in it to the river, where he submerged it to a depth that covered his wife's body but left her pillowed head above the surface. The family huddled together there all night and survived.

Still another man, realizing he was too far from the river to make it, decided to take refuge in a horse watering trough. He was boiled alive.

Terrified cattle stampeded through the streets, trampling some people. A hysterical man, rather than face death by fire, killed his wife and children and then slit his own throat. Another fastened a noose around his neck and hanged himself in his well. Seventy people huddled together in the middle of a cornfield were burned to death. And on the banks of the Peshtigo River that night, several pregnant woman gave premature birth.

The fire raged till dawn, unchecked. T. J. Teasdale, one of the survivors gave his story to the *Marinette and Peshtigo Eagle*:

When the fire struck the town it seemed to swallow up and drown everything . . . a fierce, devouring,

pitiless rain of fire and sand, so hot as to ignite
everything it touched . . .

Within three hours of the time the fire struck,
Peshtigo was literally a sand desert, dotted over with
smoking ruins. Not a hencoop or dry goods box was
left . . . Cattle and horses were burned in their stalls.
The Peshtigo Company's barn burned with over fifty
horses in the stable. A great many men, women and
children were burned in the streets, and in places so
far away from anything combustible that it would
seem impossible they should burn. But they were
burned to a crisp. Whole families, heads of families,
children were burned, and remnants of families were
running hither and thither, wildly calling and looking
for their relatives after the fire.

Peshtigo was no more. Monday morning dawned
silently. No dogs barked, no cows mooed, no birds
sang. Even the fish in the river were dead and floating
on its surface.

By afternoon, a steamer from nearby Marinette,
which had miraculously escaped the fire, arrived with
food and clothing and the news that 23 other towns had
been destroyed by the same inferno – Casco, DePere,
Shite Rock, Ahnepee, Elm Creek, Forestville, Little
Sturgeon Bay, Lincoln, Brussels and Rosiere among
them.

That night, it began to rain. It was more than the
usual rain that follows a fire storm. It would be the
beginning of 15 years of the most bountiful rainfall in
the history of Wisconsin.

The survivors in Peshtigo set about rebuilding their
city and retilling their land. Within three years, the
town would be rebuilt as a dairy center, which it is
today. But the worst forest fire in the history of the
nation would claim 1,182 lives in Peshtigo alone, and
1,500 others in the state of Wisconsin – an unenviable,
unbroken record.

Maritime Disasters

The Worst Recorded Maritime Disasters

* Detailed in text

Atlantic Ocean
* * *Andrea Doria/Stockholm* (1956)
* *Guiding Star* (1855)
* * *Lusitania* (1915)
* *Monarch of the Sea* (1866)
* * *Morro Castle* (1934)
* * *Titanic* (1912)

Baltic Sea
* * *Wilhelm Gustloff* (1945)

Bay of Gibraltar
* * *Utopia* (1891)

Belgium
* Zeebrugge
* * *Herald of Free Enterprise* (1987)

Canada
* Nova Scotia
* Halifax
* * *Atlantic* (1873)
* * *Mont Blanc* (1917) (see EXPLOSIONS)
* Sable Island
* * *La Bourgogne* (1898)
* Wingo Sound
* * *St. George/Defence* (1811)
* Quebec
* St. Lawrence River
* * *Empress of Ireland* (1914)

Cape of Good Hope
* * *St. James* (1586)

Caribbean Sea
* Near Veracruz, Mexico
* * *Grand Fleet* (1591)

Chile
* Valparaiso
* *L'Orriflame* (1770)

China
* Chusan Islands
* * *Hsin Yu* (1916)
* *Tai Ping* (1949)
* Manchuria
* Chinese Army vessel (1949)
* Swatow Harbor
* * *Hong Koh* (1921)
* Woosung
* * *Kiangya* (1948)
* Yangtze River
* Chinese troop carrier (1926)
* *Hsin Hsu-tung* (1928)

Egypt
* Safaga
* * *Salem Express* (1991)

English Channel
* * Spanish Armada (1588)

France
* La Rochelle
* * *Afrique* (1920)

Great Britain
* England
* London
* * *Marchioness* (1989)
* Spithead
* * *Royal George* (1792)
* Woolwich
* * *Princess Alice* (1878)
* Scotland
* * Rockall
* *Norge* (1904)

Gulf of Finland
  Leffort (1857)
Gulf of Mexico
  Flota de Nueva Espana
  (1590)
Haiti
  Port-au-Prince
  * *Neptune* (1993)
Hispaniola
  Spanish fleet (1502)
Holland
  Texel River
  * *Minotaur* (1810)
Hong Kong
  River steamer (1945)
India
  Indian Ocean
  Blenheim (1807)
  Madras
  * *Camorta* (1902)
  Manihari Ghat
  * Passenger ferry (1988)
Italy
  Leghorn
  * *Queen Charlotte* (1800)
Japan
  Hakodate
  * *Toyo Maru* (1954)
  Hokkaido
  Indigirka (1939)
  Sasebo
  Mikasa (1905)
  South coast
  * *Ertogrul* (1890)
  Kichemaru (1912)
  Tokyo Bay
  * *Kawachi* (1918)
Java Sea
  * *Tumponas II* (1981)
Labrador
  Egg Island
  * English Armada (1711)
Martinique
  French-Dutch convoy
  (1776)

Mexico
  Veracruz
  Flota de Neuva Espana
  (1600)
  *Neustra Senora de la
  Concepcion* (1732)
Myanmar (Burma)
  Gyang River
  * Ferry (1990)
New Zealand
  Auckland
  * *Cospatrick* (1874)
North Sea
  * *Scandinavian Star* (1990)
  York (1803)
Philippines
  Tablas Strait
  * *Dona Paz/Victor* (1987)
Romania
  Galati
  * *Mogosoaia* (1989)
Turkey
  Constantinople
  Neiri Shevket (1850)
United States
  Florida
  Coast
  * *Capitanas* (1715)
  Gulf of Florida
  Narvaez expedition (1528)
  Keys
  Spanish convoys (1622)
  Tampa
  Spanish expedition
  (1559)
  Illinois
  Chicago
  * *Eastland* (1915)
  New York
  New York
  * *General Slocum* (1904)
  Tennessee
  Memphis
  * *Sultana* (1865) (see
  EXPLOSIONS)

Venezuela
    Aves Island
    French fleet (1678)

West Indies
    Mona Passage
    Sisters (1787)

Chronology

* Detailed in text

1502
July
    Hispaniola
    Spanish fleet
1528
Sept. 22
    Gulf of Florida
    Narvaez expedition
1559
    Tampa, Florida
    Spanish expedition
1586
    Cape of Good Hope
    * *St. James*
1588
August–October
    English Channel
    * Spanish Armada
1590
July
    Gulf of Mexico
    Flota de Nueva Espana
1591
Aug. 10
    Caribbean Sea near
        Veracruz
    * Grand Fleet
1600
Sept. 12
    Veracruz
    Flota de Nueva Espana
1622
Sept. 6
    Florida Keys
    Spanish convoys

1678
May 3
    Aves Island, Venezuela
    French fleet
1711
Aug. 22
    Egg Island, Labrador
    * English Armada
1715
July 31
    Florida coast
    * Capitanas
1732
January
    Veracruz
    *Nuestra Senora de la
        Concepcion*
1770
    Valparaiso, Chile
    L'Orriflame
1776
Sept. 6
    Martinique
    French-Dutch convoy
1787
    Mona Passage, West
        Indies
    Sisters
1792
Aug. 29
    Spithead, Great Britain
    * *Royal George*
1800
Mar. 17
    Leghorn, Italy
    * *Queen Charlotte*

1803
North Sea
York

1807
Feb. 1
Indian Ocean
Blenheim

1810
Dec. 22
Texel River, Holland
* *Minotaur*

1811
Dec. 24
Wingo Sound, Nova
Scotia, Canada
* *St. George/Defence*

1850
Oct. 23
Constantinople, Turkey
Neiri Shevket

1855
Jan. 9
Atlantic Ocean
Guiding Star

1857
Sept. 23
Gulf of Finland
Leffort

1865
Mar. 26
Memphis, Tennessee
* *Sultana* (see EXPLOSIONS)

1866
April 3
Atlantic Ocean
Monarch of the Sea

1873
April 1
Halifax, Nova Scotia
* *Atlantic*

1874
Nov. 17
Auckland, New Zealand
* *Cospatrick*

1878
Sept. 3
Woolwich, Great Britain
* *Princess Alice*

1890
Sept. 19
South coast, Japan
* *Ertogrul*

1891
Mar. 17
Bay of Gibraltar
* *Utopia*

1898
July 4
Sable Island, Nova Scotia
* *La Bourgogne*

1902
April
Madras, India
* *Camorta*

1904
June 15
New York, New York
* *General Slocum*
June 28
Rockall, Scotland
* *Norge*

1905
Sept. 10
Sasebo, Japan
Mikasa

1912
April 14
Atlantic Ocean
* *Titanic*
Sept. 28
Mikasa, Japan
Kichemaru

1914
May 29
St. Lawrence River,
Quebec
* *Empress of Ireland*

1915
May 1
    Atlantic Ocean
  * *Lusitania*
July 24
    Chicago, Illinois
  * *Eastland*
1916
Aug. 29
    Chusan Islands, China
  * *Hsin Yu*
1917
Dec. 30
    Halifax, Nova Scotia
  * *Mont Blanc* (see
     EXPLOSIONS)
1918
July 12
    Tokyo Bay, Japan
  * *Kawachi*
1920
Jan. 12
    La Rochelle, France
  * *Afrique*
1921
Mar. 18
    Swatow Harbor, China
  * *Hong Koh*
1926
Oct. 16
    Yangtze River
    Chinese troop carrier
1928
Aug. 15
    Yangtze River, China
    Hsin Hsu-tung
1934
Sept. 8
    Atlantic Ocean
  * *Morro Castle*
1939
Dec. 12
    Hokkaido Island
    Indigirka

1945
Jan. 30
    Baltic Sea
  * *Wilhelm Gustloff*
Nov. 8
    Hong Kong, China
    Chinese river steamer
1948
Dec. 3
    Woosung, China
  * *Kiangya*
1949
Jan. 27
    Chusan Islands, China
    Tai Ping
1954
Sept. 26
    Hakodate, Japan
  * *Toyo Maru*
1956
July 25
    Atlantic Ocean
  * *Andrea Doria/Stockholm*
1981
Jan. 27
    Java Sea
  * *Tamponas II*
1987
Mar. 6
    Zeebrugge, Belgium
  * *Herald of Free Enterprise*
Dec. 20
    Tablas Strait, Philippines
  * *Dona Paz/Victor*
1988
Aug. 6
    Manihari Ghat, India
  * Indian passenger ferry
1989
Aug. 20
    London, England
  * *Marchioness*
Sept. 10
    Galati, Romania
  * *Mogosoaia*

1990
April 7
North Sea
* *Scandinavian Star*
April 7
Gyang River, Myanmar
(Burma)
* Ferry

1991
Dec. 14
Safaga, Egypt
* *Salem Express*
1993
Feb. 21
Port-au-Prince, Haiti
* *Neptune*

Maritime Disasters

For those who could afford it, there was no more romantic or peaceful way to travel abroad than on a transatlantic ocean liner. Those leviathans of the North Atlantic and the South Pacific were self-contained cities, and like the great cities of the world, each had its own personality. The Cunard Line, for instance, was definitely British and guarded the doors between first, cabin and tourist class. On the French Line, sybaritic considerations – a shortage of men for the after-dinner revels in first class, for instance – sometimes relaxed those same barriers. The Italian Line was similarly relaxed, as was the round-the-world Moore-McCormick Line.

But what distinguished these liners from the dull world as it was, was a sense of opulence married to a sense of fun. Although the present resurgence of cruise liners is a welcome testament to people's need for the sea, they are really pale imitations of the real thing. Floating summer camps, they cannot begin to approximate the dignified feeling of comfort and relaxation unto relief that life aboard the grand transatlantic liner offered its passengers.

Perhaps it was the long tradition of sailing that reaches back to the Phoenicians that made it so comfortable and even insular. There was a feeling of being cared for that was almost familial, and perhaps that was necessary, for the sea has been, and always will be, the master of all it surveys, borders on, or floats.

Aboard one of these posh, floating metropolises, one never really felt threatened by the sea, only occasionally tormented. Storms at sea were only fun for the very stalwart, and there were those to whom even the gentle sway of the grand saloon was too much for their centers of equilibrium. Seasickness is not fun, as anyone who has experienced it will attest.

But that was the only drawback to this supremely romantic and restful way of travel.

Still, disasters did occur at sea, and this section details the worst of them.

The criterion for inclusion in this section was mainly a mathematical one. Since most passenger ships carry upwards of 3,000 passengers, a cutoff figure of 100 deaths was employed in the majority of cases (one exception is the 1956 sinking of the *Andria Doria*, which is included in this book despite a lower number of fatalities.) Sadly enough, there were more than enough maritime disasters that fit within that parameter.

As in other categories of man-made catastrophes, wartime sinkings were, with one exception, not recorded. The one exception, the torpedoing of the German transport *Wilhelm Gustloff* by an unidentified Soviet submarine in the waning years of World War II (see p. 271), is so monumental in its all-time record toll of human life that no book which pretends to be comprehensive could ignore it, despite the fact that, to this day, little more than the bare statistics are available.

ATLANTIC OCEAN
July 25, 1956

The Andrea Doria *sank to the bottom of the Atlantic Ocean on July 25, 1956 after the SS* Stockholm *rammed it. Forty-three passengers, all aboard the* Andrea Doria, *died.*

ATLANTIC OCEAN
May 1, 1915

A torpedo from a German U-boat sank the Cunard liner Lusitania *on May 1, 1915 in the Atlantic Ocean off the coast of Ireland. One thousand one hundred ninety-eight drowned or were killed by the explosion.*

The transatlantic steamship companies vied with one another throughout the lush years of transatlantic ship travel to win the 'Blue Riband' for having the fastest ship afloat. In the early years of the century, the 'riband' floated back and forth between Germany, America and Great Britain. In 1903, the German Lloyd Lines possessed it, and it was then that the British Admiralty helped the Cunard Line to build two of the most luxurious and fastest liners afloat. In return, Cunard agreed to include fittings that would allow the ships to be taken over by the Admiralty and used as armed cruisers during wartime.

The first of the two ships was the *Lusitania*, which began its maiden voyage on September 7, 1907 from Liverpool. She was the largest ship afloat at the time and one of the most luxurious. And by the end of her second westbound voyage, on October 5, 1907, she was also the fastest. At an average speed of 23.99 knots, from Queenstown to Ambrose Light, she had clearly won the Blue Riband for England.

In November 1907, the *Lusitania*'s sister ship, the *Mauretania*, was launched, and proved to be the *Lusitania*'s only serious competition. The two passed the ribbon back and forth until 1909, when the *Mauretania* won it and kept it for the next 22 years.

In May 1913, as war drew closer in Europe, the *Lusitania* was secretly refitted. The number one boiler room was converted to a powder magazine, and a second magazine was carved out from part of the mail room. The shelter deck was adapted to accommodate four six-inch guns on either side. When war broke out, in September 1914, the *Lusitania* entered the Admiralty fleet as an armed auxiliary cruiser but continued to make the Liverpool–Queenstown–New York run on a monthly basis.

During the last few days of April, she was loaded, at New York, with 1,248 cases of three-inch shrapnel shells, 4,927 boxes of cartridges, 1,639 ingots of copper, 74 barrels of fuel oil and several tons of food supplies. She was obviously not setting out on an exclusively peaceful ocean crossing, and most of the 2,165 passengers were blissfully unaware of the lethal and dangerous cargo upon which they were sitting, sipping their bouillon.

The ship left New York at noon on May 1, 1915 with Captain William Thomas Turner on the bridge. It was her 101st crossing. All went well and serenely until May 6, when Captain Turner received bulletins from the Admiralty advising him of German submarine activity off the Irish coast. The captain ordered all of the lifeboats hanging on davits to be swung out and lowered to the promenade deck, doubled the watch on the bridge, bow and stern and blacked out all of the passenger portholes.

The cruiser *Juno* was supposed to escort the *Lusitania* from the vicinity of the Irish coast to home port, but for some unexplained reason, she was never ordered out.

On Friday afternoon, May 7, 1915, Kapitan-Leutnant Walter Schwieger gazed through the periscope of his submarine, *U-20*, and spotted the *Lusitania*, steaming straight ahead at a conservative 18 knots. At 2:10 P.M., the *U-20* fired one torpedo, which struck the *Lusitania* on its starboard side, squarely behind the ammunition-loaded number-one boiler room. Within seconds, there was a larger explosion as the ammunition cache ignited.

The *Lusitania* immediately began to list to starboard, rendering her lifeboats on that side useless. Passengers scrambled to the usable lifeboats, but there were far too few to take the passengers off the fast-sinking ship. It only took 18 minutes for the *Lusitania* to go down off Old Head at Kinsale, Ireland. Out of 1,159 passengers and 702 crew members, only 374 passengers and 289 crew members survived. One thousand one hundred ninety-eight were either drowned or killed in the twin explosions.

Survivors sued Cunard for negligence, but on August

23, 1918 a court in New York exonerated the line, stating: 'The cause of the *Lusitania* sinking was the illegal act of the Imperial German government, through its instrument, the submarine commander.' By then, the *Lusitania* had become a rallying cry of indignation, particularly useful in convincing those in the United States not inclined to join the war in Europe that it was a necessity.

ATLANTIC OCEAN
September 8, 1934

Negligence on the part of the crew and the ship line was responsible for the fire that eventually sank the Morro Castle *in the Atlantic Ocean on September 8, 1934. One hundred thirty-seven died.*

ATLANTIC OCEAN
April 14, 1912

Overconfidence in design and a collision with an iceberg caused the sinking of the 'unsinkabe' Titanic *on April 14, 1912. One thousand five hundred seventeen died.*

A virtually unsinkable ship.

The *Titanic*, announced the British White Star Line, would not only be the most luxurious liner afloat. Its individual watertight compartments would also make it virtually impossible for the new and giant liner to sink at sea. The company of course knew that if more than five of the watertight compartments were breached at once, the *Titanic* would sink. But the odds against that were astronomical, and so the maiden voyage of this truly titanic liner – 882.5 feet long, 92.5 feet broad and 104 feet high, capable of a cruising speed of 30 knots, with crystal chandeliers and sweeping staircases, inlaid wood in first class, a special lounge for the servants of the wealthy and the most up-to-date marine machinery available – was perfection at sea. However there were not enough lifeboats.

That was only one of many human failings that caused the terrible tragedy of the sinking of the *Titanic*, which has been recounted over and over in books and on film. Its last hours were packed with enough foolishness, bravery and cowardice to fill at least half a shelf of adventure novels. And the lessons learned from them would make transatlantic travel considerably safer for future voyagers.

The *Titanic* made ready for its maiden voyage on April 10, 1912. Its itinerary: Southampton to Cherbourg to Queenstown to New York. Its complement after leaving Queenstown: 322 passengers in first class, 277 in second class, 709 in third class and a crew of 898. Total: 2,206. Its lifeboat capacity: 20 lifeboats with a total capacity of 1,178.

The passenger list was democratic enough: Third class contained immigrants; second class contained the middle class; and the first-class list was packed with the world famous and the wealthy.

The beau monde was eager to try new inventions, such as the radio. Thus, on Sunday, April 14, as the *Titanic* was nearing the end of its silken smooth and memorable maiden voyage, the radio room aboard the *Titanic* was flooded with personal messages to be forwarded to Cape Race and on to America. John Phillips, the wireless operator, was inundated with them, so much so that he grew careless about the repeated warnings sent by ships in the area about the presence of icebergs.

It had been a warm winter, and an unusual number of icebergs had broken off the polar cap and were floating southward. Still, the White Star Line had charted a course for the *Titanic* that they felt would carry it safely away from the ice and its dangers. At noon, Phillips received a message from the *Baltic*. 'Have had moderate variable winds and clear fine weather since leaving,' it read. 'Greek steamer *Athenai* reports passing icebergs and large quantities of field ice today in Latitude 41.51 degrees north, Longitude 49.52 degrees west.'

In the first in a string of stupidities, the message was passed, not to the bridge, but to White Star president Bruce Ismay, who was aboard for this celebratory voyage. He showed it around to the ladies in the first-class lounge but then stuffed it into his pocket and forgot it until 7:15 that evening, when he finally delivered it to the chartroom.

More messages poured into the radio room from the passengers, and these missives took precedence over two receptions from two other ships, either one of which might have saved the *Titanic*. At 7:30, the freighter *Californian* radioed the *Antillian*, reporting three large icebergs. At 9:30, the *Meshaba* contacted the *Titanic* directly, warning that 'much heavy pack ice and a great number of large icebergs' lay ahead. Neither of these messages was delivered to the bridge.

At 11 P.M. the *Titanic* received one last warning. Just before he shut down his radio for the night, the radioman aboard the *Californian* directly contacted the *Titanic* to announce that the *Californian* was totally hemmed in by ice and had stopped engines. It was close enough to the *Titanic* to see its lights. Radioman John Phillips, his patience worn to a nub by the mountain of transmissions he had made that day, snapped back, 'Shut up, shut up, I am busy!' – thus sealing the fate of the *Titanic* and the 2,000 aboard.

Meanwhile, Captain Edward Smith, denied the information he should have been receiving, was working on the instinct that had made him an experienced and respected captain. Sensing the sharp drop in temperature, he posted six lookouts to watch for ice and kept the speed at a steady 22.5 knots. First Officer William Murdock also kept sharp eyes out for ice.

At 11:40 P.M., lookout Frederick Fleet yelled out, 'Iceberg! Right ahead!'

Murdock snapped out the order to Quartermaster

Hitchens, 'Turn the wheel hard-a-starboard!' Then he yanked the engine-room telegraph to full speed astern and pushed the button closing all of the watertight doors.

Silent seconds passed. Nothing occurred. And then a telltale shudder ran through the ship, sending it trembling from bow to stern. The ship had missed colliding directly with the iceberg. But an underwater knifelike edge of ice had struck the *Titanic*'s steel plates on her starboard side, and sliced a gash beneath the water line long enough to flood the first six compartments, which included the number-five and number-six boiler rooms.

Passengers in third class felt the collision, knew what had happened and panicked. Those in second class were moderately alarmed. Some were amused. Some who had left their portholes open found chunks of ice on their bunks. In first class, the passengers still up and about merely watched the iceberg glide by and went back to playing cards.

Captain Smith, conferring with Thomas Andrews, the designer of the *Titanic*, immediately knew the worst had happened. The ship could have stayed afloat if up to four of her watertight compartments flooded. But with *six* flooded and filling, there was no hope. She would definitely sink.

At 11:50, Captain Smith ordered radioman Phillips to send out the CQD international call for help. Second operator Bride suggested to Phillips that he also tap out the new SOS signal. Phillips did, and the *Titanic* became the first vessel in distress to use the new code.

The North German Lloyd steamer *Frankfurt* answered first. Shortly after this, the Cunard Liner, *Carpathia*, some 58 miles away, received the distress call and immediately changed course, stoking her boilers to the bursting point and disregarding her own safety by steaming full speed toward the ailing *Titanic*. It would be the *Carpathia* that would rescue most of the survivors.

Meanwhile, the icy Atlantic was pouring into the

Titanic at frightening speed. In the first 10 minutes, the water rose 14 feet above the keel.

At 12:10, Captain Smith ordered the lifeboats to be uncovered and women and children to be placed in them first. There had been no lifeboat drill; no instruction in donning life jackets had been given. The passengers were bewildered. But only the top officers and Bruce Ismay knew the worse truth: There were 1,028 fewer spaces in the lifeboats than there were people aboard. The outlook was catastrophic. Before the night was out, more than half the persons climbing toward what they fully expected would be rescued would be dead.

Fifth Officer Harold Lowe was in charge of guiding passengers onto lifeboats, and by all accounts, he was unable to maintain the kind of even-handed calmness necessary to bring about an orderly and efficient evacuation. The first lifeboat, number 14, was launched with 55 people aboard. But it would be one of the fuller boats. Number one carried only 12 people – Sir Cosmo and Lady Duff Gordon, her secretary, two Americans, six stokers and Symons, one of the lookout men. And so it went, with an average of 40 people per lifeboat that should have carried 65.

The first-class passengers, first at the lifeboats, were treated with preference. Only four of the women in first class died, three of them by choice when they refused to leave their husbands. Of the 93 women in second class, 15 survived; out of 179 women in third class, only 81 were saved. In fact, at one point, the doors between the third-class section and the upper-class sections were locked. Eventually, the rioting third-class passengers broke through.

There was an almost eerie calmness about the way some passengers met their deaths. Mr. and Mrs. Isador Straus, two millionaires, sat side by side as the ship went down; John Jacob Astor saw his wife safely into a lifeboat and then settled into a chair in the sumptuous first-class lounge to face his fate; Benjamin

Guggenheim and his valet went to their cabins, donned evening dress and sat in splendor as they awaited the inevitable.

Only after the last first-class woman was in a boat were the third-class passengers allowed onto the boat deck. Some leaped from escape ladders into the water. Others milled about without direction.

Meanwhile, down below, last, frantic efforts were being made to pump out two of the watertight compartments. They failed, and shortly after midnight, the captain ordered the crew to abandon ship. The last lifeboat, a collapsible one, carried four crewmen and 45 passengers, including White Star president Ismay, who leaped into the boat at the last minute, despite the fact that there were still women and children who had not been taken into the lifeboats.

One thousand five hundred seven passengers were still aboard the ship, and some of them now leaped into the frigid water. Captain Smith had ordered distress rockets to be launched into the sky, and the *Californian*, a mere 20 miles away, saw them and did nothing. Its captain thought they were celebratory.

Chaos continued on the ship and in the sea. Most of the half-empty lifeboats did nothing to rescue those who were struggling, drowning, and freezing in the water. In lifeboat number five, the women refused to allow the officer to search for survivors, despite the fact that they were in the midst of them. In lifeboat number six, just the opposite occurred; women pleaded with crewmen to try to rescue survivors in the water, but the crewmen rowed stoically away from the *Titanic*. Only Fifth Officer Lowe apparently made a concerted effort to rescue the drowning swimmers. He tied his lifeboat to three others and a collapsible craft and circled around to pick up whomever he could. But he was one of the last to leave the ship, and he only plucked four survivors from the icy Atlantic. Only 13 were pulled out of the water by 18 partially loaded lifeboats.

At 2:20 A.M., the *Titanic* began her final dive. The boilers exploded and, loosed from their anchoring supports, rushed forward. With the sound, according to one survivor, of a long freight train leaving the tracks, the huge, unsinkable ship pointed her bow toward the bottom, rose almost perpendicular to the surface of the black water around her and slid beneath the surface. Her decks were full of passengers; her band, who had tried to maintain calm by playing ragtime tunes during the evacuation, struck up the Episcopal hymn 'Autumn'; Captain Smith, who had decided to retire from the sea after this voyage, remained on the bridge and went down with his ship.

A whirling vortex was created, drowning some of the swimming survivors. The rest, who would live, pulled on the oars of their lifeboats, away from the spot where the *Titanic* once sailed.

Within an hour, the *Carpathia*, with all of her lights ablaze, arrived on the scene. Between 4:45 and 8:30, she rescued 705 survivors from the lifeboats. There were no survivors left alive in the sea.

At 5:40 A.M., the radio operator aboard the *Californian* opened his radio channels and learned, to his horror, what had happened less than 20 miles away.

Bruce Ismay, who had locked himself up in the doctor's cabin as soon as he had been brought aboard the *Carpathia*, was later exonerated by the British board of inquiry, although he was severely chastised by the American one. The blame for the *Titanic*'s sinking was placed on the captain and his senior officers for failure to take notice of the four ice warnings that had been received. None of them could answer the charges; all had gone down with the ship.

The captain of the *Californian* was also blamed for not going to the aid of the *Titanic*, even though the radio was, as was the custom in 1912, shut down for the night when the distress calls went out.

The horrific tragedy did produce some positive safety measures for future transatlantic passengers. The required number of lifeboats was revised to accommodate the maximum – rather than the minimum – number of passengers aboard. Boat drill became mandatory. And most important, international regulations requiring radios to remain open and functioning 24 hours a day were instituted, so that cataclysms like that of the *Titanic* could never occur again.

The story of the *Titanic* did not end with the official inquiry. Full of irony, cowardice, bravery and noble self-sacrifice, it became not only the model for seagoing adventure stories for decades to come but also the object of speculation for adventurers. On September 1, 1985, a team of American and French researchers, jointly sponsored by the American Woods Hole Oceanographic Institute and the French Insitute for Research and Exploitation of the Sea, finally reached the wreck of the *Titanic*, 73 years after it plunged 13,000 feet to the bottom of the North Atlantic. Murky television and still pictures revealed a ravaged but impressive hulk. Eleven more dives in 1986, in the submersible *Alvin*, revealed that the *Titanic* had split in two on its way to the bottom. Both pieces of the ship were standing upright on the ocean bottom, with the 300-foot bow section embedded in 50 feet of mud some 1,800 feet away from the stern, and both of them in such total darkness that hardly any marine life lived on or near them.

Even now, intrigue and controversy swirl around the *Titanic*. Talk of salvage has arisen on one side of opinion. Relatives of those who perished argue that the wreck is really a gigantic tomb, the final resting place of 1,517 people, and should remain undisturbed.

The oceanographers have refused to reveal the exact location of the wreck, lest fortune hunters try to rob the ship of the staggering wealth that supposedly sank with it. And so, the *Titanic* continues to generate its own unique and legendary aura, a mysterious, glamorous source of stories and speculation.

**BALTIC SEA
January 30, 1945**

*The most tragic and underreported maritime disaster in
history occurred on January 30, 1945 when an unidentified Soviet submarine torpedoed the* Wilhelm Gustloff,
*loaded with refugees, in the Baltic Sea. Five thousand
three hundred forty-eight people died – some records say
7,200.*

Inexplicably, the worst, most tragic maritime disaster
of all time, one that may have killed nearly five times
the number of those drowned in the *Titanic* tragedy and
more than the sinking of the entire English and Spanish
armadas in the 16th century, has gone virtually unrecorded. Missing from all but a few histories of World
War II, it is given a glancing reference every now and
then in stories of other, lesser sinkings. It took place
during World War II, but even exhaustive studies of
naval warfare of that period fail to mention it. It is
almost as if the world has drawn a curtain of shame
around this, possibly the most tragic of all disasters that
ever occurred at sea.

The *Wilhelm Gustloff* was a passenger liner that
belonged to Germany's Labor Front. Named after
Wilhelm Gustloff, the Swiss official of the Nazi Party
who was murdered on February 2, 1936, it was
launched on July 25, 1937. An imposing ship, weighing
25,484 tons, it was 695 feet long and 78 feet wide, had
10 decks and accommodated 1,465 passengers and a
crew of 417.

Before it could be put into service as a passenger
liner, the *Wilhelm Gustloff* was absorbed by the navy of
the Third Reich and did not sail on its maiden voyage
until March 23, 1938. Fitted out as a hospital ship and
troop carrier, it was berthed in Gotenhafen, in the
north of Germany, on the Baltic Sea.

By 1945, as World War II was drawing to a close,
the sea war between Germany and the Allies was

largely over. The Soviet fleet had not been particularly effective. Its main force, bottled up in the Gulf of Finland by the German Navy, did manage, nevertheless, to delay the Nazi advance through Poland and the eastern USSR. In the Baltic Sea it launched raids on small surface vessels and aircraft, mosquito fleets of motor-torpedo boats and other light craft and some submarines.

By late January 1945, the *Wilhelm Gustloff* had been repeatedly bombed and repaired and pressed back into service.

At 7 P.M. on January 30, 1945, she left the harbor of Gdynia, Poland, a few miles north of Danzig (now Gdansk). Jammed on all 10 of its decks, including the open ones, were German military personnel, technicians, female merchant sailors and an enormous number of civilian refugees trying to escape the advance of the Russian troops toward Danzig.

She must have rested extremely low in the frigid January water. Various reports said that she had up to 10,000 passengers and crew aboard. The official German estimate, reported in *Das Groose Lexicon Des Zweiten Welterkriegs*, was 6,600 – which seems more plausible, considering that she was originally designed to carry a total of 1,882, including crew.

It was a bitterly cold night; one can only imagine the monumental discomfort of those crammed on the open deck. Their only comfort was the knowledge that the voyage was to be a short one, to Kiel-Flensburg, on the sheltered peninsula of Germany that juts up and almost joins Denmark.

Two hours from Gdynia, barely into the Baltic, and off Stolpmunde, the *Wilhelm Gustloff* was torpedoed by an unidentified Soviet submarine. At precisely 9:08, she received the full force of the submarine's torpedoes. There was no hope for most of the passengers. One thousand two hundred fifty-two of them did manage to find spaces in lifeboats and rafts (some accounts, broadcast by Finnish radio, said that only 900 did), and these survived.

But the crammed decks and compartments of the hapless ship were jammed with far more people than there were spaces in the lifeboats. The ship sank swiftly. The temperature at the time was −18 degrees centigrade, or slightly less than 0 degrees Fahrenheit.

According to German historians 5,348 (or 7,700 according to other historical sources) passengers were left stranded on its ice-encrusted deck, without a means of escape. They perished instantly and passed into a black abyss of almost totally un-recorded history.

BAY OF GIBRALTAR
March 17, 1891

A storm-caused collision with the British battleship Amson *caused the sinking of the steamer* Utopia *on March 17, 1891 in the Bay of Gibraltar. Five hundred seventy-six passengers and crew died.*

BELGIUM – ZEEBRUGGE
March 6, 1987

One hundred eighty-eight people drowned and 97 were hospitalized when the Channel ferry Herald of Free Enterprise *capsized on the night of March 6, 1987, just after leaving Zeebrugge, Belgium for Dover. Human error and corporate carelessness were the causes of the disaster.*

'From top to bottom, the body corporate was affected with the disease of sloppiness,' said Lord Justice Sir Barry Sheen, as he concluded the official investigation of the *Herald of Free Enterprise* disaster. The captain of the 7,951-ton Channel ferry was suspended for one year; the first officer for two. Townsend Car Ferries Ltd. was soundly thrashed in the international press for corrupting the meaning of the name of the ship and bringing on more apparently necessary governmental regulations.

On Friday evening, March 6, 1987, the ship – a car and passenger ferry, and one of the new, fast, 'roll on, roll off' superships capable of generating increased revenue by moving people and vehicles off and on rapidly – carried 543 passengers on three decks and 84 cars and 36 trucks in its huge, hangarlike bay below. Passengers drove their vehicles onto the boat through huge doors in the deck and stern, then ascended to the passenger levels.

The *Herald of Free Enterprise* normally made the Dover-to-Calais run across the English Channel, but in March of 1987, she had been shifted to the Dover-to-Zeebrugge, Belgium route because of the refitting of other vessels and a change in the winter schedule.

It was company policy to leave with the bow-loading doors open, and then close them before the boat cleared the shelter of the port. This was the procedure that was followed as the ferry left Zeebrugge at 7 p.m. on a calm and clear night. But something went woefully wrong. The bow doors failed to close. The crew member normally in charge of securing them had been relieved, and was dozing in his cabin. That, too, was routine. If he was not available, others took on the task.

Those others were observed by some horrorstricken passengers to be frantically pounding on the giant hydraulic doors with sledge hammers, trying to force them to close before the *Herald of Free Enterprise* hit the open sea.

The captain plowed on, full speed ahead, past the breakwater. And as he did, the *Herald of Free Enterprise*, like a thirsty whale, gulped in tons of water. The sea roared into the cavern of the vehicle compartment, flinging cars and trucks and crewmen against the thin bulkheading. Within moments, the weight of the constantly increasing intake of water and the displaced cars and trucks tipped the boat to port. It heeled over rapidly and capsized, submerging its passenger decks.

'All the glasses were flying [around the dining room],' said survivor Susan Hames to reporters afterward. 'As the ship went over there were people falling, and there was so much glass.' Walls became floors; ceilings became walls; people piled up on each other, and careening furniture threatened them. Crewmen pulled distraught passengers up improvised ladders; other passengers swam into the icy waters, holding on to anything they could find.

'They came flying down, tumbling on top of me, screaming,' said William Cardwell, a port-side passenger. 'I thought I was going to die, it was over.'

It took slightly over a minute for the *Herald of Free Enterprise* to dig herself into 30 feet of water just outside the breakwater of Zeebrugge. 'It was terrible,' said a port worker who received the first survivors. 'There were women crying because they couldn't find their husbands. There were children clinging to life preservers. Some were in terrible shock.'

And some were trapped in the boat, and would remain there for days. It had all happened within twenty minutes of leaving the dock, less than a mile from the port, on a starry night in clear, calm seas.

The rescue effort would go on for days. Four hundred eight people were saved, 97 were hospitalized. One hundred eighty-eight hapless passengers drowned, all because of a failure to put human safety before business profits and perceived efficiency.

CANADA – NOVA SCOTIA, HALIFAX
April 1, 1873

A huge storm, shortage of fuel and a foundering on reefs converged to cause the sinking of the liner Atlantic *near Halifax, Nova Scotia on April 1, 1873. Five hundred sixty died.*

CANADA – NOVA SCOTIA, SABLE ISLAND
July 4, 1898

Collision in a heavy fog with the British steel bark Cromartyshire *off Sable Island, Nova Scotia on July 4, 1898 sent the French liner* La Bourgogne *to the bottom of the North Atlantic. Five hundred sixty died.*

CANADA – NOVA SCOTIA, WINGO SOUND
December 24, 1811

Heavy storms off the Baltic station in Wingo Sound caused the sinking of the British warships St. George *and* Defence *on December 24, 1811. Two thousand died.*

CANADA – QUEBEC, ST. LAWRENCE RIVER
May 29, 1914

The collision in a fog with the Norwegian collier Storstad *sank the* Empress of Ireland *in the St. Lawrence River on May 29, 1914. One thousand twenty-seven died.*

CAPE OF GOOD HOPE
1586

A combination of reckless sailing and cowardice combined to sink the Portuguese sailing ship St. James *off the Cape of Good Hope in 1586. Four hundred fifty died.*

CARIBBEAN SEA – NEAR VERACRUZ, MEXICO
August 10, 1591

A major hurricane sank the Spanish grand fleet in the Caribbean Sea near Veracruz on August 10, 1591. Five hundred died.

CHINA – CHUSAN ISLANDS
August 29, 1916

Collision in a deep fog off the Chusan Islands between the cruiser Hsin-Yu *and the cruiser* Hai-Yung *sent the* Hsin-Yu *to the bottom on August 29, 1916. One thousand Chinese soldiers aboard died.*

CHINA – SWATOW HARBOR
March 18, 1921

Fighting among passengers aboard the steamer Hong Koh *in Swatow Harbor sank the ship on March 18, 1921. More than 1,000 died from drowning or fighting.*

Violent animosity between the residents of two Chinese cities caused one of the grisliest maritime disasters of all time on March 18, 1921.

The steamer *Hong Koh*, under British command and captained by Captain Harry Holmes, approached the port of Swatow at low tide that day. Its public rooms and decks were packed with Chinese residents of Amoy and Swatow. Fistfights and arguments had already broken out between the residents of the two cities, and a general feeling of ill will pervaded the voyage. Captain Holmes welcomed the harbor pilot aboard with a sense of relief.

But his peace was short-lived. The pilot announced in no uncertain terms that a sandbar would not allow the *Hong Koh*, which drew 22 feet, to reach the harbor of Swatow. And he would not, under any circumstances, attempt to take the ship across the bar.

The captain announced to the disgruntled passengers that the ship would have to proceed to Amoy, unload and then return to Swatow. The Swatow residents rioted, smashing furniture and portholes.

The captain ordered his crew to station themselves in the bow of the ship with guns and a hot-water hose aimed at the rioting passengers. 'On the count of three, we will fire!' announced Captain Holmes, his entire concentration and that of his crew on quelling the insurgence aboard his ship. What nobody realized was that the *Hong Koh* was drifting toward a razor-edged reef. Within moments, it piled up on the rocks with a terrible sound of metal scraping against stone. And within seconds, the reef had opened a gash beneath the waterline of the steamer, causing her to list to starboard.

The momentarily chastened passengers, refueled by fear, now began to set upon one another in earnest, each fighting for a place in the lifeboats that were being lowered. Knives, hatchets and axes flashed and fell, as hundreds of people scrambled for the lifeboats. Hundreds were murdered on the spot, and the decks were covered with blood.

The demoralized Captain Holmes ordered his crew to fire over the heads of the rioting crowds. It made no difference whatsoever. People were hacked to pieces as they tried to climb into boats; those in the boats were swamped by overwhelming crowds trying to take their places. Lifeboats tangled in their halyards and spilled their human contents into the water. Others were smashed to kindling against the side of the ship.

Captain Holmes was the only British citizen aboard the *Hong Koh*. He ordered his officers to remain with him as the ship began to slip beneath the waves, but none did. They managed to crowd, unscathed, into the last lifeboat. Captain Holmes accompanied his ship to the bottom of Swatow Harbor. Around the sinking ship floated the bodies of over 1,000 people.

CHINA – WOOSUNG
December 3, 1948

The overloaded and ancient steamer Kiangya, *bearing refugees, collided with an unexploded Japanese mine near Woosung on December 3, 1948. The mine detonated, sinking the ship and killing 2,750 passengers.*

EGYPT – SAFAGA
December 14, 1991

*Four hundred sixty-two passengers, most of them Mus-
lim pilgrims returning from Mecca, were drowned when
the* Salem Express, *a Red Sea ferry, rammed coral reefs
six miles from its destination in Safaga, Egypt shortly
before midnight on December 14, 1991. One hundred
eighty survived.*

The 1,105-ton Red Sea ferry *Salem Express* set sail
from Jidda, Saudi Arabia on December 13, 1991,
loaded with nearly 700 passengers and crew. Most of
the passengers were Egyptians, headed for the Red Sea
port of Safaga, 293 miles southeast of Cairo. The vast
majority of these were Muslims, returning from *unrah*,
a pilgrimage to Mecca held outside the regular pilgrimage season. The other Egyptian passengers were workers in Saudi Arabia coming home either for a holiday
because their contracts had ended, or because they
were being deported by the Saudis.

Most of the 36-hour trip was uneventful. But late on
Saturday evening, December 14, the ship ran into
heavy weather. Forty-mile-an-hour winds whipped up
10-foot waves. The ship, for all its tonnage, bobbed
sickeningly in the pounding seas.

Whether the captain was blown off course by the
storm, or went off course in an effort to make a run for
the safety of Safaga, will never be known. Shortly
before midnight, the *Salem Express* struck a coral reef
a mere six miles from Safaga, and immediately began
to break up and sink.

It all happened in a matter of minutes, too short a
time for any of the lifeboats to be lowered. Some
passengers who survived swore that crew members
shoved them away from escape routes and saved themselves. 'They wore life preservers and left us and even
pushed us aside to escape,' said Abdel-Aaiti Hassan, a
survivor.

The facts dispute this. The captain went down with his ship; his body was discovered on the bridge two days later. Only 10 of the 70 crew members survived.

It would be dawn before fullscale rescue efforts could be launched; the raging storm and darkness prevented ships from entering the area. The American and Australian navies sent in rescuers; helicopters brought those who escaped drowning to hastily erected tent shelters in Safaga.

Four hundred sixty-two people drowned; 118 of the survivors were hospitalized. It was one more tragedy that consumed the lives of Muslim pilgrims either in or returning from Mecca. (see pp. 40 and 95).

ENGLISH CHANNEL
August–October, 1588

A succession of hurricane-force winds, faulty decisions and the wounds of war sank the Spanish Armada between August and October 1588 in the English Channel. At least 4,000 died.

'God has seen fit to direct the course of events other than we would have wished,' wrote Don Alonzo Perez de Guzman, duke of Medina Sidonia, as the once proud Spanish Armada shambled home, half its ships sunk and anywhere from 4,000 to 10,000 of its men dead. That final discrepancy is possibly a testament to the disarray of everything about Philip II's plan to invade England, overthrow the Protestant Elizabeth I and establish himself as ruler of England.

Preparations for the invasion began in 1586, under the direction of the Marques de Santa Cruz, but the course of events to which Medina Sidonia later referred began to take a hand in 1567, with a surprise attack by Sir Francis Drake. This delayed the evolution of the attack plans, and the unexpected death of Santa Cruz delayed them still further.

Still, Philip, goaded by Pope Pius V, was determined. He appointed Medina Sidonia to head up the armada – a peculiar choice, considering that the duke was schooled in neither navigation nor naval warfare, and he confessed to violent seasickness every time he left land. Perhaps it was not God who determined the course of events at all.

In any case, the 130 ships and 30,000 sailors and soldiers set out from Lisbon in May 1588 bound for Flanders, where they were to meet the army of Alessandro Farnese, duke of Parma and, combining forces, overwhelm England. However, a series of skirmishes with the English, combined with the ordinarily foul weather of the English Channel, scattered the armada, which never did make contact with the duke of Parma and his forces.

Disgruntled, down by four ships, Medina Sidonia put his lack of navigational skills to immediate use and determined to sail home via Scotland and the west coast of Ireland. The first fatality of that decision was the *Gran Grifon*, the *capitanas* of the armada. It foundered on the rocks of Fair Isle, taking 1,000 men to the bottom.

The ragtag remnants of the armada sailed on, its ships patched and its supplies running low. Somewhere out of the Hebrides, Medina Sidonia ordered all animals on board any of the ships flung overboard – an odd order, considering that the animals could have been slaughtered for food for his starving men.

The winds blew steadily and relentlessly, tattering the already torn sails of some of the ships of the armada. The *Santa Maria de la Rosa*, vice-flagship of the fleet and a huge galley, powered by sails and galley slaves – mostly captured British seamen – was in particularly bad shape by September, with half her crew down with disease and most of her hull leaking from the cannon holes in her sides.

Her captain, Martin de Villafranca, determined that she would never make it to Spain and endeavored to find shelter and a harbor off Kerry. The winds rose to hurricane force and drove his hapless ship ashore near Dunmore Head, between Great Basket Island and Beginish. Two other Spanish ships, the *San Juan de Portugal* and the *San Juan* were already at anchor and slowly sinking into the shallow water of the harbor when the *Santa Maria de la Rosa* skidded into sight, firing its guns for assistance. Her sails were in shreds, her mast splintered. She dropped anchor, but the wind and sea had done their worst. Marcos de Aramburu, the commander of the *San Juan*, wrote in his ship's log, 'In an instant we saw she was going to the bottom while trying to hoist the foresail and immediately she went down with the whole crew, not a soul escaping – a most extraordinary and terrible occurrence.'

He was not quite right. Three hundred soldiers and sailors did perish as the ship went down, but one Genoese seaman, Giovanni de Monana, rode a plank to shore, where he was captured by the English.

The *San Juan de Portugal* did send raiding parties ashore, captured some provisions and again set sail for Spain. It reached home, but before it did, 200 of its crew died on board of disease and starvation.

Meanwhile, at Killybegs, Admiral Alonso Martinez de Leyva, having lost his own ships, the *Santa Ana* and the *La Rata Santa Maria Encoronada*, in storms off Loughros Bay of Donegal, put his and other men to work patching up the giant galley *Girona*. The harbor was littered with the wrecks of the ships of many nationalities, and the admiral did admirable work. He rebuilt its masts, patched its decks and hull and loaded on cannons, stores and 1,300 men.

On October 26, 1588, the *Girona* sailed out of Killybegs, north to Scotland and back down the channel. And the next day, October 27, an enormous hurricane hit her. Her rudder split in two, she foundered side to the wind and went down off what later became known as Port-na-Spagna. Every one of the

1,300 men aboard, including Admiral de Leyva, drowned.

Sixty-three ships of the Spanish Armada sank during the three months of their ill-fated voyage. Sixty-five, in horrendous shape, made it home. At least 4,000 men died at sea. And Elizabeth remained on the throne in England. It was not one of Spain's finest hours.

FRANCE – LA ROCHELLE
January 12, 1920

A combination of engine trouble and heavy seas sank the French steamer Afrique *near La Rochelle, France on January 17, 1920. Five hundred fifty-three died.*

GREAT BRITAIN – ENGLAND, LONDON
August 20, 1989

The pleasure boat Marchioness, *on a Thames river cruise, collided with a barge on August 20, 1989 and sank. Quick rescue work saved most of the passengers aboard the* Marchioness, *but 51 drowned.*

GREAT BRITAIN – ENGLAND, SPITHEAD
August 29, 1792

Gross and fatal misjudgment by workmen caused the sinking of the battle frigate Royal George *while it was in port at Spithead on August 29, 1792. More than 900 died.*

One of the worst marine disasters in history took place, ironically enough, in port.

The *Royal George*, England's most celebrated and valuable battle frigate, had a long list of admirals at its helm and an array of 100 guns stationed on either side of its multiple masts. On August 29, 1792 it was in port at Spithead undergoing routine repairs. A small pipe beneath the waterline on the starboard side had ruptured, and while workmen crawled through the ship, sailors lounged about and merchants sold their wares to the admiralty aboard the *Royal George*. While this was happening, the ship was tipping dangerously to port.

A brisk breeze suddenly picked up, a momentary squall that would ordinarily have no effect on an upright *Royal George*. In port, however, she was at the mercy of swells that poured unchecked into her open portside gun ports. Tons of water cascaded into the vessel within minutes, and she sank like a stone, taking the 1,300 men aboard with her. Four hundred managed to swim to safety, but more than 900 drowned, trapped in the giant hull of the *Royal George*, which sank in a lethal whirlpool in shallow water in the port of Spithead.

GREAT BRITAIN – ENGLAND, WOOLWICH, RIVER THAMES
September 3, 1878

The excursion steamer Princess Alice, *loaded with celebrants, collided with the steam collier* Bywell Castle *near Woolwich on the River Thames on September 3, 1878. Six hundred forty-five died.*

Steamer excursions were popular pastimes in the late 19th century, and the regally appointed river steamer *Princess Alice* was one of Britain's most popular excursion boats. Berthed at North Woolwich pier, the steamer regularly made day trips from London Bridge to Gravesend and Sheerness. Those aboard were entertained by music on its deck, games in the parlors or tippling in its oversized saloon, reserved, in the 1870s, for men only.

On the morning of September 3, 1878, the *Princess Alice* left London Bridge with 700 holiday-minded merrymakers bound for Gravesend.

At 6:00 P.M., the ship blew several blasts on its whistle and pulled back into the Thames to begin the sail home to North Woolwich pier. Captain William Grinstead decided to hug the south side of the river to avoid a two-knot ebb tide that was working against the ship midstream.

This particular night, the maneuver put the *Princess Alice* on a collision course with the steam collier *Bywell Castle*. There were no regulations in 1878 regarding the proper order of passing (port to port is the regulation today), but it was generally agreed that passenger ships had the right of way.

The *Bywell* moved to port, toward the shore, expecting the *Princess Alice* to pass it in midstream. Instead, the excursion steamer continued to hug the shore, heading directly for the *Bywell Castle*. Too late, both pilots spun their wheels, trying to avert a collision. Both ships unleashed huge blasts on their horns; lanterns waved hysterically; shouts and screams were exchanged.

And then, with a horrific shriek, the *Bywell Castle* plowed into the *Princess Alice* directly amidships, crumpling her, splintering her decks and ripping an enormous hole in her hull from top to bottom. The steamer split in two and started to sink immediately.

The force of the impact catapulted screaming passengers into the water, where they were soon joined by others frantically trying to escape from the sinking vessel and by the bodies of those who had drowned instantly below decks.

No one was wearing a life preserver; rescue lines were flung over the side of the *Bywell Castle*, but few survivors from the steamer reached them. Within two minutes, the *Princess Alice* had sunk to the bottom of the Thames, carrying 645 persons to a watery death.

Two boards of inquiry were held. One placed the blame on Captain Grinstead for 'improper starboarding.' The second placed the responsibility on both captains.

GREAT BRITAIN – SCOTLAND, ROCKALL
June 28, 1904

Faulty judgment by the captain was responsible for the sinking of the liner Norge *after it ran on the rocks of Rockall, Scotland on June 28, 1904. Five hundred fifty died.*

The Scandinavian-American Line steamship *Norge* was an old but reliable liner, acquired from Thingvalla, another Danish line that cruised the North Atlantic. Launched in 1881 as the *Pieter de Coninck*, it served that line for eight years and then was sold to the Scandinavian-American Line, which renamed it and put it into service between Stettin, Copenhagen, Christina, Christinsand and New York.

She was a small ship, capable of carrying 1,100 passengers (50 in first class, 150 in second class and 900 in steerage) at a very conservative top speed of 11 knots.

On June 22, 1904, the *Norge* left Copenhagen with 700 emigrants and a crew of 80. Six days later, she had only made the coast of Scotland, near Rockall Island. The weather was foggy, and that night she ran onto the rocks that ring the island. The ship was not extensively damaged at first, but the captain, attempting to free the ship by reversing her engines, ripped several huge holes in both sides of her hull.

The *Norge* immediately sent out distress signals, but before help could arrive, she sank, taking 550 persons, most of them emigrants who were trapped below decks, down with her.

HAITI – PORT-AU-PRINCE
February 17, 1993

Nine hundred passengers drowned when the passenger ferry Neptune *overturned in a rain squall on a trip from Jeremie to Port-au-Prince, Haiti in the early morning*

hours of February 17, 1993. The death toll was attrib-
uted to panic, overloading, and the total absence of
lifejackets, lifeboats, and government regulation of
safety equipment.

The government of Haiti seems to care little about the
fate of most of its population. The city of Port-au-
Prince, with a population of over 2,000,000, has one
fire house. At any one time, fewer than a handful of
traffic lights work. The minuscule public school system
educates only the children of the powerful and wealthy,
who pay almost no taxes.

And so the poor, who make up the majority of the
population, must do what they can to survive, and the
peasants living on the western end of Haiti's southern
peninsula, because of nonexistent roads, must rely on
one ferry to take them from Jeremie, that region's only
city, to Port-au-Prince, where they can sell their produce and wares.

Normally, two three-tiered ferries make the 100-mile
run. But on Tuesday, February 16, 1993, one of the
ferries was in drydock for repairs. Only the 163-foot
Neptune was running that day. It was an old ship,
uninspected by the government, and bereft of either
lifejackets or lifeboats. Hours before sailing time,
hundreds of peasants, leading livestock, bearing boxes
of produce and carrying bags of charcoal, paid their
fares of between $2.00 and $4.50, and swarmed aboard
the vessel. As sailing time neared, more and more
peasants pushed their way on deck, often shoving their
way aboard without paying. The army was called from
the nearby Jeremie garrison to restore order, but
failed. Even after the ferry pulled away from port,
canoes carried last-minute passengers to the overloaded boat, now bearing nearly 1,500 passengers and
who knew how many head of cattle. It was chaotic, but
the poor people of Haiti were used to chaos.

At 2:30 A.M. on July 17, when three-quarters of the
run was completed, the *Neptune* ran into a rain squall.

It was not a particularly vicious storm, but it was enough to cause the ancient rusty hulk of the ferry to sway in the swells. Those who were on the open decks shoved their way to sheltered areas. Others, feeling the deepening of the yaws the boat was making from side to side, panicked. The captain shouted over a megaphone to the passengers not to gather on one side of the boat.

But it was too late. Overloaded, unbalanced by a surge of passengers to the rail away from the wind, buffeted by waves, the *Neptune* capsized, spilling its passengers and cargo into the water, instantly drowning the trapped inhabitants of the sleeping cabins on the lower of its three decks.

'The sea was full of people,' Madeline Juilen, a survivor, later told reporters. 'I kept bumping into drowned people.' She and others saved themselves by clinging to floating bags of charcoal. Others survived by holding onto the carcasses of drowned and floating animals. But they were in the minority. 'There were lots of children on the boat, more than 100. They all died,' said Moise Edward, another survivor. Fewer than 600 passengers were rescued, most of them by U.S. Coast Guard helicopters and boats. Over 900 drowned, making this one of the worst maritime disasters in world history.

HOLLAND – TEXEL RIVER
December 22, 1810

Driven inland by a hurricane, the British frigate Minotaur *broke up on the banks of the Texel River in Holland on December 22, 1810. Five hundred seventy died.*

INDIA – MADRAS
April 1902

A cyclone sank the British steamer Camorta *in the Gulf*

*of Martaban near Madras, India in April 1902. Seven
hundred thirty-nine died.*

The British India Steam Navigation Company was
formed in 1862 to service passengers and mail between
India and England. It proved successful, and this
service was later expanded to Australia, East Africa
and the Persian Gulf.

In 1880, the iron-hulled steamer *Camorta*, built in
Glasgow, joined the fleet. Capable of making 11 knots,
she was a reliable, hardworking ship that plied the
India-England route from 1880 to 1883, made one trip
to Australia in 1883, was transferred in early 1886 to
the Netherlands India Steam Navigation Company and
then was transferred back again to the British India
Company in late 1886, where she remained.

In April 1902 (the precise date is unavailable from all
existing records), the *Camorta* departed from Madras
with 650 passengers and a crew of 89 bound for
England. She did not get far. In the Gulf of Martaban
(now called Mannar), between Ceylon (now Sri Lanka)
and India, the *Camorta* ran into a giant killer cyclone.

The ship barely had a chance to send out a distress
signal before being overwhelmed by the storm-whipped
sea. She went down with the entire ship's complement.
There were no survivors, and no trace ever found of
her.

INDIA – MANIHARI GHAT
August 6, 1988

*An overloaded passenger ferry capsized near Manihari
Ghat, India on August 6, 1988. More than 400 died.*

A passenger ferry overcrowded with more than 565
pilgrims set out from Manihari Ghat, a city in the state
of Bihar, 200 miles northwest of Calcutta, to reach a
religious site of the Hindu god Shiva on Saturday,

August 6, 1988. There had been days of monsoons, and the Ganges River was swollen and turbulent.

Still, the officers and crew of the ferryboat allowed it to be dangerously packed with hundreds more than it could safely accommodate.

The ferry was in midstream when the waters seemed to wrest control of the boat away from its crew. Within seconds of reaching the halfway point of its short voyage, it tilted, held a precarious balance for a moment and then capsized, spilling its passengers into the roaring river waters.

It was over in an instant, and all aboard were left to their own will and strength to survive. One hundred fifty people swam to safety or were rescued by frantic witnesses who set out in small boats to try to fish the flailing swimmers out of the monsoon-swollen Ganges.

The following day, the Indian government sent divers from New Delhi to recover the bodies of the more than 400 who drowned. Cranes freed the hulk of the ferry, which was broken into several pieces. Scores of the drowned were trapped within the wreckage of the ferry itself. Others washed up at various places on the banks of the Ganges miles from the accident site. Still others were never found.

ITALY – LEGHORN
March 17, 1800

A carelessly thrown match started the fire that caused the sinking of the British frigate Queen Charlotte *near Leghorn, Italy on March 17, 1800. Seven hundred died.*

JAPAN – HAKODATE
September 26, 1954

Bad judgment sent the giant passenger ferry Toyo Maru *out from Hakodate into the teeth of a typhoon in the Sea of Japan on September 26, 1954. The ferry sank, drowning 794.*

JAPAN – SOUTH COAST
September 19, 1890

A plot to assassinate a Turkish political figure sent the ramshackle ship Ertogrul *out in adverse weather off the south coast of Japan on September 19, 1890. It sank, drowning 587.*

JAPAN – TOKYO BAY
July 12, 1918

An unexplained explosion sent the battleship Kawachi *to the bottom of Tokyo Bay on July 12, 1918. Five hundred died.*

JAVA SEA
January 27, 1981

A fire in its hold led to the sinking of the Tamponas II *in the Java Sea on January 27, 1981. Five hundred eighty died.*

LABRADOR – EGG ISLAND
August 22, 1711

Storms off Egg Island, Labrador were responsible for the sinking of the English Armada on August 22, 1711. Two thousand British sailors died.

The English Armada passed into history ignominiously, the victim of bad judgment, deliberately dangerous navigation and heavy storms off Egg Island, Labrador.

It all began on April 29, 1711, when the enormous British fleet of 61 warships and transports carrying nearly 10,000 sailors, troops and their families set sail from England under the command of Admiral Sir Hovendon Walker. Sealed orders from Queen Anne revealed that the armada was to attack and capture the most heavily protected stronghold in the Western

Hemisphere, the fortress at Quebec. It was to be a sneak attack.

Given the size of the fleet and the presence of General John Hill, it seemed a mission destined for success and glory, which would be a total turnaround from the humbling defeats the British had heretofore suffered in previous attacks against Quebec.

The armada stopped first in Boston for provisions and then headed up the Massachusetts coast. Part way there, the first misstep occurred. The fleet overtook a French sloop, the *Neptune*, commanded by a Captain Paradis. She was on her way to Quebec, and with almost unbelievable naivete, Admiral Walker decided that Paradis would be their ideal guide to Quebec, just the man to guide them through the treacherous waters of St. Lawrence Bay.

Counseled against it, Walker persisted and paid Paradis 500 pistoles for his piloting expertise.

So, at breakneck speed, the armada, led by a loyal Frenchman, headed toward an encounter with Frenchmen. At approximately 10 P.M. on the night of August 22, 1711, a heavy fog descended upon the fleet, scattering its normally tight formation. By the time the fog was blown away by gale-force winds and a biting storm, the eight transports of the armada had been blown onto the razor-sharp reefs that surrounded Egg Island.

Every one of the eight transports was dashed upon the rocks, which split the wooden ships asunder. Within minutes, pounding surf smashed them apart still further, and more than 2,000 women, children, sailors and soldiers were swept into the black and freezing waters. Most of the bodies were later discovered washed up on the shore.

The warships and Admiral Walker were luckier. Faster and more maneuverable than the transports, they had missed the reefs and the island. But Paradis, the Frenchman, had fled, and there were no longer enough troops to safely mount an attack on the French garrison at Quebec, which had probably already been alerted.

In ignominy and defeat, Walker turned his remaining ships around and headed back to England, where he would fall into disgrace and be forced to spend the rest of his days in the colonies.

There were some survivors of the wrecks, apparently. Along with the skeletons on the shore, French inhabitants a year later discovered other skeletons huddled in hollow tree trunks and in shelters constructed of branches of shrubs. None survived long enough to leave Egg Island alive.

MYANMAR (BURMA) – GYANG RIVER
April 7, 1990

On the same night that the Scandinavian Star *burned in the North Sea (see below), a double-decker passenger ferry sailing from Moulmein to Kyondo in Myanmar – formerly Burma – overturned during a gale. Two hundred forty were aboard; only 25 survivors were fished from the roaring waters. Two hundred fifteen drowned.*

NEW ZEALAND – AUCKLAND
November 17, 1874

Faulty navigation worsened a fire aboard the Cospatrick *near Auckland, New Zealand on November 17, 1874. Four hundred sixty-eight died.*

NORTH SEA
April 7, 1990

The 10,000-ton Scandinavian Star, *a Danish passenger and car ferry carrying 495 passengers and crew from Oslo, Norway to Frederikshavn, Denmark caught fire at 2:30 A.M. on April 7, 1990. Two blazes trapped sleeping passengers in their cabins, killing 110 of them.*

PHILIPPINES – TABLAS STRAIT
December 20, 1987

Allowing an apprentice officer to pilot the monumentally overcrowded passenger ferry Dona Paz *through the crowded Tablas Strait in the Philippines on December 20, 1987 caused one of the worst maritime disasters in history, the collision of the ferry with the tanker* Victor. *Both ships were set afire, and at least 3,000 died.*

It was Sunday, December 20, 1987 when the 2,215-ton ferry *Dona Paz*, owned by the Sulpicio Lines, left Tacloban, on Leyte Island, horrendously overloaded with Filipinos anxious to spend Christmas in Manila with their relatives and friends.

As night fell, the 3,000 passengers that crowded the cabins and three decks of the *Dona Paz* (she was designed to carry 1,424 passengers and 50 crew members) attempted to make themselves comfortable. It was not an easy task. Up to four people shared individual cots; hundreds sprawled on mats they had laid out in the ship's corridors; hundreds more sat, shoulder to shoulder, on the decks of the ship.

It was a dark, moonless night, but an uneventful one for 265 miles of the 375-mile trip from Tacloban to Manila. According to the Coast Guard inquiry, by 10 P.M. only an apprentice officer was on the bridge, piloting the boat through the busy Tablas Strait, 110 miles south of Manila. The other officers were watching television or drinking beer.

At 10 P.M., the ferry was just off Mindoro Island, in the busiest part of the strait. And at precisely that hour, the *Dona Paz* collided head-on with the 629-ton Philippine tanker *Victor*, bound for Masbate Island with 8,300 barrels of oil. Within seconds, the heavier, more powerful ferry had ripped into the hull of the *Victor*, peeling open its compartments and smashing into the oil it was carrying.

Barely a minute later, the *Victor* exploded with a

horrendous roar, sending flaming oil onto the *Dona Paz* and igniting the surface of the water surrounding the two foundering ships.

'I went to a window to see what happened, and I saw the sea in flames,' one of the survivors, 42-year-old Paquito Osabel, told a reporter later. 'I shouted to my companions to get ready, there is fire. The fire spread rapidly and there were flames everywhere. People were screaming and jumping. The smoke was terrible. We couldn't see each other and it was dark. I could see flames, but I jumped.'

Both ships sank, almost instantly. Many of those passengers who did not drown were burned. Even those who jumped into the water were soon coated with flaming oil and perished. Pampilio Culalia, who leaped into the water, leaving his 14-year-old daughter, 10-year-old niece and his brother behind, sobbed, 'I saw the ship in flames and [as I swam away] I wanted to kill myself. But God shook me and woke me.'

Of the more than 3,000 passengers aboard the *Dona Paz*, only 24 survived. Of the 13 crewmen aboard the *Victor*, two were fished from a sea that was littered with the charred corpses of those who had tried to escape. All were suffering from serious burns.

For seven hours, the *Don Eusebio*, a passenger ship, circled the area, searching in vain for survivors. A search mission of five commercial vessels, two naval patrol craft and three U.S. Air Force helicopters covered a wide area, looking for signs of life. They found nothing either.

The next morning, decomposing bodies began washing ashore on Mindoro Island, and for the next week, as Christmas came and went, hundreds of charred, bloated bodies began to float to the surface. But thousands more would never be recovered.

'This is a national tragedy of harrowing proportions,' said Philippine president Corazon Aquino. 'Our sadness is all the more painful because the tragedy struck with the approach of Christmas,' she added.

ROMANIA – GALATI
September 10, 1989

The Romanian pleasure cruiser Mogosoaia, *carrying 179 tourists on a Danube river excursion, collided with the Bulgarian tugboat* Peter Karaminchev, *which was towing a convoy of barges, on September 10, 1989. The pleasure boat capsized and sank immediately, drowning 161 of its passengers and crew. Only 18 survived.*

UNITED STATES – FLORIDA COAST
July 31, 1715

A hurricane off the coast of Florida sank the twin capitanas, *the two leaders of a Spanish flotilla, on July 31, 1715. More than 1,000 died on the two ships.*

UNITED STATES – ILLINOIS, CHICAGO
July 24, 1915

Faulty design, greed and an unequal distribution of passengers combined to capsize the excursion steamer Eastland *at its dock in Chicago on July 24, 1915. Eight hundred fifty-two picnickers died.*

UNITED STATES – NEW YORK, NEW YORK
June 15, 1904

A wholesale disregard of safety measures, coupled with mindlessness, caused the fatal burning of the steamer General Slocum *in New York Harbor on June 15, 1904. One thousand thirty-one people died, according to the New York City Police Department.*

Nuclear and
Industrial Accidents

The Worst Recorded Nuclear and Industrial Accidents

* Detailed in text

Germany
  * Oppau
    Badische Anilinfabrick Company (1921)

Great Britain
    England
  * Cumberland
    Windscale Plutonium Plant (1957)

India
  * Bhopal
    Union Carbide Pesticide Plant (1984)

Japan
  * Tsuruga
    Nuclear power plant (1981)

Switzerland
    Lucends Vad
    Underground reactor (1969)

United States
    Alabama
    Brown's Ferry Nuclear power plant (1975)
    Idaho
  * Idaho Falls
    Idaho Nuclear Engineering Laboratory (1961)
    Michigan
    Detroit
    Sodium cooling plant (1966)
    Minnesota
    Monticello
    Nuclear power plant (1971)
    New York
    Rochester
    Ginna Steam Plant (1982)
    Oklahoma
  * Gore
    Sequoyah Fuels Corporation Plant (1986)
    Pennsylvania
  * Middletown
    Three Mile Island Nuclear Power Plant (1979)
    Tennessee
    Erwin
    Nuclear fuel plant (1979)

USSR
  * Kasli
    Nuclear waste Dump (1957)
  * Pripyat
    Chernobyl nuclear power plant (1986)

Chronology

* Detailed in text

1921
Sept. 20
  * Oppau, Germany;
    Badische Anilinfabrick
    Co.

1957
  * Kasli, USSR; Nuclear
    waste dump
Oct. 10
  * Cumberland, England;
    Windscale Plutonium
    Plant

1961
Jan. 3
  * Idaho Falls, Idaho; Idaho
    Nuclear Engineering
    Laboratory

1966
Oct. 5
    Detroit, Michigan;
    Sodium cooling plant

1969
Jan. 21
    Lucends Vad,
    Switzerland;
    Underground reactor

1971
Nov. 19
    Monticello, Minnesota;
    Nuclear reactor

1975
Mar. 22
    Brown's Ferry, Alabama;
    Nuclear reactor

1979
Mar. 28
  * Middletown,
    Pennsylvania; Three
    Mile Island Nuclear
    Power Plant
Aug. 7
    Erwin, Tennessee;
    Nuclear fuel plant

1981
Mar. 8
  * Tsuruga, Japan; Nuclear
    power plant

1982
Jan. 25
    Rochester, New York;
    Ginna Steam Plant

1984
Dec. 3
  * Bhopal, India; Union
    Carbide Pesticide Plant

1986
Jan. 4
  * Gore, Oklahoma;
    Sequoyah Fuels
    Corporation Plant
April 16
  * Pripyat, USSR;
    Chernobyl nuclear
    power plant

Nuclear and
Industrial Accidents

Ever since Enrico Fermi put one of Albert Einstein's theories to work, the world has experienced a steadily increasing and intensifying series of nuclear accidents. The worst so far is the latest; the very worst is, alas, yet to come.

In a positive sense, nuclear disasters have made us more cautious. Three Mile Island, for instance, put the brakes on the proliferation of nuclear power plants; the Chernobyl disaster brought it to a virtual standstill. Without arguing the relative virtue of atomic power, the very fact that huge public outcries have followed each of these disasters forces government and industry to concentrate more on safety practices than ever before and to be more public about these practices or the lack of them.

For if there is a single thread that runs through all the industrial and nuclear accidents of this section, it is a failure to pay proper attention to safety precautions.

In each case, human error was the trigger that brought about the cataclysms that ensued. And if the similarity in cause and effect of man-made catastrophes has proved anything, it is that human error is at the root of virtually every man-made disaster. With industrial and nuclear disasters, this human error is compounded, all too frequently, by human greed, by political and governmental expediency, by economic considerations and by deliberate misinformation or withholding of information.

Admittedly, some of this has come from ignorance. But an equal amount has also come from governmental design, explained away as a desire not to create panic in the populace. This policy has resulted in hundreds of lawsuits against governments by the families of victims who have died agonizing and puzzling deaths long after the incident that had been passed off as posing little or no danger to the public at large. And until this pervasive policy is changed, casualty figures from nuclear accidents will continue to multiply as governments continue to use nuclear power, which is cheap and abundant, without spending the proper amount of time on researching methods of preventing disasters and their consequent effects.

The criteria for inclusion in this section were based on the effect the disaster had on the innocent. Industrial accidents are a frequent occurrence, and that is regrettable and recordable. In the case of each of the included industrial and nuclear accidents in this section, huge numbers of innocent people who had either nothing or very little to do with the industry were victims of the disaster. And that was the reason for that happening's inclusion.

GERMANY – OPPAU
September 20, 1921

An error in mixing chemicals, producing explosive gas, caused the giant explosion in the Badische Anilinfabrick Company plant in Oppau, Germany on September 20, 1921. Five hundred died; 1,500 were injured, many seriously.

GREAT BRITAIN – ENGLAND, CUMBERLAND
October 10, 1957

The overheating of uranium cartridges releasing radio-active iodine caused widespread radioactive contamination surrounding the Windscale Plutonium Plant, Cumberland, on October 10, 1957. Thirty-three cancer deaths have occurred; more are expected. There was a

temporary suspension of the milk and beef industries of
northwestern England.

The Windscale plutonium factory in Cumberland
manufactured plutonium for use in nuclear reactors and
atomic bombs and produced certain by-products that
were used in medicine. Powered by the nearby Calder
Hall atomic power plant, it was thought to be, in 1957,
a model of clean and efficient productivity.

But the accident that took place on October 10,
1957, which was England's first nuclear accident – and
one of the first in the peacetime world – was the
forerunner of hundreds of nuclear accidents that would
release radioactivity into the atmosphere. In 1957 the
world was naive to the hazards, and little space was
given to the accident. But as its aftermath extended and
deepened, so did the awareness of its significance.

At 4:15 P.M. on Thursday, October 10, 1957, the
number-one pile of uranium at Windscale overheated,
and as its temperature rose, it released radioactive
iodine-131 vapor and some oxidized uranium particles
into the air. It would be 15 minutes before the red-hot
uranium pile would be discovered; that part of the
plant had been shut down for maintenance.

Shortly after it was discovered, workers wearing gas
masks and other protective equipment were assigned to
use carbon dioxide to extinguish the fire. It was ineffectual.

A sense that this was no ordinary fire began to
grow. All of the plant's off-duty safety workers were
called back, and all of the roads to the plant were
blocked off. By 5:15, safety experts issued concilia-
tory statements to the press, claiming that all danger
had departed.

By 9:00 A.M. on the 11th, it was decided to use water
to damp down the fire. Two plant officials and a local
fire chief hauled a hose to the top of the containment
dome and aimed it at the fire. No one knew quite what
would happen, and plant workers all over the complex

crouched behind steel and concrete barriers.

Fortunately, the water worked, but it also released huge clouds of radioactive steam through the stacks and into the atmosphere. The worst was over, everyone thought; there had been neither an explosion nor a meltdown.

By midday of October 11, nearly all of the 3,000 workers at the plant and the nearby Calder Hall atomic energy plant were sent home. They had been exposed to radiation, and it was obvious that a reevaluation of the situation was needed.

Significant quantities of radioactive iodine-131 had been released into the atmosphere over a 200-mile radius, and at 2 A.M. on Sunday, October 13, police began to knock on the doors of the farmhouses in Cumberland. The milk from their cows, the police warned them, might be radioactive.

By Tuesday the 15th, the milk ban was extended from a 14-square-mile area to 200 square miles, including 600 dairy farms. Approximately 30,000 gallons of milk, worth $11,000, were dumped into the Irish Sea each day until the end of October, and all distribution of milk from the contaminated area was immediately halted.

Beyond that, hundreds of cows, goats and sheep were confiscated, shot and buried. Farmers who slaughtered their animals for meat were told to send the thyroid glands to the Atomic Energy Commission for testing.

Farmers in the area now began to make public the tales they had exchanged among themselves: Even before the accident, sterilization had occurred in their cattle. W. E. Hewitson, a dairy farmer in Yottenfews, stated that he had changed bulls four times in four years, but only a third of his cows either calved or gave milk.

Then it became apparent that the radioactive iodine-131 that safety experts first said had drifted out to sea had not done so at all. There was a marked increase in the radioactivity of the atmosphere after the accident at the Windscale plant.

Several months later, British officials conceded to a United Nations conference at Geneva that nearly 700 curies of cesium and strontium had also been released into the air over England and northern Europe, in addition to 20,000 curies of iodine-131. The iodine dose represented more than 1,400 times the quantity American officials later claimed had been released during the 1979 accident at Three Mile Island (see p. 315)

INDIA – BHOPAL
December 3, 1984

The worst industrial accident in history, the explosion at the Union Carbide Pesticide Plant in Bhopal, India on December 3, 1984, was caused by a combination of faulty maintenance, laxity in management, outdated equipment, faulty judgment and social factors. At least 2,000 died; 200,000 were injured.

Although Western industries find that locating their plants in Third World countries is profitable because labor is cheap, there are also trade-offs. The labor is usually both cheap and unskilled. And because of the distance from the source, some equipment that exists in these plants goes too long without updating, replacement or even maintenance. Finally, there is the danger that a kind of casualness, a slowing down of the metabolism that is more in tune with the pace of ancient life than of modern life, works against the constant, concentrated vigilance that can prevent industrial disaster by preparing for it.

This was at least a factor in the complex series of events that led up to the worst industrial accident in the history of the world early in the morning of December 3, 1984. The disaster took place in the Union Carbide Pesticide Plant in Bhopal, a small city in the north central region of Madhya Pradesh, in India, midway between New Delhi and Bombay.

The plant, a boon to this economically depressed city, was located in its slum section, a community called Jai Prakash Nagar.

At 2:45 P.M. on Sunday, December 2, while children played in the dirt outside the huts crammed together near the plant's entrance, about 100 workers reported for duty for the eight-hour late shift.

The plant, which manufactured the pesticide Sevin, had been closed down for some time and had been reactivated only a week before. It was still working at a partial pace, carrying through the process of making the pesticide, which consisted of a mix of carbon tetrachloride, methyl isocyanate and alpha-napthol.

The methyl isocyanate, MIC, was stored in three partially buried tanks, each with a 15,000-gallon capacity.

One of the tanks, number 610, was giving the workers trouble. For some reason they could not determine, the chemical could not be forced out of the tank. Nitrogen was pumped into the tank to force the MIC into the Sevin plant, but each time this was done, the nitrogen leaked out.

There was a greater problem with tank number 610, however, and this, plus a leak that had not been repaired in seven days, would set the stage for a major catastrophe.

First of all, MIC must, to maintain stability and be nonreactive, be kept at a low temperature. A refrigeration unit designed to keep it at that temperature had, for a still-unexplained reason, been turned off. The chemical was thus warmer than the four degrees Fahrenheit recommended in the plant's operating manual, but just how much warmer was impossible to tell, since the instruments monitoring it were old and unreliable.

In addition, the money-losing plant had undergone further cost-cutting procedures in the past months, and this included the curtailment of maintenance on the noncomputerized, behind-the-times equipment. And

The beginnings of the Great Chicago Fire, according to accepted belief. This contemporary lithograph captures the moment, on the evening of October 8, 1871, when Mrs. O'Leary and her cow first worked their mischief. (*Lithography Collection, Smithsonian Institution*)

The wind-whipped flames of the Great Chicago Fire advance on the fleeing refugees in this contemporary painting of the event. (*Library of Congress*)

Firemen at work controlling the worst theater fire in U.S. history, Chicago's Iroquois Theatre fire on December 30, 1903. (*New York Public Library*)

The interior of Boston's Cocoanut Grove Night Club after the horrendous fire of November 28, 1942, which claimed 491 lives. (*American Red Cross*)

Terrified escapees from the devastating forest fire that destroyed one-third of the town of Hinckley, Minnesota on September 1, 1894 run from a burning evacuation train and fling themselves into a swamp. Some were burned to death by the hot mud, but most survived. (*Frank Leslie's Illustrated Newspaper*)

On Sunday, June 30, 1900, a horrible fire engulfed the Hoboken docks, New Jersey and four German Lloyd ships. Three hundred twenty-six sightseers, passengers, firemen and crew members died in the tragic conflagration. (*Frank Leslie's Illustrated Newspaper*)

Harry S. Murdock, Kate Claxton and two unidentified actors plead vainly with panicking audience members to stay calm during the Brooklyn Theatre fire on December 5, 1876. (*Frank Leslie's Illustrated Newspaper*)

Firemen try desperately to bring the Windsor Hotel fire on March 17, 1899 under control. The holiday crowds, a stubborn policeman and a carelessly thrown match combined to totally destroy the famous New York City hotel. (*New York Public Library* (*Brown Brothers*))

The bodies of young women burned to death in the Triangle Shirtwaist fire of March 25, 1911 in New York City are lined up in the morgue for identification. (*New York Public Library* (*Brown Brothers*))

The stern of the *Andrea Doria* tips to starboard just before the ocean liner sinks beneath the surface of the Atlantic after its collision with the SS *Stockholm* on July 25, 1956. (*Library of Congress*)

The gigantic hole ripped in the hull of the *Lusitania* by a torpedo from a German U-boat on May 1, 1915. (*Illustrated London News*)

A contemporary painting depicts survivors of the *Lusitania* disaster floating in the North Atlantic. One thousand one hundred ninety-eight passengers aboard the luxury liner were either drowned or killed by the explosion. (*Illustrated London News*)

The *Morro Castle* burns out of control off the coast of New Jersey on September 8, 1934. Sweeping safety reforms for ships at sea resulted from this tragedy caused by careless crew members. (*Library of Congress*)

A contemporary newspaper illustration captures survivors in lifeboats and the *Titanic* poised before its final plunge to the bottom of the North Atlantic on the night of April 14, 1912. (*Daily Sphere*)

The steamer *Utopia* after its collision with the British battleship *Amson* in the Bay of Gibraltar on March 17, 1891. Five hundred seventy-six passengers and crew died in the tragedy. (*Illustrated London News*)

The Channel ferry *Herald of Free Enterprise* capsized on the night of March 6, 1987 just after leaving Zeebrugge, Belgium; 188 people drowned and 97 were hospitalized. (*Rex Features*)

A Currier and Ives lithograph captures the *Atlantic* foundering on a reef near Halifax, Nova Scotia on April 1, 1873. (*New York Public Library*)

Lifeboats from the French liner *La Bourgogne* go over the side after its collision, in a heavy fog, with the British steel bark *Cromatyshire* off Sable Island, Nova Scotia on July 4, 1898. The bark limped home; the liner sank, drowning 560. (*Illustrated London News*)

Between August and October 1588, the Spanish Armada was pummeled by hurricane-force winds in the English Channel. By the end of October, it had been totally destroyed, with a loss of life of at least 4,000. (*New York Public Library*)

The tragic collision of the excursion steamer *Princess Alice* and the steam collier *Bywell Castle* near Woolwich on the River Thames on September 3, 1878. Six hundred forty-five died in one of the worst steamship wrecks in history. (*Illustrated London News*)

The capsized hulk of the *Eastland* lies on its side in the Chicago River while rescuers search for survivors. Eight hundred fifty-two died in this 'accident that never should have been allowed to happen.' (*Library of Congress*)

An artist's rendering of the horrendous burning of the steamer *General Slocum* in New York Harbor on June 15, 1904. One thousand thirty-one people died, according to the New York City Police Department. (*New York Public Library*)

A soup kitchen is set up and utilized by survivors and families of victims of the gigantic explosion at the Badische Anilinfabrick Company plant in Oppau, Germany on September 20, 1921. Five hundred died; 1,500 were injured, many seriously. (*Library of Congress*)

A train of the Great Western line of Canada plunged through a rickety bridge and into the Des Jardines Canal, near Hamilton, Ontario, on March 17, 1857. Sixty died. (*Illustrated London News*)

A lithograph captures the first recorded major railway disaster in the world: the rear-end collision of two excursion trains leaving the celebration of King Louis Philippe's birthday in Versailles, France on May 8, 1842; 54 were killed. (*New York Public Library*)

A view from the storm-damaged Tay River Bridge near Dundee, Scotland following the plunge into the river of the Edinburgh express on December 28, 1879. (*Illustrated London News*)

The burned-out hulk of one of the cars of a troop train that collided with a passenger train near Gretna Green, Scotland on May 22, 1915. Two hundred twenty-seven were killed and 223 injured in the wreck, caused by a signalman's faulty judgment. (*Illustrated London News*)

The overcrowding of trains in India contributes greatly to the abnormally high death tolls in that country's train wrecks. (*United Nations*)

One of the oddest of all railway wrecks took place as a result of the collision of two bridges – one wrecked by floodwaters, one an innocent bystander over an arroyo near Eden, Colorado. Trestle and train were both flung into the floodwaters on August 7, 1904. (*Frank Leslie's Illustrated Newspaper*)

American newspapers fed the insatiable appetite of the public for months following the collision of two excursion trains in Revere, Massachusetts on August 26, 1871. (*Frank Leslie's Illustrated Newspaper*)

Rescue workers struggle to pull survivors from the Pennsylvania Railroad wreck in Woodbridge, New Jersey in February 1951. Wheels and shattered cars are strewn over the embankment from which the train hurtled when a temporary wooden trestle buckled. (*American Red Cross*)

Human error, inadequate signals and missed schedules conspired to cause this monstrous head-on collision of an excursion and a passenger train near Camp Hill Station, Pennsylvania on July 17, 1856. Sixty-six children on the excursion train were killed. (*Frank Leslie's Illustrated Newspaper*)

The shattered, twisted, burned-out remains of the last car of the number six train of the Lehigh Valley line excursion of the celebrating Total Abstinence League in Mud Run, Pennsylvania on October 10, 1888. Most of the 64 victims of the crash were crushed in this last car when train number seven rear-ended it. (*Library of Congress*)

Apollo astronauts (*left to right*) Gus Grissom, Ed White and Roger Chaffee shortly before the tests on the launchpad that ended in their deaths by fire on January 27, 1967. (*NASA*)

The ill-fated *Challenger* crew (*left to right, front row*) Michael J. Smith, Francis (Dick) Scobee and Ronald McNair; (*rear*) Ellison Onizuka, Christa McAuliffe, Gregory Jarvis and Judith Resnik. (*NASA*)

finally, new supervisors and operators were in key positions.

As a result of this laxity, tank number 610, besides having a faulty valve and not being maintained at the proper temperature, was also overfilled.

Other pieces of the scenario began to come together. At about 9:30 P.M. that night, a supervisor ordered a worker to clean a 23-foot section of pipe that filtered crude MIC before it went into the storage tanks. The worker did this by connecting a hose to the pipe, opening a drain and turning on the water. It flowed into the pipe, out the pipe drains and onto the floor, where it entered a floor drain. It flowed continuously for three hours.

All of the workers and presumably the new supervisor knew that water reacts violently with MIC. They also knew that there was a leaky valve not only in tank number 610 but also in the pipe that was being washed. Rahaman Khan, the worker who washed out the pipe, later told the *New York Times*, 'I knew that valves leaked. I didn't check to see if that one was leaking. It was not my job.'

It is generally conceded that it was the water flowing from the hose that triggered the horror that was to follow.

At 10:30, a pressure reading was taken on tank 610. It was two pounds per square inch, which was normal.

At 10:45, the next shift arrived. The water was still running.

At 11:00 P.M., the pressure had climbed to 10 pounds per square inch, five times what it had been a half hour before. Something was obviously wrong. But no one did anything about it, because it was still within acceptable limits. In fact, some workers later testified that that was the usual temperature and pressure of the MIC at the plant.

Then, too, there was the problem of the instruments. Shakil Qureshi, the MIC supervisor on duty, later noted that he thought that one of the readings was probably wrong. 'Instruments often didn't work,' he said. 'They got corroded. Crystals would form on them.'

But by 11:30 P.M., the eyes and noses of the workers informed them that something was indeed wrong. Their eyes began to tear. They knew MIC was leaking, but this happened on the average of once a month. They often relied on these symptoms to inform them that a leak had occurred. Suman Dey, a worker, later told reporters, 'We were human leak detectors.'

V. N. Singh, another worker, discovered the leak at approximately 11:45 P.M. He noticed a drip of liquid about 50 feet off the ground, which was accompanied by some yellowish white gas. Mr. Singh informed his supervisor, Mr. Qureshi, who said that he would look into it after his tea break.

The tea break began for everyone at 12:15. And while this ancient custom went on for 20 minutes, the disaster continued to unfold unchecked.

From 12:40 A.M. on December 3, events began to take place with lightning rapidity. The smell of gas rose alarmingly. Workers choked on it. The temperature gauge on tank number 610 rose above 77 degrees Fahrenheit, the top of the scale. The pressure gauge was visibly inching upward toward 40 pounds per square inch, a point at which the emergency relief valve on the MIC tank was scheduled to burst open.

At 12:45 P.M., the pressure gauge read 55 pounds per square inch, 15 points from the top of the scale. Supervisor Qureshi ordered all the water in the plant turned off, and it was only then that the water in the hose that had been running for three hours was finally found and turned off.

But it was far too late. The water reacted with the MIC, and the leak burst forth. Panicked workers dashed to and fro, blinded and coughing.

An alarm sounded, and within minutes the fire brigade arrived to place a water curtain around the escaping gas. But the curtain reached only 100 feet in the air. The top of the stack through which the gas was now spewing into the atmosphere was 120 feet high, and the gas fountained another 10 feet above that.

A vent gas scrubber, a device designed to neutralize the escaping gas, was turned on. But its gauges showed that no caustic soda was flowing into it. Or, perhaps, the gauge was broken. Who knew at this point? In either case, the gas, instead of being neutralized, was shooting out of the scrubber stack and was being carried on the high winds southward from the plant into the surrounding slums.

There were four buses parked by the road leading out of the plant. Drivers were supposed to man them in an emergency and load and evacuate workers and people who lived near the plant. But no drivers appeared. They, along with the terrified workers, were running from the plant.

At 1 A.M., Mr. Qureshi had run out of ideas. He called S. P. Choudhary, the assistant factory manager, who instructed him to turn on the flare tower, which was designed to burn off escaping gas.

But, explained Mr. Qureshi, with all that gas in the air, turning on the flare would cause a huge explosion. At any rate, a four-foot, elbow-shaped piece of pipe was missing from the flare. It had corroded and was due to be replaced as soon as the part arrived from the United States.

An alternative would have been to dump the MIC into a spare storage tank. There were two spares that were supposed to be empty. But they were not. Both contained MIC.

The workers who remained and tried to control the leak now donned oxygen masks. It was the only way they could breathe. Visibility was down to one foot. The supervisor, unable to find a mask, he said, opted to run away from the plant. He found a clear area, scaled a six-foot fence topped by barbed wire, vaulted over it and fell to the other side, breaking his leg. He was later transported to a hospital, with many, many others.

The gas poured unchecked out of the leak until 2:30 A.M. Jagannathan Mukund, the factory manager, arrived at 3 A.M., and only then, because, he later stated, the telephones were out of order, did he send a man to inform the police about the accident. The company had a policy, he said, of not involving the local authorities in gas leaks.

And to be fair, the sleeping populace *did* hear the emergency sirens going off, but they sounded so often in false alarms, that the people in the surrounding slums ignored them and went back to sleep – some of them for the last time.

Outside the factory, people were dying by the hundreds, some in their sleep. Others, panicked, choking, blinded, ran into the cloud of gas, inhaling more and more of it until they dropped dead. Thousands of terrified animals perished where they stood.

The outside temperature was only 57 degrees Fahrenheit which kept the lethal cloud of gas close to the ground, rather than allowing it to rise and dissipate into the atmosphere, as it would have under warmer conditions.

The gas crept into open shacks, killing the weak and the frail immediately. Others woke, vomited and groped blindly to get outdoors, where they filled their lungs with the searing chemical vapor.

'I awoke when I found it difficult to breathe,' said Rahis Bano to a reporter afterward. 'All around me my neighbors were shouting, and then a wave of gas hit me.'

She fell down, vomiting, and her two sons, whom she was carrying, rolled on the floor. She revived herself and grabbed one son. He and she would survive; the son she left behind would die.

Rivers of humanity, tens of thousands of people, stumbled about. Some were trampled. Others simply gave up and sat down. As the cloud spread southeastward, it enveloped the Bhopal railroad station. Ticket takers, trainmen and passengers died where they stood.

A hill was located in the center of the city, and thousands rushed toward it, thinking they could climb above the gas. 'There were cars, bicycles, auto rickshaws, anything that would move on the road trying to get up the hill,' said one survivor. 'I saw people just collapsing by the side of the road.'

New hazards presented themselves; many of the fleeing refugees were run over by cars and buses and emergency vehicles. The police, instead of helping, heightened the panic by roaring through the crowds, their police van loudspeakers shouting, 'Run! Run! Poison gas is spreading!'

Hospitals were immediately filled. Doctors and nurses tried to save as many as they could, but Hamida Hospital recorded a death a minute until it finally gave up trying to keep count. Dr. N. H. Trivedi, deputy superintendent of the hospital, told the *Times*, 'People picked up helpless strangers, their best friends, their relatives, and brought them in here. They did far more than the police and official organizations.'

Most hospitals placed two stricken people in one bed, until there was finally no more room, and emergency clinics were set up in stores and on streets.

When dawn finally broke over Bhopal, it lit a scene of cataclysmic destruction. Thousands of bodies – human and animal – littered the streets. No birds sang. The only movement was from trucks sent out to pick up the dead and to search houses for more dead and dying.

Between 2,000 and 2,500 had died, and more than 200,000 would be afflicted for years, possibly for the rest of their lives, with the aftereffects of the Bhopal tragedy. Some were permanently blinded. Others could not sleep, had difficulty breathing or digesting food and had trouble functioning.

For a week, the suffering continued in Bhopal's hospitals and clinics. Children between one and six years old seemed to suffer most. The tragedy was made worse by the inability of either medical specialists or parents to do anything. Relatives watched mutely from doorways as doctors placed intravenous feeding tubes in the children's arms and oxygen tubes in their noses and mouths.

For weeks, sirens wailed, cremations took place one after another and bodies were buried in mass graves. The worst panic took place 10 days after the accident, on December 13, when Union Carbide announced that it would start the plant up again on Sunday, December 16 to neutralize what remained of the MIC.

Bhopal, normally a city of 900,000, was already depleted. Besides the 2,000 dead and the 200,000 injured, 100,000 others had fled after the disaster. Now 100,000 more took to trains, buses, cars, planes, auto rickshaws, two-wheeled tongas and their own feet to put a distance between themselves and what they perceived to be the site of another possible catastrophe.

Two thousand paramilitary troops and special armed police officers were brought in by the Indian government to supplement the local police force in an effort to prevent the looting of vacated homes and to maintain order in the clinics and refugee camps.

Most of the dead came from Jai Prakash Nagar and Kali Parade, the two slum neighborhoods adjacent to the plant, but the brisk night breeze carried the fatal fumes much farther than that.

A year after the accident, residents of Bhopal who had been affected by MIC were still suffering. According to authorities in India, an estimated 10 to 20% of the 200,000 people injured were still seriously affected. Many were having trouble breathing, sleeping, digesting food and undertaking simple tasks, just as they had right after the leak occurred.

They suffered memory loss, nausea, nerve damage, including tremors, and damage to kidneys, liver, stomach and spleen. A year later, 40% of those afflicted were in the same condition, 40% had improved and 20% had worsened. Medical studies predicted that these would be long-term, perhaps lifelong, afflictions.

The relief effort had become bureaucratic and sometimes contradictory. Cortisone injections were given by one medical team; cough medicine and aspirin by another. One health expert, Rashmi Mayur of the Urban Institute in Bombay, averred that he had come across one victim who had been able to get 250 pills in one day from seven different doctors.

What ultimately became apparent in the tragic unfolding of this disaster was that ignorance was also a culprit. Even as people were dying, Union Carbide factory doctors were telling local physicians that MIC, which is used in 20 to 25% of all the world's pesticides, only caused lung and eye irritation. And none of these company doctors had informed the local medical workers ahead of time that a simple antidote for the effects of the chemical was to merely cover the face with a wet cloth. 'Had we known this,' police superintendent Swaraj Puri later told reporters, 'many lives might have been saved.'

Six months before the accident, the National Academy of Sciences had said that little or nothing was known about the health effects of most of the 54,000 chemicals used in commercial products, thus making treatment and prevention difficult at the very best.

Afterward, concerted efforts were made to find causes and blame, and there was more than enough to go around. Officials of Union Carbide were arrested when they arrived in India and then freed. They were later charged with criminal negligence, as was the plant supervisor. The government of India filed suit against Union Carbide in the federal district court in Manhattan, seeking compensation for the victims of the disaster. The suits are still pending.

It was generally acknowledged that the seeds of the tragedy were planted in 1972 when, under government pressure to reduce imports and loss of foreign exchange, the company proposed to manufacture and store MIC at the plant in Bhopal. Both the local government and the company agreed, at that time, that the risks would not be high.

Dr. S. R. Kamat, a prominent Bombay expert on industrial health and the hazards of development, probably summed it up most succinctly and accurately: 'Western technology came to this country but not the infrastructure for that technology,' he told the *New York Times* on February 2, 1985. 'A lot of risks have been taken here,' he went on. 'Machinery is outdated. Spare parts are not included. Maintenance is inadequate. Bhopal is the tip of an iceberg, an example of lapses not only in India but by the United States and many other countries.'

JAPAN – TSURUGA
March 8, 1981

A leak from a disposal building at the nuclear power plant at Tsuruga, Japan on March 8, 1981 caused widespread radiation contamination. Fifty-nine workers were exposed to radiation, and Japan's fishing industry was temporarily suspended.

UNITED STATES – IDAHO, IDAHO FALLS
January 3, 1961

Sabotage was suspected but never proved in the chemical explosion that blew apart the reactor core at the Idaho Nuclear Engineering Laboratory in Idaho Falls on January 3, 1961. Three died.

UNITED STATES – OKLAHOMA, GORE
January 4, 1986

Faulty judgment was the culprit in the chemical leak at the Sequoyah Fuels Corporation Plant at Gore, Oklahoma on January 4, 1986. One died.

UNITED STATES – PENNSYLVANIA, MIDDLETOWN
March 28, 1979

The worst nuclear disaster in the history of the United States was blamed on human error, which was in turn caused by design flaws. No deaths or injuries occurred at the plant; there is still contention over infant and fetus mortality after the radiation spread. The chief casualty was the growth of the National Atomic Power Program.

The worst nuclear disaster in U.S. history occurred in one of America's youngest nuclear power plants. The Three Mile Island Unit Two Nuclear Power Generator, owned by the Metropolitan Edison Company and located on an island in the Susquehanna River, approximately 11 miles south of Harrisburg, Pennsylvania, began operation on December 28, 1978. According to a letter sent by consumer advocate Ralph Nader to President Jimmy Carter, the plant was rushed into service in order to obtain a tax break of $40 million, despite the fact that, during its initial break-in period, the reactor was experiencing mechanical failures and other problems.

Nader was, and still is, opposed to public nuclear power, and that undoubtedly skewed his evaluation of the birth of the plant. Still, there must have been a basic core of truth in his accusations, for just slightly more than three months after it began operating, the Three Mile Island generator showed its flaws in a dramatic and terrible way, by leaking radiation over an enormous area and by narrowly missing that most dreaded of nuclear accidents, a reactor meltdown.

At 3:58 A.M. on Wednesday, March 28, 1979, the first of a chain of mishaps occurred at the plant. A pump that provided steam to the electric turbines broke down. This in turn shut down another pump that circulated water through the reactor, which in turn raised the temperature of the reactor, which opened a relief valve designed to bleed off the increased pressure brought about by the rise in temperature. Within the reactor, some of the cladding, or sheaths around the fuel rods, melted. The uranium pellets in them apparently did not.

By this time, alarms were sounding in the control room, and operators, unschooled in this sort of unprecedented emergency, began to make wrong decisions, while the system itself malfunctioned. The relief valve failed to close, and consequently pressure in the reactor dropped low enough to allow the water to vaporize.

Then, a major error was committed. An operator opened a valve allowing water from this system to enter a waste tank where it created enough pressure to rupture the plumbing. Sixty thousand gallons of radioactive water flooded the reactor to a depth of eight feet.

A second human error followed rapidly. The emergency core cooling system kicked in, but an operator shut it off.

Now, a pump flooded an auxiliary building with contaminated water, causing a release of steam. Within moments, radioactive steam poured up the vent stack and into the atmosphere.

Inexplicably, it would take operators almost three hours to act on these events. It would be 7 A.M. before state authorities would be informed and another hour before the authorities would declare a 'general emergency.'

Even this general emergency was, as in the Windscale disaster (see p. 302) minimized, presumably to prevent panic. Margaret Reilly, of Pennsylvania's Department of Radiation Protection, in one of the most monumental understatements of all time, likened the escape of radiation, to 'a gnat's eyelash.'

However, authorities were aware that a minimum of a million millirems per hour of radiation was present inside the reactor building at Three Mile Island, a lethal dose for anyone directly exposed to it. Monitors

1,000 feet from the vent stacks, where the radioactive steam was spewing into the air, showed levels of 365 millirems of beta and gamma rays per hour.

Three months later, Albert Gibson, a Radiation Support section chief who would coauthor the Nuclear Regulatory Commission's final report on Three Mile Island emissions, testified, 'All radiation monitors in the vent stack, where as much as 80 percent of the radiation escaped, went off the scale the morning of the accident. The trouble with those monitors is they were never contemplated for use in monitoring accidents like Three Mile Island.'

Besides the beta and gamma emissions, there were bursts of strontium and iodine-131, which characteristically settles on grass, is eaten by cows and thus enters the milk supply.

On Thursday, holding tanks filled to overflowing with radioactive water were opened, pouring 400,000 gallons of water containing xenon-133 and xenon-135 into the Susquehanna River, while federal nuclear officials assured the public that the gases posed 'little hazard to persons living downstream of the . . . plant.'

By the end of Thursday, March 29, detectable levels of increased radiation were measured over a four-county area, and officials at the plant admitted that, contrary to their early assessment, 180 to 300 of the 36,000 fuel rods in the reactor had melted.

At 9 A.M. on Friday, March 30, the Pennsylvania Emergency Management Agency reported that there had been a new, 'uncontrolled release' of radiation – a puff of contaminated steam.

Because of intense radioactivity within the reactor, the temperature had risen high enough in places to break up the water molecules into hydrogen and oxygen, forming a large bubble of hydrogen, which, if large enough, could prevent further reduction, therefore inhibiting the ability of the circulating water to cool down the fuel rods.

Thus, a meltdown was possible, and becoming more probable.

Now, Governor Richard Thornburgh issued a directive that advised pregnant women and small children to evacuate and stay at least five miles away from the Three Mile Island facility.

In 23 schools, children were pulled from classes, crammed into cafeterias and ordered not to open windows. From these gathering points, they were transported in sealed school buses to other schools 10 to 15 miles away. ('It was sure hot in that bus with all those windows up,' said nine-year-old Kim Hardy, from Etters, a community within the five-mile radius.) Parents were then informed of their children's whereabouts.

Fright, but no panic, abounded. An air-raid siren shrieked in Harrisburg shortly before noon, setting off a midday traffic jam of jittery state employees. The alarm was explained away by the governor's office as either a malfunction or the overzealous response of a civil defense official to Governor Thornburgh's directive.

Meanwhile, towns near the plant, such as Goldboro, had been emptying out ever since the beginning of the accident. A small leak of people from the villages had turned into a torrent by Friday, the 30th. Gasoline stations were jammed; telephone switchboards were so overloaded that callers received nothing but busy signals.

Fifteen mass-care centers were established in counties surrounding the Middletown area.

Back at the plant, officials were tensely monitoring the bubble of hydrogen, trying to decide whether to allow it to sink to the bottom of the containment vessel by drawing off water – and thus risking a further increase of temperature and the consequent possibility of a meltdown – or starting up the reactor again and trying to saturate the bubble with steam, which would break it up.

A third, venting method was tried, and on Saturday, the 31st, the bubble was reduced enough so that a combination of safety rods and water could hasten the 'cold shutdown' of the reactor. The danger of a melt-down passed.

By Monday, April 9, the Nuclear Regulatory Commission (NRC) declared the Three Mile Island crisis at an end and said it was safe for pregnant women and young children to return to their homes, despite the fact that the reactor was still leaking small quantities of radiation into the air and that readings of radiation emissions were still above average.

Schools were reopened, government offices returned to business as usual and the civil defense forces were taken off full alert. It would be months before the reactor would be entirely shut down, and further instrument failure would lengthen that process, too.

But the book on Three Mile Island was not closed, by any means. First, there was the business of assigning responsibility for the accident. On May 11, 1979, the NRC issued a report blaming the operators for 'inadvertently turn[ing] a minor accident into a major one because they could not tell what was really happening inside the reactor.' This juxtaposition of human, instrument and design error ran through the NRC report like a fugue.

The accident began when someone forgot to reopen a set of valves, and operators failed to notice the mistake. Operators apparently paid attention mainly to the pressurizer water indicator, which was misleading them, and failed to watch other instruments that should have informed them that something was wrong. Operators apparently failed to follow the procedure for dealing with a stuck-open pressure relief valve, and so forth.

But in its conclusions, the NRC removed some of the onus from the operators. 'Human factors engineering has not been sufficiently emphasized in the design and layout of the control rooms,' it admitted in its summary.

In February 1984, Metropolitan Edison Company pleaded guilty to charges that it knowingly used 'inaccurate and meaningless' test methods at the Unit Two reactor prior to the accident. The company then disciplined 17 employees – among them a former vice president, shift supervisors, control room operators, shift foremen and managers – for manipulating records of the tests. The penalties ranged from letters of reprimand to the loss of two weeks' pay.

Another aspect of the continuing story of Three Mile Island was the effect on the surrounding population.

As in practically every nuclear accident, there was no evacuation plan in place when the disaster occurred. To compound this, reports released during and after the accident were, either deliberately or inadvertently, misinformation. Despite the admirable motivation of preventing needless panic, the 'gnat's eyelash' analogy seems irresponsible in light of the later findings of other scientists and investigators.

Although the NRC continued to maintain that there had been and was still no significant intensification of radiation as a result of the Three Mile Island accident, Dr. Ernest Sternglass, a University of Pittsburgh Medical School professor of radiology, in a paper presented at the Fifth World Congress of Engineers and Architects at Tel Aviv, Israel in 1980, stated that figures from Harrisburg and Holy Spirit hospitals showed that infant deaths in the vicinity of Three Mile Island had *doubled*, from six during February through April 1979 to 12 in May through July.

Furthermore, Dr. Sternglass observed, data from the U.S. Bureau of Vital Statistics showed that there were '242 [infant] deaths above the normally expected number in Pennsylvania and a total of 430 in the entire northeastern area of the United States.' He based his linkage on the large amounts of iodine-131 released into the atmosphere and the peaking of infant mortality within a matter of months after the release of the I-131.

Dr. Sternglass went on to charge that, as NRC investigator Joseph Hendrie had confirmed on March 30, 1979, individual areas where the steam plume touched the ground were 'husky' and in the range of 120 millirems per hour or more, which was easily enough to cause severe damage to fetuses in the womb.

In addition, Dr. Sternglass noted that doses of I-131 had impacted people in the path of the plume in Syracuse, Rochester and Albany, New York, and each city had suffered rising infant deaths.

'My daughter got real sick,' Becky Mease of Middletown told an NRC panel. 'She had diarrhea for three days straight and headaches and she became anemic. I didn't know what to do. My little girl is still getting colds and sinus problems. Now if that's not because of that power plant, you tell me what it is.'

Deaths in the Middletown area from thyroid cancer (the thyroid gland is particularly affected by iodine-131) are still monitored by families and organizations. No absolute link has been established, but those who were affected feel that the cause was the accident and the radiation it released into the Pennsylvania countryside. Some cancer victims have sued the Metropolitan Edison Company.

And finally, the third reason for the continued interest in Three Mile Island is the ongoing impact it has had on the nuclear energy industry in America. Prior to Three Mile Island, antinuclear activists were relatively quiescent. On May 6, 1979, after the accident, a crowd of 65,000 demonstrators arrived at the Capitol in Washington, D.C. to demand the cessation of building and the closing of nuclear power plants in the United States.

The Three Mile Island disaster opened the door to an escalation of protest activity that became rocket powered after the Chernobyl disaster (see p. 322). It was responsible for the abandonment of the Shoreham Nuclear Energy plant on Long Island, and the virtual halt in construction of nuclear power plants nationwide in the 1980s.

USSR – KASLI
1957

Military and Soviet secrecy has muffled the details of an explosion in a nuclear waste dump near Kasli, in the Ural Mountains of the USSR, sometime in 1957, but a chemical or steam explosion has been theorized as its cause. Hundreds were said to have died; tens of thousands were afflicted.

USSR – PRIPYAT
April 26, 1986

The worst recorded nuclear accident in history, that of the Chernobyl nuclear power plant in Pripyat, USSR on April 26, 1986, was the result of human error in conducting a test of the system. Thirty-one died in the explosion and fire; more than 100,000 were evacuated from the vicinity of the plant, and casualties are yet to be finally calculated.

'An accident has occurred at the Chernobyl nuclear power plant as one of the reactors was damaged. Measures are being taken to eliminate the consequences of the accident. Aid is being given to those affected. A government commission has been set up.'

Two days after the stupendous disaster at the Chernobyl nuclear power plant, located 70 miles north of Kiev, the capital of the Ukraine, the Soviet government released this terse, businesslike and uninformative announcement.

Some of the facts and some of the effects of this, the worst nuclear disaster in history, had already drifted out of the Soviet Union, on winds bringing radioactive waste to Scandinavia, then eastern Europe, then western Europe and finally to the rest of the world, including the United States.

The situation at Chernobyl was frightening. With four 1,000-megawatt reactors in operation, it was one of the largest and oldest of the Soviet Union's 15 or so civilian nuclear stations. There, a cascade of awesome human errors had set in motion, as surely as uranium brought about a chain reaction, a series of events the likes of which the world had yet to experience.

At 1 A.M. on Friday, April 25, operators of the number-four reactor, which had gone on line in 1983, began to reduce its power in preparation for an operations test. The test was designed to measure the amount of residual energy produced by the turbine and generator after the nuclear reactor had been shut down. The conclusion of the test would tell these engineers how long the turbine and generator would be able to run if, in some sort of emergency, the reactor were shut down.

It was a routine test. The valves on the main steam line between the reactor and the turbine were to be closed, thus stopping power to the turbine, and the residual energy would then be measured until the turbine stopped.

While this was happening, steam would still be produced by the reactor, which would be slowly reduced to a fraction of its potential power. That steam could either be released into the atmosphere through bypass valves or condensed back to water in a cooling unit. If the operators decided to rerun the test, they could open the valves to the turbine and close the bypass valves.

The difficulty with the process was that, if the reactor continued to operate, certain 'perturbations,' as nuclear experts euphemistically call them, could take place in the reactor, which could in turn increase the pressure and cause the unit to be automatically shut down. Or, they could reduce the pressure, causing the automatic flooding of the reactor with emergency cooling water.

In other words, no one could tell just what would happen in the reactor under these circumstances, but the operators at Chernobyl, determined to carry through their test without a shutdown of the reactor, *shut off all of the emergency safety systems.*

As astounding as that seems, this is exactly what happened at 2 P.M. on Friday, the 25th, as the reactor was reduced to 7% capacity. The reactor's emergency cooling system was shut off. Then the power regulating system and the automatic shutdown system were disconnected. It was a little like a fire department responding to a burning fire and then dismantling the fire alarms and fire escapes and going home.

What the operators did was in violation of regulations, but they did it anyway – as countless other operators in other industrial and nuclear accidents had and would – and continued with their routine testing through the afternoon and evening. And all the while, the 'perturbations' went on in the reactor.

Some time during this process, a reactor operator received a computer printout that indicated the reactor was in extremely serious danger of overheating unless it was shut down immediately. He ignored it.

Control rods were withdrawn, lowering the power in the reactor below the minimum required by the unit's operating manual. Xenon gases began to build up as the temperature rose in the reactor.

At 1:22 A.M. on Saturday, April 26, these same operators noticed that the power level had risen to the point at which, had the emergency system been engaged, it would have shut down. The operators noted it and kept on testing. If they had stopped at that moment, if they had heeded the warnings the instruments were clearly giving them and reengaged the safety system, the disaster would not have occurred. But they blundered on, ignoring the obvious.

Exactly one minute and 40 seconds later, the reactor blew. There was a loud bang as the control rods began to fall into place. At that instant, the operators knew exactly what was about to happen. They desperately tried to drop the rest of the control rods to stop the runaway chain reactions that were taking place in the reactor, the splitting by radiation of superhot water and the reactions caused by the superheating of its graphite shell.

But it was too late. The control rods drop by gravity, and that takes time, and the operators of the reactor had used up all the time there was. Twenty seconds later, the fuel atomized. Three explosions tore through the reactor, blowing off its top, sending its 1,000-ton steel cover plate rocketing into the air and ripping off the tops of all 1,661 channels, which were attached to the cover plate and contained the nuclear fuel. The channels became like '1,000 howitzers pointed at the sky,' according to Dr. Herbert J. C. Kouts, the chairman of the Department of Nuclear Energy at Brookhaven National Laboratory on Long Island. Powered by these nuclear howitzers, a huge fireball shot up into the sky. The graphite caught fire and burned, fiercely and wildly. The reactor was completely out of control and beginning to melt down.

Flames continued to shoot over 1,000 feet into the air. This would continue for two days and nights. The operators within the building were doomed. Emergency alarms went off all through the complex, in which 4,500 workers were employed.

Miles away, a startled populace witnessed a gigantic fireworks display of hot radioactive material being flung into the night sky and onto the winds that would eventually carry this material far enough to contaminate a huge nearby area and, eventually, to a much lesser and varying degree, much of the rest of the world.

The reactor continued to burn, while emergency teams hauled off the dead and the radiated. Others, their boots sinking in molten bitumen, uselessly attempted to battle the blaze. But, as in other nuclear accidents around the world, evacuation of the populace was delayed, while scientists debated the seriousness of the situation.

Finally, at 1:50 P.M., on Sunday, April 27, fully 36 hours after the accident, the local radio station at Pripyat announced that a full-scale evacuation was to begin immediately. The city of 40,000 was to be totally abandoned, and 1,100 buses, some of them commandeered from Kiev, undertook the task. To prevent panic, rallying points were not used. The city was emptied within two hours and 20 minutes.

The countryside around Pripyat, a region of wooded steppes, small villages and moderately productive farms, was less thickly populated. Between Pripyat and Chernobyl lay the Kiev reservoir, fed by the Pripyat River. And at this point, radioactive matter was falling like lethal rain onto the thinly settled countryside and into this reservoir that supplied water to the 2,500,000 people of Kiev, Russia's third largest city.

Meanwhile, at the plant, workers were shutting down the other three reactors. The fire continued to burn unchecked. Twenty-five percent of the radiation leaked in the accident was released in the first 24 hours of the fire. The fire would continue for eight days.

On Monday morning, April 28, Swedish monitoring stations detected unusually high levels of xenon and krypton and concluded that, considering the prevailing winds, an atomic accident had occurred in the Soviet Union. Sweden demanded that the Soviets comply with international agreements to notify other nations immediately after a nuclear accident that might threaten those countries with radiation.

It was not until 9 P.M. that night that the Soviets released the terse statement quoted at the beginning of this entry, a masterpiece of noninformation.

But the truth began to seep out. On Tuesday, Soviet diplomats in Europe and Scandinavia approached private nuclear agencies, asking advice on fighting graphite fires. United Press International, frustrated by the silence from official sources, quoted a Kiev woman who communicated with them by telephone. 'Eighty people died immediately and some 2,000 people died on the way to hospitals,' she told UPI. 'The whole October Hospital in Kiev is packed with people who suffer from radiation sickness.'

A Dutch radio operator reported a message received from a Soviet ham broadcaster. 'We got to know that not one, but two reactors are melted down, destroyed and burning. Many, many hundreds are dead and wounded by radiation, but maybe many, many more,' he said, ending with a plea. 'Please tell the world to help us,' he concluded.

This was clearly at odds with the official version of events, which placed the dead at two and the injured at 197.

Now, the heavier products of radiation, the ones that the atmosphere could not dissipate easily and were lethal to human beings, were beginning to fall on Europe. Among a score of elements detected in the fallout were cesium-134 and iodine-131, both easily assimilated by the body and both thought to cause cancer.

By Wednesday, April 30, European countries began to take steps to preserve their own people. In Austria, mothers in the province of Carinthia were being advised to keep infants and small children indoors. The Polish government banned the sale of milk from grass-fed cows and issued iodine tablets to infants, children and pregnant mothers in order to protect the thyroid gland against poisoning from iodine-131. In Sweden, officials warned people not to drink water from casks that collected rain water for summer cottages and banned the import of fresh meat, fish and vegetables from the Soviet bloc countries. Evacuation plans were activated for citizens who were traveling or working in the area within 200 miles of Chernobyl. A group of American students studying in Kiev boarded planes for Moscow, then London, then the United States.

By Thursday, May 1, the Soviet bulletins noted that 18 people were in critical condition and that the fire was cooling down. In an effort to control it still further, civil defense forces began to drop bags of wet sand from helicopters hovering over the gaping hole in the top of the reactor. The radioactivity levels within the building were still too high to allow human beings, even in protective gear, to enter.

International help came swiftly. Dr. Robert Gale, the head of the International Bone Marrow Transplant Registry, left Los Angeles for Kiev on May 1. Two days later, his associate, Dr. Richard Champlin, and Dr. Paul Terasaki, a tissue-typing expert, joined him. They would have much work to do with the hundreds hospitalized from the accident.

Wind patterns were affecting the radiation levels reported in various European countries. In Sweden, it fluctuated between normal and five times the normal amount. Traces of iodine-131 were detected in rainwater samples in the Pacific Northwest region of the United States, but they were not deemed dangerous.

By Monday, May 5, the Soviet government announced that dikes were being built along the Pripyat River to prevent potential contamination and that the leakage of radiation from the plant had virtually stopped.

This was not the case, as later studies would indicate. In a report released the following September, a study prepared by the Lawrence Livermore National Laboratory in California asserted: 'The nuclear disaster at Chernobyl emitted as much long-term radiation into the world's air, topsoil and water as all the nuclear tests and bombs ever exploded.' Cesium, a product associated with health effects such as cancer and genetic disease, does not break down into a harmless form for more than 100 years, and it was sent into the atmosphere in quantities, the study estimated, that were as much as 50% more than the total of hundreds of atmospheric tests and the two nuclear bombs dropped on Japan at the end of World War II.

On May 9, the Soviets began the monumental task of encasing the still smoldering wreck of a reactor in concrete. It involved tunneling under the reactor, in order to prevent a 'China syndrome' style of meltdown, which would immediately contaminate the groundwater near the reactor. The massive job was begun by dropping thousands of tons of sand, boron, clay, dolomite and lead from helicopters into the graphite core. Then the huge sarcophagus of concrete was poured and erected.

As May gave way to June, Soviet authorities attempted to protect citizens from the continuing effects of exposure to radiation. On May 15, 25,000 students in the Kiev area received an early vacation when all of the elementary schools and kindergartens were closed early for the summer.

Officials told residents of Kiev to keep their windows closed, mop floors frequently and wash their hands and hair often to reduce the chance of radiation contamination. And for the first time, these authorities acknowledged the dissemination of radiation over the rest of Europe.

The Russian children would be transported by the state to 'Pioneer' camps scattered from the Moscow suburbs to the Crimea. More than 60,000 children, in fact, joined the first evacuees from Pripyat, who, like 12-year-old Olya Ryazanova, remembered a fire-blackened nuclear power plant, 'a sort of mist, a misty cloud around it,' and booted workers washing down the road in front of her home.

On May 15, the day the schools closed, the radioactive cloud had, after first blowing north to Scandinavia and Byelorussia, reversed itself and was hovering over Kiev. Crowds had formed at railroad stations and airports, most of them women and children, and the government had added extra trains and flights out of the city.

As more accurate information began to filter out of the Soviet Union, the scope of the disaster continued to grow. Hans Blix, the head of the International Atomic Energy Agency, confirmed that at least '204 persons, including nuclear power station personnel and firefighters, were affected by radiation from the first degree to the fourth degree.' The government newspaper *Izvestia* revealed that more than 94,000 people had been evacuated. Eventually, the official number of dead would be set at 31.

It was learned that a full month before the disaster, a Ukrainian journal had reported management failures and labor dissatisfaction at Chernobyl. Because coal was becoming scarce in the Soviet Union, construction at the plant was speeded up in 1984, and it was suggested that this haste – a fifth nuclear reactor was already under construction at the time of the accident – was partially responsible for the tragedy.

But ultimately, the blame was focused on human error, and in June, *Pravda* announced that the director and chief engineer of the plant had been dismissed for mishandling the disaster and that other top officials were accused of misconduct ranging from negligence to desertion.

As with any nuclear catastrophe, the story of Chernobyl had no quick ending. Today, nearly a decade after the accident, Pripyat is a ghost town, a place from which everyone has departed forever, and the sarcophagus that encases the 171 tons of coagulated and resolidified uranium fuel is becoming outdated. Its contents will remain radioactive and dangerous for at least 150 years, and the 20-story-high cube of concrete and steel that was hastily executed to bury that radiation has a life span of only 25 years.

The exploded generator's tortured and twisted mass of nuclear fuel can be viewed through special periscopes. According to a reporter for the *New York Times*, it resembles a 'nightmarish cave, of great uranium magma oozings solidified into what workers already are nicknaming "elephant's feet" of deadly radioactive permanence.'

In addition to the rebuilding of the gigantic sarcophagus, scientists, workers and officials are faced with the problem of the 800 burial pits of other contaminated material, including trees, topsoil and even entire houses. Some of them are close to Pripyat's water supply, and if the city is ever to live again, these pits will also have to be encapsulated with clay, concrete and steel, or perhaps decontaminated. But scientists are still uneasy about disturbing the now quiescent nuclear debris.

In recent years, the independent Soviet republics have demanded that three nuclear power generators still operating at the Chernobyl plant be closed by 1995.

Today, the long-term effects of the radiation are just beginning to manifest themselves. Data show that 150,000 people, many of whom used the obviously contaminated Kiev water system, are suffering from some sort of thyroid illness. Sixty thousand of these are children, and of these, 13,000 have what is termed 'very serious' problems requiring ongoing treatments.

Power plant workers now live in a new town, Slavutich, located 35 miles east of the plant, where even the tree bark has been scrubbed clean of radiation. Still, hot spots have been discovered here and there in the new village, and workers must change their clothes three times en route, twice a day, as they traverse the 18-mile 'hot-zone' around the plant.

Near Chernobyl, 500 tons of dangerously irradiated beef have been stored in 40 refrigerated boxcars ever since the disaster. No one knows what to do with it.

Alarming medical data are being gathered. Sickness rates are reported up 45% over 1988, and the death rate is even higher. No conclusive evidence of linkage has been released, however.

Officials from Pripyat have been quoted in Radio Liberty's 'Report on the USSR' as saying that the death toll in the cleanup was probably more than 300. But the official total still stands at 31. Even so, all experts agree, this figure will continue to rise for years, perhaps generations, to come.

Railway Disasters

The Worst Recorded Railway Disasters

Chronology

* Detailed in text

1833
Nov. 11
    Hightstown, New Jersey
1842
May 8
    * Versailles, France
1853
May 6
    * South Norwalk,
        Connecticut
1856
July 17
    * Camp Hill, Pennsylvania
1857
Mar. 17
    Hamilton, Ontario
1864
June 29
    * St. Hilaire, Quebec
July 15
    * Shohola, Pennsylvania
1867
June 26
    Bhosawal, India
Dec. 18
    * Angola, New York
1871
Feb. 25
    St. Nazaire, France
Aug. 26
    * Revere, Massachusetts
1876
Jan. 8
    Odessa, Russia
Dec. 29
    * Ashtabula, Ohio
1879
Jan. 11
    Philippopolis, Turkey
Dec. 28
    * Dundee, Scotland

1881
June 24
    * Cuartla, Mexico
1882
July 13
    Tcherny, Russia
1887
Aug. 10
    * Chatsworth, Illinois
1888
Oct. 10
    * Mud Run, Pennsylvania
1889
June 12
    * Armagh, Ireland
1891
June 14
    * Basel, Switzerland
Dec. 8
    Lahore, India
1895
Feb. 28
    Mexico City, Mexico
1896
July 30
    * Atlantic City, New Jersey
1899
Aug. 24
    Mapocho River, Chile
1902
Sept. 11
    Madras, India
1903
June 27
    San Arsenslo, Spain
Aug. 10
    Les Couronnes, France
Dec. 23
    * Laurel Run, Pennsylvania
1904
Aug. 7
    * Eden, Colorado

Sept. 24
  * Hodges, Tennessee
1907
Sept. 19
  Encarnacion, Mexico
1908
May 8
  Moradabad, India
1910
Mar. 1
  Wellington, Washington
1913
Dec. 6
  Costesi, Romania
1915
Jan. 18
  * Guadalajara, Mexico
May 22
  * Gretna Green, Scotland
1916
Nov. 19
  Behesa, Mexico
1917
Dec. 12
  * Modane, France
1918
July 9
  * Nashville, Tennessee
Oct. 15
  Bucharest, Romania
Nov. 2
  * Brooklyn, New York
1919
Oct. 5
  Mexico City, Mexico
1920
Dec. 22
  Petrograd, Russia
1925
June 16
  * Hackettstown, New
      Jersey
1926
Mar. 15
  Virilia River, Costa Rica

1933
Dec. 23
  * Lagny, France
1935
Sept. 24
  Loyang, China
1937
July 16
  * Patna, India
1938
April 5
  Yencheng, China
1939
Dec. 22
  * Magdeburg, Germany
1940
Jan. 28
  Osaka, Japan
1944
Mar. 2
  * Salerno, Italy
Nov. 7
  Aguadilla, Spain
Dec. 31
  * Ogden, Utah
1945
Feb. 1
  * Cazadero, Mexico
1946
Mar. 20
  * Aracaju, Brazil
1947
July 10
  Canton, China
1949
April 28
  Orlando, South Africa
Oct. 22
  * Nowy Dwor, Poland
1950
April 6
  * Tangua, Brazil
May 7
  Jasidih, India

Nov. 22
* Queens, New York
1951
Feb. 6
* Woodbridge, New Jersey
April 4
Sakuragicho, Japan
June 8
Nova Iguacu, Brazil
1952
Mar. 4
* Pavuna River, Brazil
July 9
Pzepin, Poland
Oct. 8
* Harrow-Wealdstone,
England
1953
Dec. 24
* Waiouri, New Zealand
1954
Jan. 21
Sind Desert, Pakistan
Sept. 24
* Hyderabad, India
1955
April 3
* Guadalajara, Mexico
1956
Sept. 2
* Mahbubnagar, India
Nov. 23
Marudaiyar, India
1957
Sept. 1
* Kendal, Jamaica
Sept. 29
* Gambar, Pakistan,
1958
May 8
* Mangueira, Brazil
1959
May 28
* East Priangan, Java

1960
Nov. 14
* Pardubice,
Czechoslovakia
1962
May 3
* Tokyo, Japan
May 31
Voghera, Italy
1963
Nov. 9
* Yokohama, Japan
1964
July 26
* Custoias, Portugal
1965
Dec. 9
Toungoo, Burma
1967
June 6
* Laangenweddingen, East
Germany
1970
Feb. 1
* Buenos Aires,
Argentina
1972
June 4
* Jessore,
Bangladesh
June 16
* Vierzy, France
July 21
* Lebrija, Spain
Oct. 9
* Saltillo, Mexico
1974
Aug. 30
* Zagreb, Yugoslavia
1981
June 6
* Mansi, India
1982
Jan. 27
Algiers, Algeria

Railway Disasters

As the first means of mechanical transportation, the railroad enjoyed a long period of unchallenged supremacy and comparative safety. Slow speeds, a conservative amount of track mileage, and a small number of passengers combined to keep the accidents and the casualty numbers low.

The very first days of rail travel were, in fact, restricted entirely to traffic in and out of mines.

It would be another three centuries before railways were used to transport people. The first railway in the world to carry fare-paying passengers was the Ostermouth Railway (also known as the Swansea & Mumbles Railway), which opened for business in April 1806 in Ostermouth, England.

By 1833, the wrecks began. By 1853, railways, particularly in America, were catastrophes waiting to happen. Whereas the English were constructing their railroads carefully and safely in the middle of the 19th century, with an eye for permanence, laying double rows of tracks and erecting substantial bridges, viaducts and tunnels and eliminating curves and grades, the American way was to put it all up quickly and expediently.

Thus, the foundation for the major categories of train wrecks was laid simultaneously with the hasty laying of track: Head-on and rear-end collisions were the result of single tracks and primitive signal systems; derailments came about through sloppy track laying and brittle wheels and axles; bridge disasters came about from poorly designed and hastily built bridges; telescopes resulted from a lethal link and pin coupling method between cars; crossing accidents resulted from lack of communication on the lines; fires resulted from a combination of superheated steam boilers in the engines and wooden cars heated by coal stoves and illuminated by oil lamps.

Many of these failings that would cause grisly accidents and terrible loss of life before the turn of the century would be corrected.

Even so, the most up-to-date technology cannot cancel out human failure. As more sophisticated signal devices were developed, signal men, conductors and engineers sometimes ignored them, resulting in catastrophe. As the possibility of higher speeds was introduced through more advanced equipment, engineers misjudged track conditions and drove their high-speed trains off the rails, into abutments or off bridges.

More recently, societal conditions have been responsible for train wrecks. The overcrowding of trains in Bangladesh and India, where poverty dictates that train and bus travel are the only means by which enormous segments of the populace can travel, has resulted in calamitous tragedies, with enormous loss of life. Inebriated train operators have also become a hazard. And drug use has necessitated mandatory random drug testing for American railroads.

Despite the hazards, railroading remains a relatively safe mode of transportation.

Like the other disaster categories in the book, events in this section were chosen in terms of human, not material, loss. An arbitrary cutoff figure of 50 deaths was used, and the only deviations from this figure occurred when historic firsts were deemed important enough to be included.

ARGENTINA – BUENOS AIRES
February 1, 1970

Human error caused the collision of an express train and a commuter train near Buenos Aires, Argentina on February 1, 1970. One hundred forty-two died; hundreds were injured.

On Sunday night, February 1, 1970, a cross-country express train of Argentina's Bartolome Mitre railroad, composed of two diesel locomotives and 21 passenger coaches containing 500 people, was nearing the end of its 1,000-mile journey from the northern city of San Miguel de Tucuman to Buenos Aires. It was traveling at 65 miles per hour and was 50 minutes behind schedule.

Ahead of it, a commuter train, packed with 700 weekenders returning to Buenos Aires from the fashionable northern suburb of Zarate, had experienced mechanical difficulty and was stalled five miles outside the Pacheco station, which was 18 miles from Buenos Aires.

A signalman, Maximo Bianco, on duty near the crash site should have warned the approaching express of the stalled commuter train. But for some reason he did not, and the express plowed into the back of the stalled local train at 65 miles an hour.

'We were going very, very fast,' said survivor Maria Isabel Algoden, 'when all of a sudden everything exploded and people went everywhere.'

The last five cars of the commuter train were crushed beyond recognition. Other cars telescoped into one another, mangling their occupants and upending some of the coaches. Wreckage was strewn over a wide area on either side of the tracks outside Pacheco.

Rescue crews were dispatched immediately. Firemen installed mobile power stations to illuminate the wreckage, and air force helicopters flew blood plasma, medical kits and surgical instruments to the macabre, floodlit scene.

Ambulances, trucks, commercial buses and private cars were pressed into service to transport the injured to an emergency hospital that was set up in the Pacheco railroad station. There, doctors from Buenos Aires labored to save whomever they could. The less seriously injured were taken into Buenos Aires and its hospitals.

The dead were first lined up along the tracks and then taken to the Pacheco and Benavidez stations, where they were displayed for identification purposes. One hundred forty-two persons died, most of them in the rear cars of the commuter train. Hundreds more were injured.

At first, authorities blamed terrorists. Only 90 minutes before the crash occurred, terrorists had attacked a railroad station three miles from the site of the collision and had made off with $400. Some link between the two incidents was thought to exist.

But further investigation led to the arrest of signalman Maximo Bianco and two of his fellow workers for failing to engage the warning signals that would have informed the engineer of the express that the commuter train was stalled in front of him. Once more, human error had caused a tragic rail accident.

BANGLADESH – JESSORE
June 4, 1972

Human error caused the collision of an express train with a standing train in the station at Jessore, Bangladesh on June 4, 1972. Seventy-six were killed on the train and the station platform; 500 were hospitalized.

BANGLADESH – MAIZDI KHAN
January 15, 1989

Bangladesh's worst train disaster, the collision of an overloaded express train with a mail train near Maizdi Khan on January 15, 1989 was caused by human error – the switching of both trains onto the same track. One hundred thirty-six died; more than 1,000 were injured.

On January 15 in Tongi, a city in central Bangladesh, hundreds of thousands of pilgrims gathered for a Muslim religious festival. The devout came from all over Bangladesh to take part in the ceremonies, and a train, filled to overflowing with more than 2,000 pilgrims, made its way north from Dhaka to Tongi and then southeast to Chittagong. Passengers were everywhere – in seats, in the aisles, on the platforms, on the roofs of the cars. It was not an unusual occurrence, but in this case it was a terribly dangerous one.

Several days before, a new signal system had been initiated on this line, and later official explanations blamed what was about to occur on railroad personnel being confused by the new system.

The express bearing the more than 2,000 pilgrims had almost reached Tongi. It was speeding at 50 miles per hour, near the village of Maizdi Khan, when suddenly a mail train appeared, headed in the opposite direction on the same track. There was no time for either train to brake, although the mail train had almost stopped. They crashed head-on.

The impact flung the diesel locomotives of both trains off the tracks, and the first two coaches of each train were carried with the locomotives. Other cars telescoped into one another, picking off the passengers on the roofs as if they were billiard balls. 'I saw coaches flying up to 15 feet as the collision occurred,' said a soldier who, with some 250 other military men, was involved in winter exercises near the tracks. 'It was a terrible scene with hundreds of passengers – men, women and children – shouting for help.'

The carnage was appalling. Bodies, some of them without limbs or heads, were strewn over the country-side. Screams and moans filled the air. The soldiers were the first on the scene, and they pulled more than 100 dead passengers from the mangled cars and laid them side by side along the tracks.

Medical teams and ambulances arrived, but the job was overwhelming. More than 1,000 were injured, 100 of them critically enough to require hospitalization. Hundreds were taken to hospitals in Tongi, five miles north of Maizdi Khan; hundreds more were taken to Chaka, the capital, 22 miles to the south.

Police were brought in to control the crowd of thousands, who thronged the fields around the wreckage trying to find loved ones among the rows of bodies. Twenty-six would die in the hospitals. A total of 136 would perish, and more than 1,000 would be injured in this, Bangladesh's worst railway accident.

BRAZIL – ARACAJU
March 20, 1946

The worst train wreck in Brazil's history occurred near Aracaju on March 20, 1946 when an overcrowded commuter train derailed. One hundred eighty-five died; several hundred were injured.

Brazil's worst train wreck also caused a bizarre aftermath. An overcrowded suburban commuter train carrying 1,000 passengers was apparently too heavy to negotiate a steep incline near Aracaju, the capital of the Brazilian coastal state of Sergipe. It derailed; its cars uncoupled, telescoped and piled up at the bottom of the incline.

Hundreds were trapped in the crushed cars; 185 died and several hundred were injured.

Grief-stricken relatives descended on the scene and discovered the surviving passengers. Enraged at the accident, they turned on the engineer. The thoroughly terrified man fled on foot and finally surrendered himself to authorities in the nearby town of Laranje-tras. Several of the survivors, blaming him for the crash, tried to lynch him, the engineer told the local police, who took him into protective custody.

BRAZIL – MANGUEIRA
May 8, 1958

Human error – a wrong switch thrown – caused the head-on collision of two commuter trains near Mangueira, Brazil on May 8, 1958. One hundred twenty-eight died; more than 300 were injured.

BRAZIL, PAVUNA RIVER
March 4, 1952

Overloading, outdated equipment and unrepaired track caused the collision of two suburban trains on the Pavuna River bridge in Brazil on March 4, 1952. One hundred nineteen died; hundreds were injured.

BRAZIL – TANGUA
April 6, 1950

A lack of warning signals and torrential rains were responsible for a passenger train plunging through a weakened bridge over the Indios River near Tangua, Brazil on April 6, 1950. One hundred ten died; 40 were injured.

CANADA – ONTARIO, HAMILTON
March 17, 1857

Failure to maintain a railroad bridge caused a train to break through the bridge and fall into the Des Jardines Canal near Hamilton, Ontario on March 17, 1857. Sixty died; 20 were injured.

CANADA – QUEBEC, ST. HILAIRE
June 29, 1864

The worst bridge disaster in North America occurred at St. Hilaire, Canada on June 29, 1864 as a result of human negligence; the engineer of a passenger train failed to stop before crossing the open St. Hilaire drawbridge. Ninety were killed; more than 100 were injured.

CZECHOSLOVAKIA – PARDUBICE
November 14, 1960

Both engineers of two passenger trains ignored speed and right-of-way regulations and collided near Pardubice, Czechoslovakia on November 14, 1960. One hundred ten died; 106 were injured.

FRANCE – LAGNY
December 23, 1933

Heavy fog and excessive speed combined to cause the collision of a Strasbourg-bound express with the stationary Nancy express and a commuter train near Lagny, France on December 23, 1933. One hundred ninety-one died; 280 were injured.

FRANCE – MODANE
December 12, 1917

A military order to move a severely overloaded troop train near Modane, France on December 12, 1917 resulted in the derailment and plunge of the train into a gorge. More than 1,000 soldiers were killed; hundreds were injured.

It would be 15 years before there would be a full accounting of one of the worst railway disasters in history. The reason: It occurred in wartime, the train was loaded with servicemen and the responsibility for the wreck lay squarely on the shoulders of the military officers in charge.

In early December 1917, a troop train was packed far beyond its safe capacity with more than 1,200 war-weary French soldiers on their way home for Christmas. The war had been going badly for the French, and this respite was seen as a necessary one for morale.

Alarmed at the weight and balance problems resulting from the overloading, the engineer refused to leave the station until the load was decreased. A French staff officer confronted the engineer, warning him that he would be court-martialed for refusing to follow orders if he did not pull his train out immediately. The engineer remained adamant, citing safety regulations. The officer produced a pistol and warned that the engineer's offense was a capital one and that he would therefore have him executed for refusing to obey wartime orders. Faced with this ultimatum, the engineer agreed to begin what would be a fatal journey.

The overweight train, loaded with celebrating soldiers, navigated the flat portion of its journey uneventfully. But part of its return trip would take it through the Alps in the southeastern corner of France. It entered the steeply graded Mount Cenis Tunnel near the village of Mondane. Partway through the tunnel, the overloaded train wrested itself away from the engineer's control and accelerated far beyond safe limits.

At the bottom of the grade at the end of the tunnel was a wooden bridge and a sharp curve. Below it was an immense and deep gorge. The train blasted the bridge to tinder, shot off the rails and fell sickeningly into the gorge below. When it struck bottom, it burst into flames, which consumed the entire train in a matter of minutes. More than 1,000 soldiers died in the crash and the flames. Hundreds were injured. Only a handful of survivors emerged from this monumental and avoidable disaster. Ironically, one of these survivors was the engineer.

FRANCE – VERSAILLES
May 8, 1842

A rear-end collision of two excursion trains in Versailles, France on May 8, 1842 killed 54 passengers. The cause was a combination of overloading and a broken axle on the lead train.

FRANCE – VIERZY
June 16, 1972

Two trains crashed into the collapsed Vierzy tunnel in France on June 16, 1972. One hundred seven died; 90 were injured.

GERMANY – LAANGENWEDDINGEN
June 6, 1967

The failure to report a defective grade crossing in Laangenweddingen, East Germany caused the collision of a commuter train and a gasoline truck at the crossing on June 6, 1967. Eighty-two were killed; 51 were injured.

The grade crossing alongside the railroad station in the little town of Laangenweddingen, located near Magdeburg, 80 miles southwest of Berlin and 20 miles from the West German border, was defective in July 1967. The barrier, which should have lowered and prevented vehicles from crossing the tracks, snagged repeatedly on an overhead telephone line and failed to close. There was a crossing guard, and it was his duty to report this sort of danger to his supervisor, who would order the proper repairs to be made. But from the time of the first discovery of the defective crossing gate, no such warning had been issued. At 8 P.M. on the evening of July 6, 1967, the lack of a report resulted in tragedy.

That night, a gasoline truck, owned by the East German state-operated oil corporation and loaded with 4,000 gallons of gasoline, approached the grade crossing. Seeing no barrier, the driver assumed that it was safe to cross the tracks and so drove ahead.

At that instant, a double-decker commuter train roared into sight. There was no time for the train to stop or the truck to dislodge itself. The train slammed full speed into the truck; it exploded in an incendiary spectacle that shot flames to enormous heights. The cars of the train were set afire; the explosion blew apart the engine and the first four coaches, which were heavily loaded with children.

Flaming gasoline poured into the cars, onto the tracks and onto the roof of the railroad station, which caught fire and burned to the ground. Inside the trains, children were burned to cinders instantly. Seventy-nine people died on the spot; three more died of their injuries later in the local hospitals at Magdeburg and Bahrendorf. Fifty-one were injured, and Red Cross volunteers, doctors, firemen and policemen labored for hours cutting away wreckage and pulling the injured and the dead from the twisted mass of fused and still-hot metal.

An investigation was immediately initiated, and five days later, the crossing operator and his supervisor were arrested and charged with manslaughter. The results of their trial were never released by the East German authorities.

GERMANY – MAGDEBURG
December 22, 1939

The ignoring of a signal by the engineer of the Berlin express caused him to crash at full speed into the rear of the Cologne express near Magdeburg, Germany on December 22, 1939. One hundred thirty-two died; 109 were injured.

GREAT BRITAIN – ENGLAND, HARROW-WEALDSTONE
October 8, 1952

Ignoring signals by the engineer of one train caused the multiple collision in the Harrow and Wealdstone station, near London, on October 8, 1952. The worst crash in the history of British Rail, to that date, it killed 112 and injured 165.

The worst crash in British Rail history took place at the worst possible time – at the height of the morning commuter rush hour. An estimated 1,000 persons jammed the platform of the Harrow and Wealdstone station, some 11 miles west of London, on the morning of October 8, 1952. Most were waiting the arrival of the local from Tring and West Hertfordshire to London, but a few had arrived early to board the many commuter shuttles that used this customarily crowded station.

The local loaded up at 8:19 and was just pulling out of the station when the Night Scot, an express from Perth to London, late and trying to make up time, roared into the station on the same track as the local. It had ignored the clear signals set by signalman A. G Armitage at Harrow number one box and, oblivious, hurtled into the rear of the local train, flinging coaches everywhere and ripping an enormous hole in a footbridge that ran beneath the tracks.

According to observers, bodies seemed to fly through the air, and some dropped through the hole in the footbridge. It was a catastrophic scene, but not the end of the carnage. Seconds later, the Manchester express, also late and trying to make up time, sped into the station on an adjacent track that was now blocked with some of the cars of the demolished commuter train. The express, powered by two enormous engines, careened into the cars. Both engines left the tracks, soared vertically into the air and came down directly on the platform, which was crowded with waiting commuters.

Scalding gouts of steam erupted everywhere. Severed electric lines rained sparks and swung lethally over the scene. Within minutes, thousands of rescuers rushed to the station, freeing those who were reachable, bandaging horribly mangled bodies, administering morphine to those who were trapped or maimed or dying.

It would be two days and nights before the two rear

coaches of the local would be reached, by cutting with acetylene torches, and there the rescue operation reached its most hopeless nadir. There were few survivors and scores of dead in these two cars alone.

One hundred twelve died; 165 were seriously injured in that morning of horror at the normally placid commuter stop of Harrow and Wealdstone.

GREAT BRITAIN – SCOTLAND, DUNDEE
December 28, 1879

Storms caused the buckling of the Tay River Bridge near Dundee on December 28, 1879. Seventy-five people were killed when a train plunged through it; there were no survivors.

The Tay River Bridge at Dundee was completed in 1877, and it was hailed worldwide as a triumph of engineering skill. The longest bridge in the world, it was also the most modern, the strongest, the most graceful.

But a mere two years after its completion, it would be the scene of one of the saddest disasters in the history of rail travel, one in which there was not a single survivor.

The train that left Edinburgh at 4:15 P.M. on December 28, 1879 was traveling in hard conditions. A raging storm with hurricane-force winds had lashed the countryside all day, battering at houses and seawalls and swelling streams and rivers. One of the rivers that was at least three times its normal depth was the Tay, and its boiling waters had been ramming the pilings of the Tay River railbridge since the storm began.

The train started to cross the multiple-span bridge at 6:15 and traversed almost half of its length before disaster struck. Midway through the central span, the train lurched as girders began to buckle beneath it. Thirteen girders gave way, pulling the structure out from beneath the wheels of the train and flinging it 88 feet into the river below.

It was only a matter of minutes before the waters closed over the train, leaving nothing in evidence but stray pieces of it, floating bits and pieces of luggage and boards from the cars that shattered on the rocks or were crushed by the steel girders that hurtled downward once the train had shaken them loose.

Seventy-five people – all the passengers and crew – died in this wreck.

GREAT BRITAIN – SCOTLAND, GRETNA GREEN
May 22, 1915

Human error on the part of a signalman caused the crash of a troop train and 2 passenger trains near Gretna Green on May 22, 1915. Two hundred twenty-seven were killed; 223 were injured.

On May 22, 1915, Great Britain's worst railway disaster took place at Gretna Green, in Scotland, reportedly the fault of one man, a signalman who threw the wrong switch.

Gretna Green is a small town in which several tracks of the Caledonian Railway intersect. At 6:00 A.M. on May 22, 1915, a troop train loaded with 500 soldiers bound for the Western front roared into view. The signalman waved it on, and into a direct collision course with a local train traveling in the opposite direction. Within minutes, both trains hit head-on, turning the engines into mangled, hissing interweavings of steel and telescoping a series of passenger cars into one another.

The signalman had no sooner left his post to try to assist in rescue efforts when the London-Glasgow express appeared. With no signal to slow it, the express rammed both trains, igniting heavy ammunition and gas cylinders that were being carried in a baggage car of the troop train.

Within an instant, the wreckage was turned into an exploding inferno in which human beings were incinerated by the score.

A horrendous consequence of the soldiers' battle dress made rescue a dangerous proposition. Each of the soldiers was wearing an ammunition belt, and the heat of the fire began to set off the belts, causing them to explode, thus killing not only the wearer of the belt but rescuers in the vicinity.

Fire brigades, swarms of rescuers, nurses and doctors toiled all day and night to try to save whomever they could. Arms and legs were set, transfusions were given, battlefield operating rooms were set up and amputations were performed on the spot. Long before they got to the war, most of this company was decimated. Out of 500 soldiers and hundreds of civilians, 227 died and 223 were wounded. It was a catastrophe of immense proportions, one of the worst of the war, and it occurred, ironically, hundreds of miles and a channel from the battlefields.

INDIA – HYDERABAD
September 24, 1954

Monsoon rains weakened a bridge over the Vasanti River near Hyderabad, India, causing it to give way beneath a train on September 24, 1954. One hundred thirty-seven were killed; 100 were injured.

INDIA – MAHBUBNAGAR
September 2, 1956

Monsoon rains weakened a bridge over a gorge near Mahbubnagar, India, and a train was flung into the gorge as the bridge collapsed on September 2, 1956. One hundred twelve were killed; hundreds were injured.

INDIA – MANSI
June 6, 1981

*The worst train wreck in India's history was caused by
an engineer's decision to brake for a cow on the tracks
on the rainy night of June 6, 1981 near Mansi. Two
hundred sixty-eight bodies were recovered; more than
300 were missing.*

Cows are sacred in India. To harm one is forbidden.
And the engineer of a nine-car passenger train passing
near Mansi, in the northeastern state of Bihar, 250
miles northwest of Calcutta, on the monsoon-whipped
Saturday of June 6, 1981 was certainly aware of this. A
devout Hindu, he would not, under any circumstances,
add further bad karma to the cycle of his lives by
harming a cow. And yet, on that rainswept night, as his
train, loaded with more than 1,000 passengers,
approached a bridge over the Baghmati River, there it
was: a cow standing on the track.

The engineer applied the brakes, too suddenly, too
fast and at just the wrong place. The momentum of the
train carried it forward; the following cars, sliding on
rain-slick rails, on a roadbed that had been made, by
the heavy rains, soft and insecure, derailed and
whipped forward. Seven of the nine coaches and the
locomotive plunged over the embankment, off the
bridge and into the whirling waters below. It was over
in an instant; the cars catapulted downward one after
the other, careening and crashing into one another
before they sank swiftly into the monsoon-swollen
river.

Survivors in the last two cars which remained on the
tracks moaned as they faced the fate of the others.
There was nothing to be done but to run for help to
take out the bodies. There was no sign of life in the
river below.

Within hours, help arrived. Fifty-nine divers, 110
soldiers and scores of villagers from Mansi and other

nearby settlements searched the wreckage and the riverbanks for miles and for days. Two hundred sixty-eight bodies were found, but more than 300 passengers from the tragically fated seven cars were missing and assumed dead. It was the worst railway wreck in the history of India.

INDIA – PATNA
July 16, 1937

A monsoon-softened track bed accounted for the derailment of a passenger train near Patna, India on July 16, 1937. One hundred seven were killed; 65 were injured.

INDONESIA – JAVA, EAST PRIANGAN
May 28, 1959

The uncoupling of several cars of a passenger train in an act of sabotage sent the cars careening into a ravine in East Priangan on the island of Java on May 28, 1959. One hundred forty were killed; 125 were injured.

Sabotage was responsible for the worst train wreck in the history of Indonesia, in which a trainload of innocent passengers plunged into a ravine in the East Priangan regency of West Java province on the island of Java.

Indonesia in 1959 was a country in ferment. Under pressure from the United Nations, the Dutch had given way to Nationalist pressure in 1949, and an independent republic of Indonesia was formed. Sukarno was elected president of a parliamentary form of government, but his administration was marked by inefficiency, injustice, corruption and chaos. Inflation soared in the 1950s, and economic depravation spawned a popular revolt. It began in Sumatra in 1958, and widespread disorders caused Sukarno to become more and more authoritarian. In

May 1959, there were numerous incidents that killed both the innocent and the involved. Sukarno would dissolve parliament in 1960.

One of these incidents was the train wreck of May 28 in West Java. The Bandjar-Bandung express was loaded with 500 passengers and, early that morning, was traveling through mountainous terrain, slashed by ravines hundreds of feet deep. The train was not moving fast; there were numerous curves and steep inclines, and it was on just such an incline that someone uncoupled the engine from the entire complement of passenger cars.

Set free, the cars rolled backward, gaining speed alarmingly. There were apparently no independent braking devices on them, and in moments the cars left the tracks, careened crazily on the edge of a precipice and then plunged hundreds of feet into a ravine.

Miraculously, some passengers escaped uninjured, but 140 were killed and 125 seriously injured in the wreck.

At first, the conductor was charged with negligence, but further investigation determined that an unidentified person (he or she would never be captured and brought to trial) had uncoupled the cars from the engine. Speculation grew that Sukarno might have invented the charges to cover up still another example of inefficiency or corruption in his government, but the dissolution of parliament in 1960 forestalled any possibility of a public inquiry.

IRELAND – ARMAGH
June 12, 1889

A faulty decision by a conductor led to the collision of two excursion trains near Armagh, Ireland on June 12, 1889. Three hundred were killed; hundreds were injured.

ITALY – SALERNO
March 2, 1944

The stalling of a train in a tunnel near Salerno, Italy on March 2, 1944 caused the death by asphyxiation of more than 400 passengers and crew.

Ordinarily, railroad wrecks are the result of head-on and rear-end collisions, derailments, collapsed bridges or switching errors. These are the most common hazards, and there are safety regulations and precautions to prevent them. But no one could predict the circumstances that would lead to one of the most tragic train wrecks in the history of European rail travel.

On March 2, 1944, at the height of World War II, a train loaded to capacity with military and civilian passengers approached Salerno, Italy. A long tunnel marks the last few meters into the city, and for a reason never explained, this train stalled midway through the tunnel. The fumes from the engine accumulated and spread through the cars, killing over 400 passengers. Trapped and asphyxiated in their seats, they had no chance of escaping the lethal contamination.

JAMAICA – KENDAL
September 1, 1957

Mechanical failure caused the derailing of a train near Kendal, Jamaica on September 1, 1957. One hundred seventy-five died; more than 750 were injured.

JAPAN – TOKYO
May 3, 1962

Human error – the running of a signal – caused the collision of a freight train and a commuter train near Tokyo on May 3, 1962. One hundred sixty died; more than 300 were injured.

JAPAN – YOKOHAMA
November 9, 1963

A cracked rail was responsible for a three-train collision near Yokohama, Japan on November 9, 1963. One hundred sixty-two died; 72 were injured.

KENYA – DARAJANI
January 30, 1993

In the worst rail disaster in Kenya's history, 200 were killed when a passenger train crashed into a 94-year-old bridge and plunged into a flood-swollen tributary of the Athi River 40 miles from Mt. Kilimanjaro. More of the train's 600 passengers would have died if an alert conductor had not detached the third-class coaches from the rest of the train.

MEXICO – CAZADERO
February 1, 1945

Human error – a faulty switch setting – caused the collision of an excursion train and a freight train in Cazadero, Mexico on February 1, 1945. One hundred died; 70 were injured.

MEXICO – CUARTLA
June 24, 1881

Faulty judgment on the part of an engineer caused the plunge of a train through a weakened bridge near Cuartla, Mexico on June 24, 1881. A fire compounded the tragedy. Two hundred sixteen died; 40 were injured.

MEXICO – GUADALAJARA
January 18, 1915

Loss of control by the engineer on a steep grade

accounted for the derailment of a train near Guadala-jara, Mexico on January 18, 1915. Over 600 died; scores were injured.

Even in the best of times, the military tends to obfuscate the precise details of incidents that result in great loss of life to that military's personnel. In 1915, Mexico was awash with civil unrest and violence. President Victoriano Huerta had resigned, partly because of U.S. military intervention under President Woodrow Wilson, and one of the revolutionaries, Venustiano Carranza, was the ostensible head of the country. But bands of brigands, led by Francisco 'Pancho' Villa and Emiliano Zapata, continued to terrorize the countryside.

Still, Carranza hoped to present a face of relative order in a country that had been split asunder by civil war, and so, when a railroad wreck of awesome proportions and horrendous fatalities occurred near Guadalajara on January 18, 1915, he and his military aides made certain that the world received no official news of it.

The only report of this tragedy came from a letter written in February 1915 by American missionary Mrs. John Howland to the American Board of Commissions for Foreign Missions.

Guadalajara province was secured by Carranza's troops on the 18th of January, and as a reward to his troops, Carranza ordered that their families be sent by train from Colima to join them. The train carried 20 cars, but this was inadequate to accommodate the number of people. 'The roofs [were] covered with men and women and many slung under the cars in a most perilous position even for ordinary travel,' wrote Mrs. Howland.

'At the top of the steepest grade, coming down,' she continued, 'the engineer lost control, the cars rushed down the long incline, throwing off human freight on both sides and finally plunging into an abyss.

'Nine hundred people were on the train and only six were unhurt. More than six hundred were killed outright,' the letter concludes, thus making this one of the most lethal train wrecks of the world.

MEXICO – GUADALAJARA
April 3, 1955

No reason was given for the derailment of a passenger train over a gorge near Guadalajara, Mexico on April 3, 1955. Three hundred were killed; hundreds were injured.

MEXICO – LOS MOCHIS
August 10, 1989

Most of the 112 people who were killed in the wreck of a passenger train that fell from the Rio Bamoa bridge into the rain-swollen San Rafael River on August 10, 1989 died from drowning. The bridge collapsed under the train, sending the engine and two passenger cars into the river.

MEXICO – SALTILLO
October 9, 1972

Drunkenness in the cab and excessive speed were the causes of the derailment of a passenger train near Saltillo, Mexico on October 9, 1972. Two hundred eight were killed; hundreds were injured.

MEXICO – TEPIC
July 11, 1982

An eroded roadbed accounted for the derailment of a train near Tepic, Mexico on July 11, 1982. One hundred twenty died; hundreds were injured.

NEW ZEALAND – WAIOURI
December 24, 1953

A swollen river caused by a volcanic eruption caused the bridge accident of a train near Waiouri, New Zealand on December 24, 1953. One hundred fifty-five died; there is no record of survivors.

The eruption of the 9,000-foot-high volcano Mount Ruapehu, near Waiouri, New Zealand, in December 1953 was described by seismologists as 'minor.' And in the scale of volcanic activities it undoubtedly was.

The eruption was, however, intense enough to send millions of gallons of water barreling down the River Wangaehu, which in turn weakened the Tangiwai Railroad Bridge. On Christmas Eve it was about to be crossed by the Wellington-Auckland express, a nine-car passenger train loaded with hundreds of well-wishers on their way to welcome Queen Elizabeth II, who was making a rare visit to New Zealand.

Partway across the span, the train broke through the sagging and swaying trestle and plunged into the roaring river. Some cars floated, momentarily, but most sank like boulders, drowning 155 hapless passengers.

PAKISTAN – GAMBAR
September 29, 1957

Inadequate signals caused the collision of a passenger train and an oil train in Gambar, Pakistan on September 29, 1957. Three hundred died; 150 were injured.

PAKISTAN – SINDH PROVINCE
January 4, 1990

Three hundred seven were killed and 700 injured when an improperly set switch sent a 16-car passenger train, the Zakaria Bahauddin, *onto a siding, where it crashed*

*head-on into a standing, 67-car freight train. It was one
of the worst railway disasters in history.*

**POLAND – NOWY DWOR
October 22, 1949**

*Excessive speed was blamed for the derailment of a
passenger train near Nowy Dwor, Poland on October
22, 1949. Two hundred were killed; 400 were injured.*

**PORTUGAL – CUSTOIAS
July 26, 1964**

*The overloading of a passenger car caused its derailment
in Custoias, Portugal on July 26, 1964. Ninety-four
died; 92 were injured.*

The worst train accident in the history of Portugal
occurred because of the overloading of one passenger
car. Designed to carry a maximum of 70 passengers,
one of the cars of the Automara express was packed
with 161 holiday revelers on their way from the seaside
resort of Povoa de Varzim to Oporto, Portugal on July
26, 1964.

A short six miles from the end of their journey, near
the village of Custoias, the overloaded car came
uncoupled, jumped the track and raced down an
embankment. It would take seven hours to excavate
the smashed debris of the car and unearth survivors and
the dead. Sixty-nine people died instantly in the accident; 92 were seriously injured, and of those, another
25 died in the hospital, bringing the total of dead to 94.

**SPAIN – LEBRIJA
July 21, 1972**

*Human error – the ignoring of a signal – caused the
collision of two trains near Lebrija, Spain on July 21,
1972. Seventy-six died; scores were injured.*

SWITZERLAND – BASEL
June 14, 1891

A collapsed bridge caused the accident of June 14, 1891 in Basel, Switzerland. One hundred twenty were killed; scores were injured.

UNITED STATES – COLORADO, EDEN
August 7, 1904

Swollen rivers caused the wreckage of one bridge to collide with another, collapsing it just as a train passed over it near Eden, Colorado on August 7, 1904. Ninety-six died; scores were injured.

Collisions of trains are not uncommon. But collisions of bridges are quite another phenomenon, destined for the record books. And such an occurrence resulted in one of the United States' more terrible train disasters.

Much of the land of the American West is scarred with arroyos – gullies that once contained a river or small stream. Pacific train number eight, which because of the St. Louis World's Fair had earned itself the nickname World's Fair Flyer, crossed a number of these arroyos on its trip from Denver to St. Louis and back again. Arroyos were usually just part of the scenery, and the bridges that forded them were maintained in a desultory manner, as were the wagon bridges, some of which were never maintained but left to age in the relentlessly extreme weather.

The beginning of August 1904 brought heavy rains to Colorado, and the normally dry arroyos were no longer unobtrusive. They overflowed with boiling mountain streams, tumbling toward valleys miles away. On the night of August 7, the World's Fair Express paused momentarily at the small mountain town of Eden and then pushed on toward St. Louis.

If its only task had been to cross Steele's Hollow Bridge, its trip would have been as serene as it usually was. But on this particular night, coincidence conspired with nature and brought about a catastrophe. Just as the seven-coach express began its traverse of the railroad trestle, an ancient wagon bridge a short distance upstream collapsed with a roar.

Propelled by the floodwaters in the arroyo, the timbers of the wagon bridge acted like battering rams and slammed into Steele's Hollow Bridge just as the train was in mid-span. Trestle and train collapsed simultaneously and were flung into the water. Nothing was left of the three main spans of the bridge. The train's locomotive, baggage car and chair and smoking cars dove into the stream together. A quick-thinking porter, seeing the disaster occurring ahead of him, grabbed the air brakes on the two sleepers and dining car, saving himself and his fellow passengers from the horrible fate of those in the rest of the train.

Frank Mayfield, the fireman of the train, was thrown clear. He landed on the embankment and was knocked unconscious. Later, his eyewitness account describing the wreck and early rescue attempts formed the basis of most news accounts of the disaster.

What he saw were pullman cars sitting serenely on the tracks, no sign of the engine, and passenger cars with their roof burst open by the impact. Passengers and wrecked cars alike were driven miles downstream by the raging floodwaters, and the army of more than 500 rescuers would spend days and nights digging debris and bodies out of the muddy river banks. Ninety-six died and scores were injured in this freak accident.

UNITED STATES – CONNECTICUT, SOUTH NORWALK
May 6, 1853

Disregard of both a signal and a speed limit caused the bridge accident over the Norwalk River near South

Norwalk, Connecticut on May 6, 1853. Forty-six were killed; 25 were injured.

UNITED STATES – ILLINOIS, CHATSWORTH
August 10, 1887

Human negligence led to the weakening of a railroad bridge, which caused an excursion train to fall through it at Chatsworth, Illinois on August 10, 1887. Eighty-two died. There is no record of injuries.

UNITED STATES – MASSACHUSETTS, REVERE
August 26, 1871

Outdated equipment was responsible for the collision of two excursion trains in Revere, Massachusetts on August 26, 1871. Thirty-two died; more than 100 were injured.

UNITED STATES – NEW JERSEY, ATLANTIC CITY
July 30, 1896

Human error was blamed for the broadside collision of the Philadelphia express with a West Jersey excursion train at 'Death Trap,' a track intersection in Atlantic City, New Jersey, on July 30, 1896. Sixty were killed; hundreds were injured.

UNITED STATES – NEW JERSEY, HACKETTSTOWN
June 16, 1925

A collision with a mudslide caused the wreck of an excursion train in Hackettstown, New Jersey on June 16, 1925. Thirty-eight died; 38 were injured.

UNITED STATES – NEW JERSEY, HIGHTSTOWN
November 11, 1833

A broken axle caused the first derailment in U.S. history in Hightstown, New Jersey on November 11, 1833. One person was killed; several were injured.

UNITED STATES – NEW JERSEY, WOODBRIDGE
February 6, 1951

Speed was the culprit in the derailing of an express train at Woodbridge, New Jersey on February 6, 1951. Eighty-four died; more than 100 were injured.

UNITED STATES – NEW YORK, ANGOLA
December 18, 1867

Defective equipment caused the derailing of the Lake Shore express near Angola, New York on December 18, 1867. Forty-three were killed; hundreds were injured.

UNITED STATES – NEW YORK, BROOKLYN
November 2, 1918

Excessive speed, outdated equipment, defective brakes and an overworked motorman combined to cause the derailment of a Brooklyn Rapid Transit train outside Malbone Tunnel in Brooklyn, New York on November 2, 1918. Ninety-seven died; 95 were injured.

UNITED STATES – NEW YORK, QUEENS
November 22, 1950

Defective equipment was responsible for the rear-end collision of two Long Island Railroad trains in Queens, New York on November 22, 1950. Seventy-nine were killed; 363 were seriously hurt.

UNITED STATES – OHIO, ASHTABULA
December 29, 1876

A collapsed bridge caused a train to plunge into a gorge near Ashtabula, Ohio on December 29, 1876. Eighty were killed; 68 were injured.

UNITED STATES – PENNSYLVANIA, CAMP HILL
July 17, 1856

Missed schedules, inadequate signals and human error were responsible for the head-on collision of two trains near Camp Hill, Pennsylvania on July 17, 1856. Sixty-six children on an excursion train died; 60 were injured.

UNITED STATES – PENNSYLVANIA, LAUREL RUN
December 23, 1903

Debris on the tracks was the initial cause of the huge train wreck of December 23, 1903 near Laurel Run, Pennsylvania. Sixty-four died; nine were injured.

UNITED STATES – PENNSYLVANIA, MUD RUN
October 10, 1888

Outdated equipment accounted for the rear-end collision of two trains at Mud Run, Pennsylvania on October 10, 1888. Sixty-four died; 100 were injured.

UNITED STATES – PENNSYLVANIA, SHOHOLA
July 15, 1864

A 13½-hour departure delay caused the head-on collision of a troop train and a passenger train at Shohola, Pennsylvania on July 15, 1864. Seventy-four were killed; there is no record of the injured.

UNITED STATES – TENNESSEE, HODGES
September 24, 1904

Human error was blamed for the collision of two trains at Hodges, Tennessee on September 24, 1904. Sixty-three died; there is no record of the injured.

UNITED STATES – TENNESSEE, NASHVILLE
July 9, 1918

Human error was responsible for the worst rail crash in number of fatalities in U.S. history, a head-on collision of an express and a workers' train near Nashville, Tennessee on July 9, 1918. One hundred one were killed and 100 were injured.

UNITED STATES – UTAH, OGDEN
December 31, 1944

An engineer's heart attack was the cause of a rear-end collision near Ogden, Utah on December 31, 1944. Fifty died and more than 80 were injured.

YUGOSLAVIA – ZAGREB
August 30, 1974

Drinking in the cab of a train caused the crash of a train at high speed into the station at Zagreb, Yugoslavia on August 30, 1974. One hundred seventy-five were killed; there was no official report of injuries.

The worst rail accident in the history of Yugoslavia took place in the station at Zagreb on the night of August 30, 1974.

A solitary passenger train, the Belgrade to Dortmund express, traveling at nearly 55 miles per hour, roared into the station at Zagreb that night, its engine at full throttle. A subsequent board of inquiry would accuse the train's two engineers of drunkenness, and to the horrified witnesses of this cataclysm, it was the only plausible explanation for the bizarre scene that unfolded before them.

Out of control, the train crashed into the station platform and derailed, splaying its cars onto the platform and adjacent tracks. Electric power cables, used for commuter lines, exploded into sparks and fell on the metal cars, electrocuting some of the occupants as they tried to escape.

It would be hours before 50 passengers, trapped by the power lines and the overturned cars, could be rescued. They were the lucky ones. A staggering 150 passengers were killed by the crash and 25 others were electrocuted. The two engineers were acquitted of drunkenness but received reprimands for speeding.

Space Disasters

The Worst Recorded Space Disasters

* Detailed in text

United States
  Florida
  * Cape
      Canaveral (1967)

  * Atlantic Ocean (1986)

USSR
  * (1967)
  * (1971)

Chronology

Space Disasters

Thankfully, this section is a brief one. In the more than two decades of its existence, modern space exploration has claimed only 15 lives – 21 if you count the six American astronauts who died in airplane accidents and other ancillary activities. And perhaps there are other casualties never reported by the Soviet space program.

Space exploration has been largely dominated by the two world superpowers – the United States and the USSR. From that monumental moment in 1957, when *Sputnik I* was launched, the exploration of space moved from the pages of science fiction stories to the front pages of newspapers and from there to the imaginations of the world. To those who had trouble flying in an airliner and who now watched astronauts on the moon, the leap in achievement seemed almost beyond comprehension. But the public loved it. Reservations for the first passenger flight to the moon sold at a brisk clip in New York City in the early 1960s.

That the race between the two superpowers to put a man in space, then men on the moon, then people on space stations, then people on Mars and other planets would eventually extract its toll in human tragedy was scarcely believable in the early days of the space race. Even the high economic cost failed to dampen the exciting, adventurous enthusiasm of scientists and non-scientists alike. Up went the satellites, space stations and space shuttles, until outer space began to resemble an ill-tended backyard, full of floating garbage left by those who played in it.

It would take a tragedy the size of the 1986 *Challenger* explosion to sober up the world, it seemed. The adolescent love affair with outer space ended for many that January day. Experiment, the world learned, carries with it danger and responsibility.

Ironically enough, one of the lessons that has been learned from the four space tragedies that have occurred so far is that, as in civilian airline travel, the most dangerous moments in any flight occur during takeoff and landing. With the exception of the fire on the launchpad at Cape Canaveral that killed astronauts Grissom, White and Chaffee, all took place in the first few seconds of blastoff or the last few seconds of landing.

Thus, as this is written, more and more launchings are being aborted on the launchpad, as we learn from our disasters. It is only the beginning for the space program. And it is only the beginning of the chronicle of its disasters and achievements.

UNITED STATES – FLORIDA, CAPE CANAVERAL
January 27, 1967

Three Apollo I *astronauts perished in a simulation exercise at Cape Canaveral, Florida on January 27, 1967 when a fire caused by a spark from a faulty wire ignited the pure oxygen in their space capsule.*

UNITED STATES – FLORIDA, ATLANTIC OCEAN
January 28, 1986

While millions watched, the Challenger *space shuttle exploded on blastoff over the Atlantic Ocean near Cape Canaveral on January 28, 1986, killing all seven astronauts aboard. A combination of low temperatures, O-rings that malfunctioned, and NASA's determination to launch the shuttle caused the disaster.*

In the age of modern telecommunication, we have become accustomed to seeing history as it happens. Millions watched while Jack Ruby killed Lee Harvey Oswald on television, live. The evening news carried the Vietnam War into our living rooms, and, as violence escalated in society, the theory was postulated that, since that time when war appeared on our TV screens as information, we had become inured to violence, numbed by actuality-as-television-drama.

But nobody who was sitting before a television set on the morning of January 28, 1986 was immune to the escalating horror they witnessed as the space shuttle *Challenger* and its seven occupants exploded in a million fragments, 74 short seconds after they had taken off from Cape Canaveral, Florida. The personal shock and loss ran like an electric current through practically everyone in the nation, for this was the famous first flight that would take an ordinary citizen into space. Schoolteacher Christa McAuliffe was the Everywoman of the 20th century, and she was also the victim of one of its worst tragedies. Not since the assassination of John F. Kennedy 23 years before had such a shared sense of loss and sadness and bewilderment united ordinary people on the street.

The *Challenger* flight was a storybook mission. The space shuttle was a known quantity. It had succeeded before; it would succeed again. America felt good about its space program. The fact that there was a predominantly civilian crew aboard *Challenger* was, of itself, a positive sign. We had turned the corner toward space travel for the common person.

Scheduled to fly the *Challenger* that January day were mission commander Francis R. (Dick) Scobee; the pilot, Commander Michael J. Smith of the Navy; Lieutenant Colonel Ellison S. Onizuka of the Air Force; Dr. Ronald E. McNair, a physicist; Dr. Judith Resnik, an electrical engineer; Gregory B. Jarvis, another electrical engineer; and science teacher Christa McAuliffe.

Behind the scenes, the scenario was a little less sanguine. Bad weather at the Kennedy Space Center in Florida had already caused two postponements in three days of the *Challenger* launching.

It had originally been scheduled to leave on Sunday morning, January 26. But the weather reports on Saturday had been ominous, predicting heavy rain, and so the Sunday launch was scrubbed. As it turned out, the weather forecasters were wrong, and it was a balmy, blissful day, ideal for a space launch. But the cancellation, once put in motion, had to stand.

On Monday, January 27, the skies clouded up, but meteorologists predicted a clearing trend, so the *Challenger* astronauts suited up and boarded the ship. But a handle on the shuttle latch malfunctioned. Mindful of the Apollo disaster (see p. 378), those in command dispatched workers to free or replace the recalcitrant handle.

It would take the workers two hours to complete the job, and by then, stiff winds had blown up and the launch was again postponed, this time to 9:38 Tuesday morning, January 28, 1986.

But even that launch date and time were the subject of long and worried conferences. The winds that had postponed the January 27 launch preceded a cold front that was about to visit Florida. The forecast, issued in mid-afternoon of the 27th, called for freezing temperatures throughout the night.

'When we saw those predicted temperatures, I just knew we had to talk about it,' recalled Allan J. McDonald, an engineer who represented Morton Thiakol Inc., shuttle contractors and the manufacturer of the booster rockets. Mr. McDonald argued vehemently that evening against proceeding with the countdown. He and other Morton Thiakol engineers were concerned about the effect of the cold weather on the solid-fuel booster rockets. Their concern was focused on the O-rings, the rubber seals that contained the booster's hot gases.

These seals were obviously critical, and they had had a history of problems. A double set of synthetic rubber Os shaped like giant washers, they fit around the circumference of the rocket casing and were intended to fill the tiny gap that remained after two steel rocket segments were bolted together. In the past, the enormous pressures during blastoff had sometimes dislodged these seals. Besides, they had never been tested at temperatures lower than 53 degrees Fahrenheit.

So when McDonald got on the phone to Utah to confer with other engineers at Morton Thiakol, he returned with a unanimous recommendation for delay. The engineers suspected that cold weather could only heighten the chances of a failure of the O-ring seals. The rubber, they argued, would harden and shrink at these low temperatures, increasing the likelihood that the seals would open up. The consequences, they concluded, could be catastrophic.

NASA took this under advisement, but NASA was under pressure to proceed with this launch. They were scheduled to conduct 15 shuttle flights in 1986, which was six more than in any previous year. This was to be the symbolic 25th flight, which would demonstrate that it was safe and that space vehicles could be reused. And it was to be the first flight with an ordinary citizen aboard.

According to later testimony, NASA brought extreme pressure on Morton Thiakol to agree to a go-ahead. Finally, Morton Thiakol reluctantly agreed.

As the weather forecast predicted, the temperature fell below freezing. At 6 A.M., it was 27 degrees on the launchpad, and the shuttle's external tank was coated with frost and ice. A special ice team checked the shuttle and boosters three times – at 1:30 A.M., 7 A.M. and 11 A.M. They noted readings of seven and nine degrees in the right-hand booster rocket, much lower than in the left booster – an indication that liquid hydrogen might have been leaking from that rocket. In fact, there were indications that temperatures on the strut connecting the rocket to the external fuel tank were as low as eight degrees below zero. All of this could have signaled danger, but the ice team's mandate was merely to check for excess ice, and so their infrared temperature readings were not reported to high-level officials who made the decision about lifting off.

At 9:07 A.M., the seven astronauts boarded the shuttle. The photograph that will remain as one of the public's permanently stored images of that day shows them smiling, cheery and waving. It was a historic occasion, and the excitement was written on each of their faces.

They climbed into the shuttle, arranged themselves at their stations and drew on extra gloves. It was cold in the spaceship.

Shortly after they settled in place, the astronauts were told that the liftoff had again been put on hold to wait for the sun to warm up and melt some of the ice on the capsule and rockets. The delay would last for two hours.

The crew waited patiently – Francis R. (Dick) Scobee, the commander, and Commander Michael J. Smith at the controls, Dr. Judith Resnik in the center of the shuttle at the flight engineer position, Lieutenant Colonel Ellison Onizuka to her right, and in the mid-deck, Christa McAuliffe, Dr. Donald McNair and Gregory Jarvis.

At T minus nine minutes, the countdown was resumed. It was 38 degrees on the launchpad, 15 degrees colder than it had been for any previous launching at the cape, or anywhere else. At 6.6 seconds before liftoff, the *Challenger*'s three main engines roared to life. At zero, the two 149-foot booster rockets ignited.

'Liftoff,' announced the commentator in Houston. 'Liftoff of the 25th space shuttle mission, and it has cleared the tower.'

Several thousand spectators, including family members of some of the crew, shivered and cheered as the boosters and the shuttle began their slow ascent into the heavens. It all looked so easy and smooth and impressive.

But less than a second into the flight, there was

trouble. A puff of black smoke shot out of the lower part of the right booster, at a location covered by a seal. And this was probably the cause of the coming tragedy. The puff of smoke went undetected at the time, and was only found when photos were examined the next day.

Twelve to 13 seconds after liftoff, the smoke, which had spread and blackened, disappeared. The computers monitoring the mission registered no warnings or problems.

At 40 seconds into the flight, when the main engines had been throttled down to 65% thrust, the shuttle encountered heavy, shifting winds. It responded by automatically pivoting the booster and main engine nozzles to maintain the correct trajectory.

At 52 seconds, the three engines began their steady throttling up to full power. 'Challenger, go with throttle up,' Mission Control radioed.

'Roger, go with throttle up,' responded Scobee, calmly.

At 59 seconds, the *Challenger* reached its maximum dynamic pressure, when the vibrations of thrusting rockets, the momentum of the ascent and the force of wind resistance combined to exert incredible stresses on the shuttle structure. At this moment, the O-rings would be tested to the extreme.

A new plume of smoke now appeared on the lower side of the right booster. The pressures, which should have been equal between the two boosters, started to diverge. The right booster's pressure dropped alarmingly, indicating a leak. The fire in the O-ring was being fed by escaping fuel. Both the primary and backup seals had ruptured, and at 73.175 seconds into the mission, there were flashes of light and a series of explosions. At 73.621 seconds, there was a sudden surge of pressure in the main engines. Intense heat shut down one of them.

Now the superheated propulsive gases set off a chain of events that led to the explosion of propellants in the huge primary fuel tank. Flames from the leak severed the struts that held the rocket's base to the fuel tank. As the booster pivoted outward, its nose swung in and ruptured the tank, releasing its hydrogen, and a fierce explosion occurred. The shuttle and its rockets were consumed in an immense fireball.

At this moment, the *Challenger* was about nine miles above the earth and seven miles out over the Atlantic Ocean from the Florida coast. Spectators looked on in horror as the shuttle, soaring so serenely against the crystalline blue of the morning sky, suddenly blew apart in a huge orange flash and then, trailing a white plume, arched over and fell back to earth. On thousands of TV screens, including the ones in Christa McAuliffe's school, the identical, horrible scene was unfolding.

From Houston, at Mission Control, there was a long, terrible pause. 'Obviously a major malfunction,' stated Stephen Nesbitt, the public relations officer describing the liftoff. 'We have no downlink,' he added, meaning that all communication with the *Challenger* had ceased. There was a long pause, and then Nesbitt came back on the line. 'We have a report,' he said, 'from the flight dynamics officer that the vehicle has exploded.'

Debris would rain down on the Atlantic for hours, making immediate salvage operations impossible. It would be March 10 before Navy divers would find the crew compartment, with its crew inside, in 100 feet of water, 15 miles northeast of Cape Canaveral. The cabin, it was learned, had remained intact until it hit the ocean, where it broke apart on impact. It is believed that the seven were alive and perhaps conscious during that long, nine-mile plunge to the surface of the ocean. It was theorized that the seven had met their deaths either through the shock of the initial blast, the sudden depressurization of the cabin or by the force of the tumbling, nine-mile descent.

In whatever way, they were gone, the U.S. space

program would be thrown into confusion and reassessment. It would be a long, long time, experts predicted, and many, many safety precautions, before another *Challenger* would be launched from the pad at Cape Canaveral into another blue sky of another clear Florida morning.

USSR
April 23, 1967

A defective parachute caused the crash of Soyuz I *on April 23, 1967 in the USSR. Vladimir Komarov, its sole astronaut, was killed in the crash.*

Vladimir M. Komarov was a Muscovite who had served in the Soviet Air Force from the age of 15 but was almost dropped from the Soviet space program because of a heart murmur. The tall, dark-haired astronaut was a jet fighter pilot with a scholarly nature that had, in 1954, won him admission to the Zhukovsky Air Force Engineering Academy in Moscow.

His training as an aeronautical engineer made him an ideal candidate for space, and in the fall of 1964, he and two companions, scientist Konstantin P. Feoktistov and doctor Boris B. Yegrow, tested the first of the eight-ton Vosknod spaceships. The three made 16 orbits of the earth that fall, and Komarov proved that his physical disability had been either exaggerated or cured.

In 1967, Komarov was selected to test the *Soyuz I*, the first Soviet-launched spaceship in two years. It would make him the first Soviet astronaut to make two trips in space.

The launchpad from which the colonel and his *Soyuz I* craft were launched was only a few yards from an obelisk marking the site of the launching of *Sputnik I*, on October 4, 1957 at Baikonur, the Soviet Union's space center in Kazakhstan, 1,200 miles southeast of Moscow.

It was the practice of Soviet astronauts not to wear

space suits in flight, and Colonel Komarov arrived on the morning of April 23 two hours before blastoff wearing a bright blue nylon pullover, sports trousers and light shoes.

The launching was a textbook one, and the colonel entered orbit easily. After the first circle of the earth, he reportedly radioed to ground control a message that sounds anything but spontaneous: 'This ship is a major creative achievement of our designers, scientists, engineers and workers,' he said. 'I am proud that I was given the right to be the first to test it in flight.'

U.S. tracking stations were monitoring the experiment closely, and partway into the flight, they were aware that all was not well aboard the *Soyuz I*. It was not responding as easily as the colonel's sanguine statement indicated, and it was clear, according to U.S. space officials, that the flight would not extend beyond 24 hours.

The experiment had actually included the launching of a second space vehicle, to dock with the colonel's ship, but that was apparently scrubbed early in the colonel's flight.

Real problems began to develop when Colonel Komarov began reentry procedures. According to U.S. observers, he tried to bring his ship in on the 16th orbit, after 24 hours of flight, but he was unable to do so because he could not maneuver it properly to fire the braking rockets.

The colonel and his craft circled the world twice more, while he fought to control the tumbling spaceship. Finally, on the 18th orbit, the retrorockets fired, and he appeared to be coming in successfully. 'Well done!' was the cry from ground control.

'Everything is working fine,' replied Komarov, who was over Africa at this moment.

When the spaceship reached 23,000 feet, its landing parachute was to be deployed. But the frantic tumbling in outer space had taken its toll. The parachute lines had become hopelessly tangled, and the parachute did not open. And the *Soyuz I* streaked toward the earth at a frightening rate of speed.

Colonel Komarov struggled to regain control of the ship, but there was no backup for an unopened parachute. He died on impact.

Moscow mourned; thousands passed his bier, which was placed on public display. Two days later, in a ceremony attended by every top dignitary in the Soviet government, his ashes were placed in an urn, and he was buried in the Kremlin wall. The Russian space program would be set back another year by this.

USSR
June 30, 1971

A faulty valve or hatch seal caused a sudden decompression during the landing of the Soyuz II *spacecraft in the USSR on June 30, 1971. All three astronauts aboard were killed.*

Bibliography

Brown, Walter R. and Norman D. Anderson. *Fires*. Reading, Mass.: Addison-Wesley, 1976.

Brown, Walter R., Billye W. Cutchen and Norman D. Anderson. *Catastrophes*. Reading, Mass.: Addison-Wesley, 1979.

Butler, Hal. *Inferno!* Chicago: Henry Regnery Co., 1975.

Butler, Joyce. *Wildfire Loose*. Kennebunkport, Me.: Durrell Publications, 1987.

'Captain X.' *Safety Last: The Dangers of Commercial Aviation*. New York: Dial Press, 1972.

Carlson, Kurt. *One American Must Die*. New York: Congdon and Weed, 1986.

Clarke, James W. *American Assassins*. Princeton, N.J.: Princeton University Press, 1982.

Davie, Michael. *Titanic*. New York: Alfred Knopf, 1987.

Demaris, Ovid. *Brothers in Blood: The International Terrorist Network*. New York: Charles Scribner's Sons, 1977.

Dobkin, Marjorie Housepian. *Smyrna 1922*. Kent, Ohio: Kent State University Press, 1988.

Dobson, Christopher and Ronald Payne. *The Never Ending War: Terrorism in the '80s*. New York: Facts On File, 1987.

——. *The Terrorists*. New York: Facts On File, 1982.

Dunbar, Seymour. *A History of Travel in America*. Indianapolis: Bobbs-Merrill, 1946.

Eddy, Paul, Elaine Potter and Bruce Page. *Destination Disaster: From the Tri-Motor to the DC-10: The Risk of Flying*. New York: Quadrangle, 1976.

Edwardes, Michael. *British India*. New York: Taplinger Publishing Co., 1967.

Emerson, Steven and Brian Duffy. *The Fall of Pan Am 103*. New York: G.P. Putnam's Sons, 1990.

Farrington, S. Kip Jr. *Railroading around the World*. New York: Castle Books, 1955.

Gadney, Reg. *Cry Hungary! Uprising 1956*. New York: Atheneum, 1986.

Garrison, Webb. *Disasters That Made History*. New York: Abingdon Press, 1973.

Godson, John. *Unsafe at Any Height*. New York: Simon and Schuster, 1970.

Grayland, Eugene C. *There Was Danger on the Line*. Auckland, New Zealand: Belvedere, 1954.

Hamilton, James A. B. *British Railway Accidents of the Twentieth Century*. London: Unwin, 1967.

Hamlyn, Paul. *Railways*. London: Hamlyn Publishing Group Ltd., 1970.

Hartunian, Abraham H. *Neither to Laugh nor to Weep: A Memoir of the Armenian Genocide*. Boston: Beacon Press, 1968.

Hooper, Finley. *Roman Realities*. Detroit: Wayne State University Press, 1979.

Howland, S. A. *Steamboat Disasters and Railroad Accidents in the United States*. Worcester, Mass.: Dorr, 1846.

Hyams, Edward. *Terrorists and Terrorism*. New York: St. Martin's Press, 1974.

Hyde, George E. *A Life of George Brent*. Norman, Okla.: University of Oklahoma Press, 1968.

Jerrome, Edward G. *Tales of Railroads*. Belmont, Calif.: Fearon Pittman Publishers, 1959.

Johnson, Thomas P. *When Nature Runs Wild*. Mankato, Minn.: Creative Education Press, 1968.

Kelner, Joseph, with James Munves. *The Kent State Coverup*. New York: Harper and Row, 1970.

Kennett, Frances. *The Great Disasters of the 20th Century*. London: Marshall Cavendish Books Ltd., 1981.

Larimer, J. McCormick. *The Railroad Wrecker*. Muskogee, Okla.: Muskogee Press, 1909.

Lattimer, John H. *Kennedy and Lincoln*. New York: Harcourt Brace Jovanovich, 1980.

Lenz, Harry M. III. *Assassinations and Executions, An Encyclopedia of Violence, 1865–1986*. New York: McFarland, 1988.

Longstreet, Stephen. *City on Two Rivers; Profiles of New York – Yesterday and Today*. New York: Hawthorn Publishers, 1975.

Marshall, John. *Rail Facts and Feats*. New York: Two Continents Publishing Group, 1974.

Marx, Joseph Laurence. *Crisis in the Skies*. New York: David McKay, 1970.

Matthews, Rupert. *The Fire of London*. New York: The Bookwright Press, 1989.

McClement, Fred. *Anvil of the Gods*. New York: J. B. Lippincott, 1964.

——. *It Doesn't Matter Where You Sit*. New York: Holt, Rinehart & Winston, 1969.

McKee, Alexander. *Dresden, 1945: The Devil's Tinderbox*. New York: E. P. Dutton, 1984.

Medvedev, Zhores. *Nuclear Disaster in the Urals*. New York: Vintage, 1980.

Meltzer, Milton. *The Terrorists*. New York: Harper and Row, 1983.

Michener, James. *Kent State; What Happened and Why*. New York: Random House, 1971.

Morris, John V. *Fires and Firefighters*. New York: Bramhall House, 1955.

Nash, Jay Robert. *Darkest Hours*. New York: Nelson-Hall, 1976.

Nock, Oswald, S. *Historic Railway Disasters*. London: Allan, 1966.

Obenzinger, Hilton. *New York on Fire*. Seattle: Real Comet Press, 1989.

Pryce-Jones, David. *The Hungarian Revolution*. New York: Horizon Press, 1970.

Reed, Robert C. *Train Wrecks*. New York: Bonanza Books, 1968.

Rolt, Lionel T. *Red for Danger*. London: Bodley Head, 1955.

Sayre, Nora. *Sixties Going on Seventies*. New York: Arbor House, 1973.

Sobel, Lester A., ed. *Political Terrorism*. New York: Facts On File, 1975.

Soboul, Albert. *The French Revolution, 1787–1799*. New York: Vintage, 1975.

Sterling, Claire. *The Terrorism Network*. New York: Holt, Rinehart and Winston, 1981.

Stover, John F. *American Railroads*. Chicago: Chicago University Press, 1961.

Wasserman, Harvey et al. *Killing Our Own*. New York: Delacorte Press, 1982.

With, Emile. *Railroad Accidents*. Boston: Little Brown, 1856.

Index